Source Book of Scottish Economic and Social History

Source Book of Scottish Economic and Social History

BY

R. H. CAMPBELL

Professor of Economic History
University of East Anglia

and the late

J. B. A. DOW

sometime Lecturer in Economic History
University of Glasgow

NEW YORK
BARNES & NOBLE
1968

First published in the United States, 1968
by Barnes & Noble Inc.
New York, New York

Library of Congress Catalog Card Number: 68 28311

Printed in Great Britain

Contents

Preface

A collection of documents to illustrate the sources used in Scottish economic and social history was first conceived by the late James Dow and myself some years ago. Both of us felt the need for such an aid in the study, and especially in the teaching of the history of modern Scotland. The aims behind the book are explained in more detail in the introduction.

Much of the material was collected before James Dow's tragic death in April 1965. Other commitments then retarded the task of the final presentation and arrangement, which fell to me. Most difficult of all was the problem of knowing what to leave out, since more than twice the number of documents used were in the first draft. Though the final decisions on such issues are mine, the principles on which they were made were frequently discussed between James Dow and myself. I do not think he would have disagreed too strongly with my decisions. The book is therefore as much his as mine and appears under our joint names.

It is a great tragedy that James Dow has not lived to see the publication of this book. His death has been an irreparable loss to economic and social history in general and to Scottish history in particular.

University of East Anglia R. H. CAMPBELL
March 1968

Acknowledgements

A large number of the extracts in this volume are transcripts of records in the Scottish Record Office and the Public Record Office, and of parliamentary papers.

Transcripts of public records in the Scottish Record Office appear with the approval of the Keeper of the Records of Scotland. The following have granted permission for the use of the private records deposited by them in the Scottish Record Office –

Carron Company for the Carron Company Manuscripts; Sir John Clerk of Penicuik for the Clerk of Penicuik Manuscripts; Col. T. A. H. Coltman for the Hamilton of Pinmore Manuscripts; The trustees of the late Lord Seaforth for the Seaforth Manuscripts.

Transcripts of Crown-copyright records in the Public Record Office appear by permission of the Controller of Her Majesty's Stationery Office.

Transcripts of parliamentary papers appear by permission of Her Majesty's Stationery Office.

Acknowledgement is made to the following for permission to use copyright material –

Scottish History Society for the use of their publications vol. 43 (Third Series) in I, A (1) and (3): vol. 39 (Third Series) in II, A (9): and vol. 2 (Fourth Series) in IV, A (3). Her Majesty's Stationery Office for II, A, (6). Associated Book Publishers Ltd. (Methuen and Co. Ltd.) for the use of the Cannan edition of A. Smith, *The Wealth of Nations* in II, A (8), IV, B (2); and for II, B (4). Oxford University Press for the use of the Oxford Standard Authors edition of S. Johnson, *Journey to the Western Islands of Scotland in 1773* in II, C (1) and VIII, A (1). *Oban Times* for II, C (12). The Scottish Council (Development and Industry) for III, D (1) and III, D (5). *The Glasgow Herald* for III, D (2) and III, D (3). His Grace the Duke of Hamilton for VII, A (8). British Railways Board for IX, C (12).

The author and publisher have made every effort to clear all copyright material. In the event of any unforeseen infringements they express their regrets and would welcome any information which would remedy such oversight in future editions.

Many others have helped by drawing attention to possible sources and by criticising my choice. Without the suggestions of several of the officers of the Scottish Record Office in particular the collection would have been much thinner. Mr. R. S. Campbell; Mr. J. K. Hay; Mr. M. Miller; Dr. J. M. Sanderson; Mr. A. Slaven and Dr. R. G. Wilson have assisted in a variety of ways. Dr. T. C. Smout, as on many other occasions, has been a generous helper and discerning critic. The typing of a difficult manuscript was successfully carried out by Mrs. P. Fulcher and Miss C. Townsend.

Introduction

Selecting a group of documents involves many problems, the chief of which is probably knowing what to leave out. More documents were rejected than were finally inserted in the present collection. It is therefore necessary to stress some of the principles which determined its compilation.

The collection is not meant to be comprehensive. To have adopted such an aim in a single volume would have been to attempt the impossible. It seemed better not to try. Nor is the collection meant to be an alternative to a textbook. A deliberate attempt has been made to limit the commentary to a minimum. If any reader requires more explanation or discussion of the historical background, he must seek it in an orthodox textbook.

The collection is an attempt to provide raw material which teachers and students of Scottish history can use for a variety of purposes. Deliberately the commentary does not explain all points of significance in the documents, not only to achieve brevity, but to give greater freedom to teachers in their use of them. Teachers may want to use them for a wide range of purposes: they may even want to encourage students to examine issues for themselves with little help in the first instance.

To facilitate the use of the collection in this way three factors governed the choice of extracts:

1. More than one extract on the same topic has sometimes been given, generally to illustrate different points of view.

2. The extracts are often lengthy, to allow an investigation of different facets of the writer's argument. Brief quotations are often so short that they are meaningless, or at best illustrate only one issue; long quotations illustrate many.

3. The insertion of several extracts on one theme, and the use of long extracts, limits the range of topics which can be covered in one volume of reasonable length. The topics chosen must inevitably display personal preferences and prejudices, but an attempt has

been made to make them represent some of the major issues of Scottish history, particularly those about which there is frequently much discussion, and which seem useful for teaching purposes.

The documents are reproduced exactly as given, though the length of a number have been reduced by making some cuts. In a few cases insertions have been made for the sake of clarity. They are indicated by square brackets.

Table of Contents

CHAPTER I

Population and Migration

A. POPULATION

B. EMIGRATION

C. IMMIGRATION

CHAPTER II

Agriculture

A. THE IMPROVING MOVEMENT

B. SUPREMACY AND COMPETITION

C. HIGHLANDS

CHAPTER III

Industry

A. TEXTILES: LINEN

CHAPTER IV

Trade and Finance

A. THE UNION AND TRADE

B. BANKING: COMMERCIAL BANKS

C. BANKING: SAVINGS BANKS

CHAPTER V

Working Conditions

A. MINES

B. FACTORIES

CHAPTER VII

Labour Movements

A. EARLY COMBINATIONS AND THE LAW

B. LABOUR ASSOCIATIONS

CHAPTER VIII

Living Conditions

A. HOUSING

B. ENVIRONMENT

C. SANITATION

D. HOUSING AND SANITARY REFORM

CHAPTER IX

Transport

A. ROADS

B. WATERWAYS

C. RAILWAYS

CHAPTER I

Population and Migration

A. POPULATION

The first official census of the population of Scotland was taken in 1801. Two earlier attempts at enumeration were by Alexander Webster around 1755 (1) and by Sir John Sinclair about 1795 (2). Neither of these eighteenth century attempts would be considered satisfactory by modern standards (though Webster less than Sinclair) but they represent the total population and its distribution with reasonable accuracy.

(1) J. G. Kyd, *Scottish Population Statistics* (1952). Scottish History Society publication no. 43 (third series). Population by county in 1755, estimated by Alexander Webster –

SCOTLAND 1,265,380

Aberdeen	116,168	Fife	81,570	Perth	120,116
Angus	68,883	Inverness	59,563	Renfrew	26,645
Argyll	66,286	Kincardine	23,057	Ross and Cromarty	48,084
Ayr	59,009	Kinross	4,889	Roxburgh	34,704
Banff	38,478	Kirkcudbright	21,205	Selkirk	4,021
Berwick	23,987	Lanark	81,726	Stirling	37,014
Bute	7,125	Midlothian	90,412	Sutherland	20,774
Caithness	22,215	Moray	30,604	West Lothian	16,829
Clackmannan	9,003	Nairn	5,694	Wigtown	16,466
Dumfries	39,788	Orkney	23,381	Zetland	15,210
Dunbarton	13,857	Peebles	8,908		
East Lothian	29,709				

(2) Sir John Sinclair, *Analysis of the Statistical Account of Scotland* (1825). Population by county around 1795 –

SCOTLAND 1,526,492

Aberdeen	122,921	Fife	87,250	Renfrew	62,858
Angus	91,001	Inverness	73,979	Ross and Cromarty	55,430
Argyll	76,101	Kincardine	26,799	Roxburgh	32,020
Ayr	75,030	Kinross	5,302	Selkirk	4,314
Banff	38,487	Kirkcudbright	26,959	Stirling	46,662
Berwick	30,875	Lanark	125,254	Sutherland	22,961
Bute	11,072	Midlothian	122,655	West Lothian	17,570
Caithness	24,802	Moray	26,080	Wigtown	20,983
Clackmannan	8,749	Nairn	6,054	Zetland (incl. Orkney)	43,239
Dumfries	52,329	Peebles	8,107		
Dunbarton	18,408	Perth	133,274		
East Lothian	28,966				

(3) Census of Scotland. Population by county at census years from 1801 – see folding plate facing page 8.

B. EMIGRATION

Though emigration from the Highlands (see below, p. 44) became a major festering sore in Scottish social and economic life, the experience of the Lowlands was not entirely dissimilar. Many Lowlanders were also attracted by the opportunities portrayed in the colonies, and landlords sometimes felt impelled to prevent rather than encourage emigration (1). In the Lowlands the emigrants came from industrial as well as from rural occupations. Changes in industrial organisation led some to seek a new life overseas, most notably the handloom weavers after the widespread adoption of power looms in the 1820s. Their distress was increased when their ranks were swollen by even poorer Irish immigrants (2). The variety of occupations of those seeking aid to go overseas confirms the nature of emigration from the Lowlands in the early nineteenth century (3).

(1) Public Record Office. (Copy in Scottish Record Office.) State Papers (Scotland), Series 2, 54/46, II, p. 253. Thomas Miller to Lord Justice Clerk, 27th October 1773 –

After transmitting My Report to your Lordship, I was called to attend a County meeting at Air, upon County business. The meeting was very fully [attended], My Lord Loudon in the Chair; And after our other bussiness was over, Sir Adam Ferguson took notice of the dangerous situation this County was in, from the various Arts used to impose upon our People, and entice them to America, and he produced to the meeting the enclosed printed paper, Copys of which had been dispersed over Ireland & this part of Scotland, and tho' we have not lost many of our People by this first attempt, yet in the neighbouring Countys of Argyll & Northward, as well as in Ireland, the Migration has been considerable. What must necessarily add to the influence of such a Publication, is the name & high sounding titles prefixed to it.

The meeting recommended it to me to transmitt this paper to your Lordship, probably you may have seen Copys of it before this time. But as the effects of it are but just beginning to appear in this County, the Meeting thought it proper that it should be transmitted to your Lordship, wishing, as I doe, that your Lordship should be acqainted with every thing that may effect the happiness of this Countrey. And I have the honor to be with the greatest regard, etc.

Tho. Miller

(2) *Third Report of the Select Committee on Emigration, 1827*, pp. 14-15 –

From this evidence, the case of Scotland appears to be that which presents the greatest difficulty. Where the evils of a superabundant population are found to exist, they are not in general under those circumstances to which Emigration could be applied as a permanent and effectual remedy; and Your Committee would beg to remind the House, that they are not prepared to offer any recommendation in favour of Emigration unless such collateral measures can be taken as would prevent the recurrence of the evils complained of. In point of fact there has not been laid before Your Committee any evidence which tends to show general or extensive distress from over-population in the agricultural districts of Scotland. In some of the islands, indeed, upon the western coast, it does appear that a case exists in some degree, but upon a smaller scale, corresponding with that of Ireland: and there is no doubt that very valuable settlers might be furnished from those parts with advantage to the islands and colonies.

The system has indeed been carried into effect, and, it is stated, with advantage by some proprietors . . . But by far the strongest case of distress appears in the state of the manufacturing districts—in that class, whose places, from the greater fluctuations in trade than in agriculture, would be the most certainly and speedily filled up. Under this impression, it appears from the concurrent testimony of all the witnesses examined, that a general disinclination would be felt in those districts to advance any sum for facilitating Emigration; and the numerous applicants who have, by their delegates, been before Your Committee, are in a state which utterly precludes any pecuniary exertion on their part.

The universal opinion expressed also, is, that even in those districts where the population is, strictly speaking, redundant, the redundancy is chiefly, if not entirely, owing to the formidable influx and competition of Irish labourers, who seem already to have in a great measure effected in the manufacturing districts of Scotland those alarming changes in the condition of the lower classes, which have been already pointed out, under the head of Ireland, as calculated to excite such serious apprehension with regard to England.

(3) *Third Report of the Select Committee on Emigration, 1827*, p. 500. Abstract of Petitions and Memorials received at the Colonial Department, from Persons desirous of Emigrating from the United Kingdom –

3.—Scotch Applicants

Date of the application		*Place of residence*	*Description*	*Number of family*	*Subject of application*
1826:					
June	5	Glasgow	weavers	140 persons	Requesting assistance to emigrate to U. Canada
	5	Paisley	paupers	50 heads of families	. . . . Ditto
	9	Uist and Barra	paupers	4 to 500 inhabitants	Applying, on their behalf, for means to join their friends, who were assisted to emigrate to Cape Breton in 1817

Date of the application	*Place of residence*	*Description*	*Number of family*	*Subject of application*
12	Paisley	Chelsea Pen[rs] late 5th Dg[n] Guards	—	For assistance to emigrate to U. Canada
16	Hebrides	paupers	300 persons	For assistance to emigrate to Cape Breton
July 15	Paisley	manufacturers	100 heads of families	.... Ditto U. Canada
19	Aberdeen	old soldier	wife	Requesting grant of land in Canada
Aug. 26	Glasgow	weavers	242 families	Having formed themselves into a society, request assistance to emigrate to U. Canada
29	Springburn	weavers	many families	.... Ditto
Sept. 4	Rutherglen	weavers	100—d°—	Having formed themselves into a society, request assistance to emigrate to U. Canada
6	Roxburghshire	farmer	wife, 6 children	Desirous of emigrating to North America
6	Glasgow	weavers	150 families	.... Ditto U. Canada
9	Glasgow	weavers	many families	.... Ditto
9	Glasgow	weavers	250 families	.... Ditto
14	—	various trades	50 families	.... Ditto
21	—	weavers	50 d°—	.... Ditto
Sept. 21	Glasgow	weavers	150 d°—	Desirous of emigrating to U. Canada
21	—	—	200 persons	Praying, on their behalf, for assistance to emigrate to U. Canada, and to be furnished with implements of husbandry
23	—	—	100 families	.... Ditto
23	—	—	50 d°—	Praying assistance to emigrate to U. Canada, and to be provided with the means of subsistence until the first crops may be gathered
25	—	—	100 d°—	.... Ditto

Date of the application		*Place of residence*	*Description*	*Number of family*	*Subject of application*
	25	—	—	100 d°—	.... Ditto
	30	—	—	50 d°—	.... Ditto
	—	Ards	Presbyter^{n} minister	many families	Applies on their behalf, and would be desirous of accompanying them, as settlers, to the borders of Lake Erie, N. America
Oct.	4	Glasgow	manufacturers	400 persons	Having received favourable accounts of U. Canada, would prefer that place for emigration, and praying assistance to accomplish their object

C. IMMIGRATION

The majority of immigrants into Scotland until very recent times were of Irish origin. The movement increased in the second quarter of the nineteenth century, when famine in Ireland coincided with the first large-scale development of the heavy industries in Scotland. The shortness and cheapness of the passage between Ireland and Scotland always encouraged seasonal migration of even the poorest labourers (1). While seasonal migration remained common, much of the movement in the middle of the nineteenth century was permanent. At the 1851 census 207,367, or 7.2 per cent of Scotland's population were Irish-born against 2.9 per cent in England and Wales. This supply of cheap labour was welcomed by many of the new industrialists in both the textile and the heavy industries (2).

(1) Evidence to the Select Committee on the State of the Irish Poor in Great Britain, 1836, Appendix G, p. 103. Evidence of George Burns, part Owner and Agent of the Belfast and Glasgow Steam-boat Company –

All the trade between Belfast and Glasgow has been in the hands of our company for more than three years, with the exception of one vessel. We have four steamers on that station, plying constantly summer and winter; the price of a passage has varied materially; before the other vessel began to sail, the prices were 20s. the cabin, and 4s. the deck. Since that time the cabin fare has been reduced to 5s., and the deck fare to 1s., and sometimes as low as 6d.

There are also steamers from Dublin and Derry to Glasgow, but the Dublin bring scarcely any deck passengers; the Derry brings a good many more than the Dublin, but not nearly so many as from Belfast.

There is a constant flow of deck passengers to and fro all the year round, but the number of those from Belfast is greatly increased at the time of harvest, viz., from the beginning of July to the middle of August, a large proportion of whom return again at the conclusion of the harvest. A large part of the deckers, who come at all times of the year, are hawkers, who bring poultry, eggs, bacon, and other provisions. Those who come at harvest, as far as their outward appearance goes, seem to be a poorer class; they carry back a good deal of money, however. This has been ascertained by the masters and collector of the ship, and is a matter of general notoriety to all concerned; the bulk of these reapers confine themselves to Scotland, and do not go into England; they usually stay about six weeks.

On board the vessels they are not more disorderly and troublesome than might be expected from so large a body of persons collected together in a small space; we are forced to use great vigilance and caution in collecting the fares, but, on the whole, they are paid pretty completely. The great majority of the harvest-men who come to Glasgow return by Glasgow. The immigration of Irish into Glasgow has been progressively increasing since the introduction of steam navigation, and it has rapidly increased since the lowering of the fares during the last two years.

According to the best computation which I have been able to make, I find that, during the year from 1st January till 31st December, 1833, for every 100 of deck passengers brought by us from Belfast, we have carried back 94. In other words, 6 out of every 100 brought to Scotland have remained or found their way back to Ireland by other routes.

I am not aware that the practice of paying the passages of poor Irish emigrants to Glasgow exists to any extent; no facts of the kind have ever come to my knowledge.

The great bulk of the Irish who come to Glasgow are able-bodied men, in search of labour or trafficking. In many instances, the junior members of a family, after obtaining a settlement here, bring over their infirm relations.

(2) Evidence to the Select Committee on the State of the Irish Poor in Great Britain, 1836. Appendix G, p. 114. Evidence of William Dixon –

The reasons why there are so many more Scotch than Irish among the boys, is that they are generally the sons of the colliers, and there are more Scotch than Irish colliers; moreover, the Irish are generally younger men, and have not been so long with us.

The Irish in the coal mines with us bear a good character; we have nothing to complain of them on that score; they are fully more obedient and tractable than the natives, and are not so much given to combine; they are lively, and sometimes, when they get drink among them, they are a little excited, but not to any extent worth speaking of. They are very much disposed to learn any thing you put them to; they do not find so many difficulties in beginning any thing new. An Irishman, who has never seen the mouth of a coal-pit in his life, has no hesitation in going down and commencing what you ask him to do. They are, perhaps, quicker at taking any thing new than the Scotch, that is, in the same class.

We find them very useful labourers, and their services are of considerable importance to us; at present we could not do without them. In this part of the country, the Scotch do not show much disposition for labouring work; they would rather go to trades. Even the hand-loom weavers, whose wages are so low, do not either themselves attempt to be labourers, or bring up their children to it. A great majority of the West Highland hands are quite useless; they are deficient in the aptitude to learn, and they do not work so heartily: in general, they are a lazy idle set; we decidedly prefer the Irish to these Highlanders. The North Highlanders are a different set altogether; they are preferable both to Irish and West Highlanders; not many of them come to Glasgow.

CHAPTER II

Agriculture

A. THE IMPROVING MOVEMENT

Though some improvements were made in Scottish agriculture before the Union, occasional dearths in the eighteenth century indicated its continuing deficiencies. Throughout the century improvements of many kinds were required. The most extensive changes came about a century after the Union, during the Revolutionary Wars, when high war-time prices provided an appropriate encouragement. The agricultural reports prepared for the Board of Agriculture between 1793 and 1816, and the accounts of parish ministers in the old Statistical Account of around 1790, provided Sir John Sinclair with much of the information which enabled him to give a comprehensive list of the deficiencies which characterised Scottish agriculture throughout most of the eighteenth century.

(1) Sir John Sinclair, *Analysis of the Statistical Account of Scotland* (1825), 1831 edn., vol. I, pp. 229-233 –

Nothing can give a more deplorable idea of the system of agriculture formerly pursued in Scotland, than the unwise and pernicious practices, described in the statistical volumes.

Run-rigg.—In every part of the kingdom, the plan of alternate ridges, cultivated by different farmers, and often belonging to different proprietors, (a mode of occupation similar to the common-field system of England), anciently prevailed. Though this plan was chiefly introduced with a view to divide the good and bad soil equally among the husbandmen, it had likewise for its object, to unite them in the common cause, when their property was in danger of depredation. As long as this injurious system prevailed, all attempts at improvement were in vain. The ridges could not be made straight, nor could either draining or inclosing be attempted. During winter, every field became a common, liable to be poached by the cattle in the neighbourhood, who wandered over it without restraint, endeavouring to glean a miserable subsistence from the *balks*, or strips of grass, interspersed among the ploughed lands, and often between the several ridges. Neither turnips, nor sown grasses were cultivated, nor was it practicable to introduce an improved rotation of crops, even had the farmer been sensible of its advantages. This mode of occupation, however, though at first general over Scotland, was got rid of in all the southern and eastern counties, by the enactment of wise and salutary laws for the division of landed property, passed by the Scottish Parliament about the close of the seventeenth century.

Personal services.—In addition to the disadvantages of the *run-rigg* mode of occupying land, farmers, more especially those, who resided in the northern and western districts, had to struggle with the burden of *personal services*, together with a variety of other exactions, not less troublesome. They were usually bound, under the significant appellation of "*master-work*," to plough and manure the home farm of the proprietor;—cut down his hay;—harvest, and carry to market his corn crops;—provide him with peats for fuel;—in short, to perform almost every kind of field work, which he might require. The females also, were obliged to spin a certain quantity of flax, or wool, for the landlady; and the males, to carry letters to a distance without remuneration, or food; while, under the name of "*customs*," they were bound to provide a number of articles for the landlord, as straw *cazzies*, or bags for carrying grain on horseback, hair-ropes for drawing his ploughs, straw for thatching his offices, etc. . . .

Thirlage.—Astriction or bondage to particular mills, is another grievance, which, though now in some degree abolished, by a recent act of Parliament, was loudly complained of in the statistical volumes. . . .

Croft and outfield land.—The distinction between *croft* and *outfield* prevailed almost universally during the old and imperfect state of husbandry in Scotland. The *croft*, or infield as it was sometimes called, consisted of a few acres nearest the farm-house, was perpetually in crop, and received the whole manure of the farm. The *outfield* was the open pasture land, which was occasionally ploughed in patches for oats, till exhausted, and then left to rest.

The whole manure of the farm being injudiciously confined to the croft land, it was necessarily enriched; but being kept continually in crop, often became so full of weeds, as to yield but miserable returns.

Joint occupation of farms.—Each farm was commonly divided among a number of small tenants; and it is well known, that work, under

the management of many, and where every one claims an equal share in the direction, can never be carried on with success.
Leases.—The leases, where any existed, were anciently short; and when a farmer has possession with certainty for only a few years, scarcely any restrictions imposed, or encouragement offered, can induce him to incur the trouble and expense of improving his farm.
Instruments of husbandry.—The ploughs were formerly of the worst description. In some districts, from their great weight, eight, ten and sometimes twelve oxen, were yoked to one plough. While in others, from the smallness and weakness of the cattle, four men and seven horses were sometimes employed to turn up the same furrow. For that purpose two horses were yoked to the *ristle*, a piece of sharp iron, shaped like a coulter, but bent farther forward, and like it fixed in a beam. It had two handles, and required two men to manage it, though intended merely for cutting the rough sward before the plough, which followed in the same line, drawn by five horses, and attended by two men.

In other districts, the ploughs were drawn by four oxen, or horses, yoked abreast; one trod constantly upon the tilled surface, another went in the furrow, and two upon the stubble or white land. The driver walked backwards, holding his cattle by halters, and taking care, that each beast had its equal share of the draught. This, though it looked awkward, was contended to be the only mode of yoking, by which four animals could best be compelled to exert all their strength. Their harrows, which had merely wooden teeth, were drawn by an ox or heifer; and their carts were tumbler sledges, with wheels of the same piece.
Live-stock.—The cattle kept under this wretched system, were generally in a starving condition. The horses, when their pasture became very bare in winter and spring, often tore up the ground with their feet to come at the roots. Many tenants kept two or three cows, which, from the poverty of their feeding, had not a calf for years together. Mention is made of one farmer, who had a cow ten years old, which never had but one calf; and of another, who, though he kept three or four cows, had not a calf for six years.
Roads.—The want of roads, and wheel-carriages, was a further obstruction to improving the soil. Till about the year 1776, even in the neighbourhood of Paisley, lime, coal, grain, etc. were generally conveyed on horseback.
Late sowing.—It was a barbarous, but a very general custom, that,

however favourable the season, the operations of husbandry should never begin till a certain day in spring, generally the 10th of March; and it was not considered too late to finish sowing barley, "*when the leaves of the ash covered the pyet's* (*magpie's*) *nest*," which seldom happened before the end of May, or beginning of June. This late ploughing occasioned a late seed-time, and of course a late harvest, accompanied by many other disadvantages, and often much loss. *Idle habits.*—In some Highland districts, it was usual to discontinue all farming operations from the time when harvest was over, (generally about the middle of October), till seed-time returned, which was often five or six months after; and then all capable of working were employed in hurrying over the work in a most superficial manner. When sowing was over, all concern about the farm was again laid aside till the harvest began. In the southern districts, however, ploughing generally commenced, as soon as the season permitted it.

The legal basis for improvements was laid down in a series of Acts prior to the Union. Several Acts, of 1661, 1669, and 1685, made provision for a process before a sheriff, whereby a proprietor could force his neighbour to pay half the cost of erecting fences along the boundaries of different holdings; in other words, these Acts provided for enclosure in the literal sense. They also encouraged the planting of trees, which was a prominent activity of the improvers in the early eighteenth century.

(2) Acts of the Parliaments of Scotland, VII, 488 (1685). Act in favours of Planters and Inclosers of Ground –

OUR SOVERAIGNE LORD with the advice and consent of the Estates of this present Parliament for the encouragement of the Inclosing of ground and planting of trees Does ratifie and approve all former Laws and acts of Parliament made in favour of Inclosers of Ground and Planters of trees and particularly the fourtie ane act Parliament first Charles the Second entituled Act for planting and enclosing of Ground and because the time preferyved in the said act is now elapsed they Statut and Ordain That the whole heads contained in the said act be observed for the Space of Nynteen years next to come Commencing from the date heirof And lykeways Ratifies and approves the seventeenth Act Parliament Second Charles the Second entituled Act for enclosing of Ground and Ordaines the same to be observed in all time coming. And furder Statuts and Ordaines that herafter no person shall cut break or pull up any tree or piel the bark of any tree under the pain of ten pound Scots for each tree within ten yeares old and tuentie pound Scots for each tree that is above the said age of ten yeares And that the havers or users of the timber of any tree that shall be so cut broken or pulled up shall be liable to the same penalty except he can produce the person from whom he got it and if the person that shall be so convicted be not able to pay the fine then he shall be decerned to work a day for each half merk contained in the said fine to the heretor whose planting shall be so cut or broken As lykeways Statuts and Ordains that no person shall Break doun or fill up any Ditch hedge or Dyke whereby Ground is inclosed and shall not Leap or suffer their horse Nolt or sheep to goe over any ditch hedge or dyke under the pain of ten pounds Scots toties quoties the half whereof to be applyed to the heretor and the other half for repairing and mending of Bridges and high ways within the paroch at the sight of the Sheriff Stewart or Justices of Peace before whom the Contraveeners shall be pursued.

An act of 1695 authorised the division of any commons, except those belonging to the King or to Royal Burghs, by a process in the Court of Session.

(3) Acts of the Parliaments of Scotland, IX, 462 (1695). Act concerning the Dividing of Commonties –

Our Soveraign Lord with Advice and Consent of the Estates of Parliament for preventing the disscords that arise about Commonties, and for the more easie and expedit deciding thereof, in time coming, Statutes and Ordains, that all Commonties excepting the Commonties belonging to the King and Royal Burrowes that is all that belong to his Majesty in property, or Royal Burrowes in Burgage, may be divided at the instance of any having interest, by Summonds raised against all persons concerned, before the Lords of Session, who are hereby Impowered to disscuss the Relevancy and to determine upon the rights and interests of all parties concerned and to value and divide the same, according to the value of the rights and interests of the several parties concerned, and to grant Commissions to Shirriffs Stuarts Baillies of Regality and their Deputs, Justices of Peace or others for perambulating and taking all other necessary probation Which Commissions shall be reported to the saids Lords, and the saids processes ultimatly determined by them And where mosses shall happen to be in the saids Commonties with power to the saids Lords to divide the saids mosses amongst the several parties having interest therein, in manner forsaid; or in case it be Instructed to the saids Lords that the saids mosses can not be conveniently divided His Majesty with consent forsaid Statutes and Declares that the said mosses shall remain common, with free ish and entrie thereto, whither divided or not, Declaring also, that the interest of the Heretors having right in the said Commonties shall be estimat according to the Valuation of their respective Lands or properties And which Divisions are appoynted to be made of that part of the Commonty that is next adjacent to each heretors property.

An Act, also of 1695, authorised sheriffs and others to allocate land held in runrig among the different proprietors.

(4) Acts of the Parliaments of Scotland, IX, 421 (1695). Act anent Lands lying Run-rig –

Our Soveraign Lord and the Estates of Parliament Taking into their Consideration the great Disadvantage arising to the whole Subjects from Lands lying run-rig, and that the same is highly prejudicial to the Policy and Improvement of the Nation, by planting and inclosing, conform to the several Lawes and acts of Parliament of before made thereanent: For remeid whereof His Majesty with the Advice and Consent of the said Estates Statutes and Ordains that wherever Lands of different Heretors ly run-rig, it shall be leisum to either party to apply to the Shirriffs, Stewarts, and Lords of Regality or Justices of Peace of the several Shires where the Lands ly; to the effect that these Lands may be divided according to their respective interests, who are hereby appoynted and authorised for that effect; And that after due and lawfull Citation of all parties concerned, at an certain day to be prefixed by the said Judge or Judges. It is always hereby Declared That the saids Judges, in making the forsaid Division, shall be, and are hereby restricted, so as special regaird may be had to the Mansion houses of the respective Heretors, and that there may be allowed and adjudged to them the respective parts of the Division, as shall be most commodious to their respective Mansion houses and Policy, and which shall not be applicable to the other adjacent Heretors: As also it is hereby Provided and Declared That thir presents shall not be extended to the Burrow and Incorporat Acres but that notwithstanding hereof, the same shall remain with the Heretors to whom they do belong, as if no such Act had been made.

The application of many improvements was limited by their high cost and by their benefits accruing only over a long period. The owners of entailed estates were in a particularly difficult position. They could not charge part of the cost of improvement on their successors, who would reap most of the gains. It was estimated, though subject to a wide margin of error, that about one-third of the land in Scotland was entailed, and so could not easily be improved. An Act of 1770 helped to remove some of the restrictions by various minor concessions, such as permitting longer leases if the tenant agreed to effect improvements, and by the major concession of allowing proprietors of entailed estates to charge to their heirs three quarters of the money laid out in improvements.

(5) 10 Geo. III, c. 51 (1770). An Act to encourage the Improvement of Lands, Tenements, and Hereditaments, in that Part of *Great Britain* called *Scotland*, held under Settlements of strict Entail –

. . . it shall and may be lawful to every Proprietor of an entailed Estate within that Part of *Great Britain* called *Scotland*, to grant Tacks or Leases of all or any Part or Parts thereof, for any Number of Years not exceeding Fourteen Years from the Term of *Whitsunday* next after the Date thereof, and for the Life of One Person to be named in such Tacks or Leases, and in being at the Time of making thereof; or for the Lives of Two Persons to be named therein, and in being at the Time of making the same, and the Life of the Survivor of them; or for any Number of Years, not exceeding Thirty-one Years from the Term aforesaid.

II. Provided always, That every such Lease for Two Lives shall contain a Clause obliging the Tenant or Tenants to fence and inclose in a sufficient and lasting manner, all the Lands so leased within the Space of Thirty Years, and Two Third Parts thereof within the Space of Twenty Years, and One Third Part thereof within the Space Ten Years, if the said Lease shall continue for such respective Terms; and that every such Lease for any Term of Years exceeding Nineteen Years, shall contain a Clause, obliging the Tenant or Tenants to fence and inclose in like Manner all the Lands so leased during the Continuance of such Term, and Two Third Parts thereof before the Expiration of Two Thirds Parts of such Term, and One Third Part thereof before the Expiration of One Third Part of such Term . . .

IX. 'And whereas it may be highly beneficial to the Public, if Proprietors of entailed Estates were encouraged to lay out Money in inclosing, planting, or draining, or in erecting Farm-houses, and Offices or Out-buildings for the same, upon their entailed Lands and Heretages: And whereas such Proprietors may be induced and encouraged so to do, if they, their Executors and Assigns, were secured in recovering a reasonable Satisfaction, for the Money expended in making such Improvements, from the succeeding Heirs of Entail;' be it therefore enacted by the Authority aforesaid, That every Proprietor of an entailed Estate who lays out Money in inclosing, planting, or draining, or in erecting Farm-houses, and Offices or Out-buildings for the same, for the Improvement of his Lands and Heretages, shall be a Creditor to the succeeding Heirs of Entail for Three Fourth Parts of the Money laid out in making the said Improvements.

One of the major improvers was John Cockburn of Ormiston, who tried to achieve a complete reorganisation of his estate. In 1734 he rebuilt the village of Ormiston and tried to encourage the linen industry by importing skilled labour from Ireland and by laying out a bleachfield. His influence was effective over a large area, as was that of other fellow pioneers.

(6) Historical Manuscripts Commission, vol. 67. Polwarth Manuscripts, vol. v (1725–1780), 208, pp. 146-147. Sir James Hall of Dunglas to the Earl of Marchmont. n.d. *c.* 1737? –

I sent three of my most knowing tenants to Ormistoun where they have learned more of labouring and improveing there grounds in two days than they have doon in all ther life. I have sent for a plewgh that two hors draws as easile as four ane ordinary plewgh. They when they follow [fallow] there grounds so turneip which does ther sheep great advantage and meliorats the grounds as they doe in England. They have all ther grounds inclosed at the tennants charge. His toun is riseing exceedingly, he having 40 [spinning] lomes and wabsters, and to every 6 lomes has 60 spinsters and all others for cairding, and the work so that thers not a boy or a girel of 7 years old but has some thing to doe that ye will not see ane in the toun except in any hour of play. Blacksmiths, shoemakers, candlemakers and baikers, maltsters, etc. make throng doeing. I was twice ther myself and very prittilie interteand, tho the first time J. Cock(burn) happened to be at Edinburgh. Ther is boths building for all thair merchandise and to be market days, and ther is 16 houses contracted for this nixt season. All those are the Great Street and to be at least two storys high or neare as they please, and in the by lains as they please, but all must be sclated or tiled. What ground he gives them off for a little yeard, they pay for the stance of the house and yeard, as it comes to 22 sh. per aiker and 25 years purchase and ane sh. sterling per year. I shall, Dear Marchmont, in a litle time be beter able to let you know more about it. I have sent for a duble of his tacks and feus. His takes are generaly for 3 lives, and when ane fails he oblidges himself and airs to give another upon the tender of a year's rent.

Apart from Cockburn, and others of renown, many little-known agriculturists were among the foremost improvers. George Robertson was a leading factor in Scotland, and in recollections written towards the close of his life he pointed out the varied sources of the improvements in two rather different areas.

(7) George Robertson, *Rural Recollections* (1829), pp. 352–355; pp. 619-620 –

Lothians

Many of these improvements have been brought in insensibly, nobody knows by whom, nor by what means. It seems probable, however,—indeed there is something like direct evidence for it—that the introduction of artificial grasses and of turnip, to which so much of the increased fertility of the soil is owing, has been by some of the great landed proprietors. In particular, Thomas, the sixth Earl of Haddington, who lived in the beginning of the last century is mentioned as actually having done so. But the great mass of improvements arising from a better mode of tillage, and system of rotation in cropping, has been owing almost entirely to the farmers themselves, with very little example set them by the proprietors. There have indeed been many instances in which proprietors have been cultivators of part of their own land, but it has been but rarely that their example, from its success, has led to imitation. Agriculture, to be well conducted, is a science, or rather an occupation that requires such increasing attention, and so much laborious industry, that few men who are in the independent circumstances of an opulent landholder can bring themselves to dedicate to it their whole talents and time ... Should they ... remain at home on their paternal estates, their attentions are commonly directed to the embellishment of their property rather than to its cultivation: they enclose—they plant—they build—they construct highways, erect bridges, or plan canals or railroads—they lay out gardens, or they erect gateways, or other rural decorations ... The proportion of lands actually in tillage-culture by the proprietors will, probably, not exceed one part in fifty of the whole. Even where their cultivation is the most correct in every point, it forms such a small proportion, and is so little in view, as hardly to attract notice.

These remarks apply chiefly to the Lothian landed proprietors, more especially to those in the county of Edinburgh [Midlothian]; with the metropolis in their immediate neighbourhood, and where the greater part of them have their chief business, either in the various departments of the law, or are connected with the several banking-companies, or in other commercial establishments; so that they are the less called upon, at any time, to dedicate their talents to agricultural pursuits. In more remote parts of the country, the proprietors are more in the habit of cultivating their own lands; and, in fact, there are many instances there, in which improvements in cultivation have been introduced by them, and have been followed from their example. This application to husbandry by the proprietor ... more generally ... occurs in cases where extra cultivation is required; as in the improvement of waste ground, or in the draining of marshy lands. There are, sometimes, such expensive undertakings as the common husbandmen is not always possessed of the means to accomplish; or, from the ordinary duration of a lease, he is not assured of being, in that time, repaid the expenses the improvement must occasion. Much of the rapid improvements that, of late, have been so manifest in many parts of Scotland, are owing to the exertions of the proprietors themselves, who are justly entitled to every credit on this account.

It has, nevertheless, been remarked, that however much they may have improved the soil and embellished the face of the country, yet they themselves have rarely made much by it in their own time; though, ultimately, their heirs may have profited from the increased fertility of the soil. The improvement of land, in almost all cases, is unavoidably attended with much expense, even in the hands of the most attentive and parsimonious husbandman . . .

Ayrshire.

Though this county cannot boast of having produced so many examples of energetic improvement, as in Kincardineshire, by the landed gentlemen, nor, as in the Lothians, by the tenants themselves, yet great praise is due to the proprietors of Ayrshire for their very successful exertions, in enclosing their lands, and in embellishing the whole country with plantations. In these respects, no county in Scotland has been more universally improved, or at so early a period, more resemblant now to an English county, than any other in North Britain. In these great points none displayed more taste, or made greater exertions, at so early a period, as Alexander, the tenth earl of Eglinton . . . To him the county is indebted for making extensive plantations all over his lands in this county, and his example was soon followed by the numerous and highly respectable other proprietors. In the improving operations of husbandry too, the country gentlemen have uniformly taken the lead. The grand change, however, of system in the rotation of cropping, seems generally to be imputed to the influence of the late Alexander Fairlie, Esq., of Fairlie . . . At what particular period it was that he introduced this more rational practice, I have no precise information; but it was during the time that he was commissioner over the great estates of Eglinton, after the death of the Earl Alexander in 1769, that he enforced it, more generally, on the tenantry.

However desirable, the changes could not be made easily. The difficulties of doing so were demonstrated by Adam Smith.

(8) A. Smith, *The Wealth of Nations* (1776) (Cannan edn.), vol. i, pp. 221–222.

The lands which were kept constantly well manured and in good condition, seldom exceeded a third or a fourth part of the whole farm, and sometimes did not amount to a fifth or sixth part of it. The rest were never manured, but a certain portion of them was in its turn, notwithstanding, regularly cultivated and exhausted. Under this system of management, it is evident, even that part of the lands of Scotland which is capable of good cultivation, could produce but little in comparison of what it may be capable of producing. But how disadvantageous soever this system may appear, yet before the union the low price of cattle seems to have rendered it almost unavoidable. If, notwithstanding a great rise in their price, it still continues to prevail through a considerable part of the country, it is owing, in many places, no doubt, to ignorance and attachment to old customs, but in most places to the unavoidable obstructions which the natural course of things opposes to the immediate or speedy establishment of a better system: first, to the poverty of the tenants, to their not having yet had time to acquire a stock of cattle sufficient to cultivate their lands more completely, the same rise of price which would render it advantageous for them to maintain a greater stock, rendering it more difficult for them to acquire it; and, secondly, to their not having yet had time to put their lands in condition to maintain this greater stock properly, supposing they were capable of acquiring it. The increase of stock and the improvement of land are two events which must go hand in hand, and of which the one can no-where much out-run the other. Without some increase of stock, there can be scarce any improvement of land, but there can be no considerable increase of stock but in consequence of a considerable improvement of land; because otherwise the land could not maintain it. These natural obstructions to the establishment of a better system, cannot be removed but by a long course of frugality and industry; and half a century or a century more, perhaps, must pass away before the old system, which is wearing out gradually, can be completely abolished through all the different parts of the country. Of all the commercial advantages, however, which Scotland has derived from the union with England, this rise in the price of cattle is, perhaps, the greatest. It has not only raised the value of all highland estates, but it has, perhaps, been the principal cause of the improvement of the low country.

Some improvers took a considerable quantity of land under their own control; when they left it in the hands of tenants, they sometimes required the acceptance of leases which ensured the cessation of harmful practices and the satisfactory farming of the land. Such improvement clauses were important in the first encouragement of improvements; later they could prove restrictive on the initiative of the tenants.

(9) H. Hamilton (ed.), *Selections from the Monymusk Papers, 1713-1755* (1945), pp. 46-48. Scottish History Society Publication, vol. 39 (third series). Copy Draft of the Lease for Farms at Monymusk February, 1751.

That the said B. shall not plow in any one year above a third of his intown land & one third of the outfield land & one third of the haughs or low land, not take above three cropts in immediate succession from any of them, excepting pease are sowen after cross faughing beside the usual tillage, in which case one cropt more may be take, also excepting 9 bolls sowing of [ ] ground, which after reasonable dunging each third year the said B. may plow for six cropts & in succession 9 bolls more in like manner of said land; but in other respects the said lands are to be subject to the forsaid General Regulations so that all the land must be at least six years in grass for each course of tillage as above, and all the tillage reasonably directed to bring it to a levell & to make the ridges straight, & with the last cropt of each course of tillage sowen with a reasonable quantity of clean grass seeds in the intown or haugh ground & hay seeds in the outfield or low lands & not above two cropts of hay to be cutt from the same ground in each course of grass. That all the tillage land as above shall lye and be connected together so as the whole fields or divisions may be regularly in grass or corn at the same time & brought into tillage in a regular order agreeable to the above Regulations, & therefore the tillage shall begin and proceed according to a plan thereof to be settled and subscribed by the said parties which shall also be deemed part of the tack.

That one rake of six horses shall be given annually to the Heritor if required for lime, the same for slate, the same for wood, four raik of six horses each for grain to Aberdeen or like distance & in same way one raik of 6 horses upon any other acc^{t}, besides usuall services to Kirk, Minister, Schoolhouse, Mill & Kilne or two shilling sterling for each deficient horse, & eight pence sterling for each deficient man, and to be subject to what general regulations by Acts of Court of the Barrony are now subsisting or shall be made for the common benefit with the consent & apporbation of two thirds of all concerned . . .

The said B. is to be allowed two crofters or grassmen if he thinks proper, they to give two days work for hay or lint to the Heritor or flax raiser w^{t}out payment and four days for payment at the rate of wadges in the countery . . .

And if in any of the particulars of this Agreement there shall arise any difference betwixt the said parties, it shall be determined by the arbitration of two persons, one to be choisen by each party and in case of varience betwixt the arbiters or if either party refuse or neglect to name arbiters, the Shirreff Depute for the time being or his substitute shall determine the same.

B. SUPREMACY AND COMPETITION

During the Napoleonic Wars high prices and profits encouraged the widespread adoption of agricultural improvements throughout Scotland below the Highland line. When prices fell after the war, arable areas in England suffered; less so those in Scotland. Wheat, which experienced the greatest fall in price, was never extensively cultivated in Scotland, except in the Lothians and in Berwickshire. The main grain crop was oats, often for feeding to livestock, not for sale as a cash crop. But the most substantial basis for prosperity lay in the efficient agricultural practices of some parts of Scotland. The Lothians became a model for others to copy, especially when they supplied many bailiffs to southern farms and estates. R. H. Greg, a Hertfordshire farmer, was so impressed by his bailiff that he went to the Lothians to investigate the reasons for its success. He published his findings in the *Manchester Guardian* 'in the hope of awakening attention to the backward state of Agriculture in many parts of England, more especially in the neighbouring Counties of Lancashire and Cheshire'. Greg believed many English farmers could survive the repeal of the corn laws only by following the example of their fellow agriculturists in the Lothians.

(1) R. H. Greg, *Scotch Farming in the Lothians* (1842), pp. 9-28 –

The general conviction which remains upon my mind is this, that with a system equal to that of the Lothians, established throughout England, landlords might receive double rents, farmers be rich and prosperous, and the country be rendered, for two generations, independent of foreign supplies, notwithstanding an abolition of all protective duties. I am confident the agricultural produce of England, Wales, and the west of Scotland, might be doubled; and that of Lancashire and Cheshire be tripled, and this without any material addition to the agricultural population . . .

The Lothian farms consist, each, of from 200 to 500 Scotch acres, the Scotch acre being one-fourth larger than the English statute acre . . .

The farm buildings are small, compact, and situated near the centre of the farm, and have always a *steam engine*, of six to eight horse power, for thrashing and other purposes. The corn is put up in stacks, in a stackyard near the thrashing machine; the stacks being of such a size, as that one may furnish a day's work for the machine.

At the entrance of the farm yard, is the dwelling of the grieve, or bailiff; for every farmer keeps a bailiff, who superintends every thing on the farm, and is cognizant of every thing that goes in, or out of the farm buildings. A fact which struck me much was, that the grieve received only one shilling a week more than the ploughman. The explanation given is equally remarkable, viz. that every man on the farm has knowledge enough for the situation of grieve, but every man has not the qualifications, which fit him for the management of other men, or, perhaps, is not sufficiently trustworthy for so responsible a situation. That the requisite knowledge for conducting a farm of 500 acres may be had for 12s. a week (the wages of a ploughman), and that 1s. extra, will command the extra qualifications for a bailiff, speak eloquently what education has done for the peasantry of this part of Scotland. I found the grieves, universally, clever, acute and sensible; and their minds open to what was passing in the world, beyond the limits of their own farm, or immediate neighbourhood.

The farmer's dwelling house is, generally, a little in front of the farm buildings, a neat, comfortable home, with kitchen and flower garden attached.

The farmers, themselves, are men of very superior education, manners, and style of living, to the, possibly, equally wealthy ones of the farming counties of England, even Lincolnshire and Norfolk, where the farms are of equal extent with those of the Lothians. As a class, however, they would compare better with the master manufacturers of Lancashire, so keen and pushing. Few of them are without a handsome phaeton, for the use of the female members of their family; they are of most hospitable habits; and I was informed, that, excepting for a month at seed time, and the same at harvest, they have company at home, or dine out, three times a week.

One feature throughout the Lothian farms may be remarked—a great uniformity in the quality of the crops. Not, as elsewhere, here, a good farmer, and there, a bad one; here a failing crop, there, a middling one; and here again, a fine one; but, nearly all the same, showing that farming is there reduced to a science, leaving nothing uncertain but the *seasons*, which, affecting all nearly alike, do not materially disturb the uniformity I speak of.

The present season has been remarkably favourable in the Lothians, as a whole, though somewhat too dry. The wheat would average about five quarters to the acre; and, in the seventy or eighty acres on the same farm, it would sometimes be difficult to point out a square yard which carried more, or fewer ears than the rest of the field.

The farms are divided into fields of from twenty, to fifty acres, each; the hedges are clipt, low and thin, and the ditches covered in, so as to occupy as little space as possible. There are no trees in the hedge-rows, and few furrows, the land being laid down flat; and thus, between one thing and another, the entire area of the farm is made productive, and the expense of fences and gates is reduced to a minimum.

Another thing worth noting is, that permanent grass, either as meadow, or pasture, is unknown, or nearly so; the only hay, or pasture, is derived from artificial grass, sown in the regular rotation of crop, which remains two years down, and is then ploughed up and followed by oats. The crops of artificial grass were extremely heavy. I counted, in one field of sixteen acres, no less than 234 sheep, from 150, to 200 of which, had been on the land since the first of April. In another field of the same size, twenty cows; and in both, the feed, chiefly white clover, was abundant, and of the finest quality.

The rent of the Lothian farms is from £3. 10s. to £5. per acre; and these high rents, the farmers not only pay, but thrive upon; indeed, a more thriving set of men I never met with. They are enabled to pay these rents, and thrive, partly, by the heavy crops, arising from skilful cultivation, and partly, by economy of management in every department. Actual wages, however, are as high as in England, namely—10s. to 11s. a week for a common labourer; 12s. for a ploughman, and ninepence a day for women, 10 hours to the day. As to the great amount of produce, it must be remembered, that all the land is under the plough. Five quarters of wheat, to the acre, are reckoned a good average; but some fields turn out six. Ten, or eleven quarters of oats, eight, to ten tons of potatoes, and twenty-six, to thirty tons of turnips, are reckoned good fair crops.

Economy of management is shown in many ways:

1. In the position and quality of farm buildings, in having no land lying idle, or unproductive, and in the use of machines and horses, instead of manual labour, wherever circumstances admit of it.
2. By confining attention to as few points as possible. Thus, instead of buying stock to feed off the grass, during the two years the land is seeded down, it is let off to stock-feeders or butchers, at about £6 per annum, the acre, and the farmer's attention and capital is, thereby, saved from distraction and division. . . .
3. Economy in the use and keep of horses. Such an abuse as three horses to a plough, except to the subsoil plough, is unknown. The universal complement for 100 acres, I found to be, two pair of horses, two ploughmen, and one labourer; the number of women and children varying with the particular crop, perhaps, six or eight, during the season.

In this small allowance of horses, it must be remembered, that the whole 100 acres is arable, there being no permanent pasture.

The winter keep of the horses is a mixture of one-half chopped straw, or chopped any thing, and one-half, steamed turnips, or potatoes; and this feed is found not only much cheaper than hay and oats, but the horses are kept in better condition, and enjoy better health. No horses could look in finer condition than they did.

All the Lothian farms are held on 19 years leases, and the rents are wholly, or partly, corn rents, rising and falling with the yearly fluctuations of the price of corn. The tendency of a corn rent, I conceive to be, to throw fluctuations in the value of a farm—that arising from an alteration of corn-laws, for example—upon the landlord, instead of the tenant.

Without a long lease, the farmers would not lay out their capital, in the free manner they now do; and with a long lease, they feel independent of their landlords, more as if they were the actual proprietors, and, altogether, hold themselves higher, and with good reason, than the most wealthy of our English farmers.

In consequence of this independence, and part ownership as it were, of their farms, men of superior rank, education, and capital, engage in the business of farming, than is the case in England, or indeed, than ever will be the case in England, under existing circumstances.

The foundation of all improvement in the Scotch farming is the system of thorough draining; and so essential is this considered, that most of the land is deemed unworthy of being farmed at all, until it has undergone this operation.

Thorough draining, or furrow draining, is a series of drains, of tiles, or broken stones, made at regular distances, from 15 to 30 feet, or more, apart, according to the nature of the soil, over the whole field. This may be called the new system of draining, as opposed to the old one of cutting a few deep drains where springs actually show themselves, and which mode of draining is now, I believe, entirely abandoned by the best farmers . . .

The general course of cropping the Lothians seems to be—wheat, after summer fallow, or not; turnips, or potatoes; barley; seeds, down for one, two, or three years, as circumstances vary; oats. When farther from town manure, and land stiffer, a crop of beans and peas is taken. In East Lothian we saw comparatively few potatoes, whilst in West Lothian it appears to be the grand crop.

The best approximation I could learn, as to the division of the gross proceeds of a farm, gives—

Rent	33	per cent
Expenses . . .	47	do
Profit and Interest	20	do
	100	

I have thus endeavoured to give, in a somewhat unconnected way, the result of my observations on the Lothian farming, where high rents, high profits, and a well-paid and contented peasantry, are all seen combined in a pleasing union.

There is as wide a difference between the system existing there, and in these parts of England, as between that pursued in the small detached spinning mills of thirty years ago, and what is now practiced in the first-rate factories.

It is an interesting question, but one I am not going to enter upon, how this improved system of cultivation can be introduced into England, particularly into our own and the neighbouring counties? Where are the landlords ready to grant a 19 years' lease? Where, the farmers of sufficient intelligence and capital to manage successfully, 500 acres, and willing and able to lay out £1,000 to £1,800 in draining alone, during the first two years of their lease? Where, the ploughmen, educated enough to convert into bailiffs, on such farms, for an extra shilling a week?

I am inclined to think the more generally diffused and more practical education of the Scotch, has been at the bottom of the improved state of things. Education has quickened the intellect, and given the knowledge which has enabled them to apply their capital with success, and to extract from the landowner the long lease, which enables them to invest their capital with safety, as well as success.

I may, in concluding, mention a suggestion repeatedly made to me, that, instead of sending for Scotch bailiffs, who have many difficulties and prejudices to contend with amongst strangers, the English landowner should send intelligent young men to Scotland, to spend a year or two upon the farms there, and who would, on their return, be better received than a stranger, and have greater facilities for introducing another system.

Even areas such as the Lothians, which had a proportion of their acreage under cash grain crops, did not suffer significantly from the repeal of the Corn Laws. But the nineteenth century witnessed the firm establishment in Scottish agriculture of livestock production, both dairy and beef stock, a specialisation which was to stand in good stead in later years. The Ayrshire was practically Scotland's only native dairy breed. Its origins are obscure, reaching back well into the eighteenth century, but it was first referred to as a distinct breed by the Highland and Agricultural Society in 1814. Its popularity increased in the mid-nineteenth century and the Ayrshire Cattle Herd Book Society was formed in 1877.

(2) Col. William Fullarton, *General View of the Agriculture of the County of Ayr* (1793), pp. 58-59 –

In Cunningham, or the northern division of the county, a breed of cattle has for more than a century been established, remarkable for the quantity and quality of their milk in proportion to their size. They have long been denominated the Dunlop breed, from the ancient family of that name, or the parish where the breed was first brought to perfection, and where there still continues a greater attention to milk cows and dairies than any other part of Scotland.

The cattle in this district appear originally to have been of the old Scotch low country kind. Formerly black or brown with white or flecked faces, and white streaks along their backs, were prevailing colours. But within these twenty years, brown and white mottled cattle are so generally preferred, as to bring a larger price than others of equal size and shape, if differently marked. It appears, however, that this mottled breed is of different origin from the former stock, and the rapidity with which they have been difused over a great extent of country, to the almost entire exclusion of the preceding race, is a singular circumstance in the history of breeding. Indeed, it is asserted by a gentleman of great skill and long experience (Mr. Bruce Campbell) that this breed was introduced into Ayrshire by the present Earl of Marchmont, and afterwards reared at the seat of the Earl of Glasgow, from whence they are said to have spread over all the country.

This breed is short in the leg, finely shaped in the head and neck, with small horns, not wide but tapering to the point. They are neither so thin coated as the Dutch, nor so thick coated and rough hided as the Lancashire cattle. They are deep in the body, but not so long, nor so full and ample in the carcase and hind quarters as some other kinds. They usually weigh from 20 to 40 English stone, and sell from £7 to £12 according to their size, shape and qualities. It is not uncommon for these small cows to give from 24 to 34 English quarts of milk daily, during the summer months, while some of them will give as far as 40 quarts, and yield 8 or 9 English pounds of butter weekly. The breed is now so generally diffused over Cunningham and Coil, that very few of the other sorts, are reared on any well regulated farm. The farmers reckon that a cow yielding 20 quarts of milk per day during the summer season, will produce cheese and butter worth about £6 per annum.

The origins of the great beef breed, the Aberdeen-Angus, are more certain. It was pioneered by two farmers in the north-east, Hugh Watson and William McCombie, and had its first great success at the Smithfield show in 1829. By about 1870 the Aberdeen-Angus ranked with the beef Shorthorn and the Hereford as the world's leading beef breeds. On the foundations of the ancient cattle trade and the new breeds of livestock the north-east of Scotland built a successful organisation, supplying meat to the country's urban markets. William McCombie described it.

(3) William McCombie, *Cattle and Cattle-Breeders* (4th edn. by James Macdonald, 1866), pp. 81-84 –

The dead-meat trade has become one of the great institutions of the country. There are hundreds engaged in the business, and it is yearly increasing . . . When the supply is short, some of our most enterprising butchers attend the Glasgow market, bring down cattle, and slaughter them in Aberdeen, and send the carcasses to London. I have known Mr. Butler bring down fifty in one week. The following table shows the number of cattle and tons of dead meat sent to London and other markets during 1865 and the six previous years; it also shows what was sent by rail and sea respectively:-

	Cattle		*Dead meat*	
Year	*Rail*	*Sea*	*Rail*	*Sea*
1859	13,130	7,282	6,905	48
1860	13,993	3,782	5,769	53
1861	8,852	8,324	8,041	127
1862	6,281	4,518	9,392	75
1863	9,623	4,163	9,395	58
1864	7,624	3,551	9,840	2
1865	9,031	4,558	10,074	61

. . . Calculating that 6 cwt. was the average weight of the cattle, this will show that 33,783 cattle were sent away from Aberdeen as dead meat, against 9,031 live cattle by rail and 4,558 by sea, so that 20,194 more cattle were sent away dead than alive . . .

The Aberdeen butchers have a higher standing than can be claimed by their brethren in any other part of the kingdom. The butchers in other cities are generally only purveyors, and never dispute the honours of the show-yard with the grazier or breeder. They buy their weekly supply at their weekly markets; but many of the chief Aberdeen butchers do not depend upon the market for their supplies, but feed large lots of fine cattle and sheep themselves to meet emergencies, upon which they can fall back. They do more than this; they are the largest and most successful exhibitors at our great annual fat shows. They are not only great purveyors themselves, but they supply a good proportion of the Christmas prize animals to the chief butchers of London, Birmingham, Liverpool, Newcastle, York, Darlington, Edinburgh, Glasgow, etc. I was the first Scotch exhibitor at Birmingham. It is now the most deservedly popular of the fat shows with our exhibitors. The names of Martin, Stewart, Knowles, etc. are celebrated not only in Great Britain, but in France,

Such men are public benefactors, and entitled to the gratitude of heir country.

The prosperity of the mid-nineteenth century did not last. A. G. Bradley had personal experience of the Lothians in the days of its renown and prosperity. In the 1860s as a young man, he was a pupil of George Hope, tenant in Fentonbarns, perhaps the best known Lothian farmer of the mid-nineteenth century. Later in life Bradley described Fentonbarns and the Lothians in general. When noting the changes which had taken place in the forty years before 1914 he felt that many might have been anticipated but were not. Though perhaps exaggerated in detail, the general impression is accurate.

(4) A. G. Bradley, *When Squires and Farmers Thrived* (1927), pp. 68-88 –

Fentonbarns was then a farm of note in the best-farmed region of Great Britain. It was there at least *primus inter pares*, and certainly a familiar name in the higher agricultural circles of England and even among leading agriculturists on the Continent, partly, perhaps, on account of the personality and position of Mr. George Hope, the occupant. For the whole country was farmed up to the highest scientific level of the day, paying in rent from £3 to £5 an acre and leaving a good margin of profit to the enterprising tenants who had produced such results. Fentonbarns was in area about six hundred acres, and let at £3. 5s. an acre on a nineteen years' lease, the then East Lothian custom. It was a clay loam of average natural fertility, but outside the area of the Dunbar red sandstone belt, the best soil in Scotland, where rents were higher. The Hope family had been there for just a hundred years. The grandfather, working in a comparatively humble way, had begun to bring the land out of the rude and undrained condition common to mid-eighteenth century Scotland, and the son and grandson had perfected it. It was the story, in fact, of many Lothian farms, the story in cameo of Scottish agriculture generally, which, far behind England when George III came to the throne, was as far ahead of it when a younger son was king. Rents had leaped from 5s. to £3, £4 and £5. Scots Lowland lairds, from being too poor to face London society, were drawing rents which made Norfolk and Shropshire look foolish.

A fine new farmhouse of red sandstone had recently been built and the old homestead handed over to the steward. Born on the farm, Hugh Bertram had risen from a ploughman to be the trusted right hand and confidential steward and friend, now this long time, of his master . . .

The homestead stood on a broad ridge commanding a considerable slice of East Lothian, and much more besides. For miles in nearly all directions there were great sweeps of tillage patterned in large, rectangular fields, the hedgerows, short and trimmed like garden fences, showing as mere straight lines. There was hardly a tree in the nearer landscape, nor a thicket, nor a patch of waste ground. It was all arable. . . . Red roofed steadings, planted at intervals about the land, shot tall brick chimneys skyward, some of them a-smoke in evidence that thrashing was going forward. For every farm had its fixed engines and machinery and its own steam-plough. No travelling thrashing machines nor peripatetic steam-ploughs went round for hire in that country . . .

This great farm . . . went like clockwork. Its fields, of from 20 to 30 acres, were all rectangular. There were no odd corners, no thickets, no hedgerow trees, no ragged, any-shaped pastures. The quickset hedges were clipped low and narrow like those of a garden . . . There were no open ditches, and the plough ran right up to the roots of the fence. The land was as clean as a well-kept garden, and the whole farm subsoil drained with tile pipes. There was not an acre of permanent grass. I do not think there was one in the whole country, outside the lairds' policies (parks) or the hill country, but only the clover and rye grass which came in rotation in the six-course shift. One shift was always potatoes, 50 to 80 acres with us, the then famous Dunbar Regent fetching the highest price in the London market for roasting at the popular steak and chop houses. The stuff put under the potato crop would make a Sussex farmer gasp. Forty load of barnyard manure, and 900 lbs. of artificials to the acre, I see by my old journals, though this may have been the Scotch acre, about one-fifth larger than the Imperial measure, as both were in use there.

And then the wheat crop that followed the potatoes, six and even seven quarters to the acre: I have seen eight! I remember Mr. Hope selling one potato crop at £50 an acre in the ground, the buyer both lifting and shifting it. Potatoes were and are, however, a bit of a gamble. Damp and close weather in early autumn for a fortnight or so carried tremors throughout East Lothian, and does still, and then perchance came that ominous whiff betoking disease. Fine pairs of Clydesdales with brisk Scotch hinds in the plough stilts behind them ran long clean furrows eight or nine inches deep. Steam ploughs were then in fashion with advanced agriculturists, though in later days they became unpopular for technical reasons not here relevant. There was not only our steamer constantly at work in the ploughing season, but the smoke of half a dozen others would be generally visible from the farm.

I daresay there were twenty or more men engaged on the place, all living in the low, one-storied, red sandstone, tile-roofed cottages of the country, always grouped around the homestead (to borrow an English term), as is customary on both sides of the Border. No long walks from distant villages worried the Scottish labourer. Wages were then paid partly in kind, the use and keep of a cow being a valuable item, and so many yards of potatoes in the field crop another. Porridge being in those days the staple though not the sole diet of the labourer, the milk supply was of immense benefit, above all to the children. As a matter of fact oatmeal was not of ancient use in South-Eastern Scotland. Pease bannocks in the eighteenth century and perhaps later had been the basic food, nourishing but nasty by universal repute. Oatmeal disappeared unfortunately from the Scottish labourers' table long before the great war, and home-baked bread went the same way. The cow and the milk was counted for cash allowance. Tea and anaemic baker's bread and the grocer's cart with tinned stuff took their place when wages in 1914 were still about 22s. a week. At the time I write of, the total weekly value was reckoned at about 14s., and a house rent free. . . .

None of these confident, cheery, deep-pocketed Lothian farmers could have guessed the fate that was hanging over them and their kind . . . Ten years later the pride of prosperity and pre-eminence still beat as high as ever in East Lothian. And then, suddenly, as it seemed to all British farmers, though they might well have foreseen it, the grain of the virgin lands from overseas burst upon the country like a flood. Wheat fell rapidly from its old comfortable, consistent figures of fifty and sixty shillings to thirty odd, with oats and barley to match.

. . . The high condition of Lothian land and its skilful management helped that country to weather in some sort the two dismal decades of the 'eighties and 'nineties, while the great potato crop, being outside foreign competition, was a further support. But all the great farming families with a few exceptions disappeared, not necessarily ruined, though much money was lost . . . On revisiting this county after 20 or odd years absence, I found that nearly all the old names had gone. The high standard of farming had carried on, but for many years at what a price no one will ever know. And then new men had come in, a rather different class, or perhaps a more varied one. Hard working grieves who had saved money, merchants' sons with capital ready to risk for a Lothian farmer's life, which had always in the past, like English gentleman farming, a glamour for the cities and even a touch of social attraction. And then things got better till the War, after which date I have nothing to say, for I know nothing. Agriculture may or may not prosper in the future, but neither in Scotland, nor in England will the days which ended, broadly speaking, with the 'seventies ever return. Only those of us who were mixed up with such things and are old enough to remember those days can fully realise the profound security and solidity then associated with the landed interest . . .

In '77 or '78 I was revisiting East Lothian as well as other counties. The great machine was running then as smoothly, unsuspiciously and proudly as of old. There was not a whisper of the coming blast. But to me it seemed so plain, indeed almost too plain to be worth discussion. And yet it seemed hidden from the people at home, the very wisest of them, and who was I to tell a crack East Lothian farmer that in 4 or 5 years he would be cursing his 19 year lease, the very sheet-anchor of the great East Lothian system.

The problems of agriculture in the later nineteenth century arose when the opening of the grain producing regions of North America at a time of improved transport led to increased imports of foodstuffs. The south-east, where a larger acreage was under arable cultivation, suffered most from foreign competition; the south-west, which had specialised in dairying, and the north-east, relying on fatstock, suffered least. Royal Commissions investigated agricultural conditions in the 1880s and 1890s. The evidence presented to them shows the differential impact of the depression. Those in dairying districts suffered least (5); the arable producers suffered most (6). A factor, giving evidence in 1896, stressed the contribution of the differential effects, which often led landlords to vary their remissions in rent according to a tenant's specialisation (7).

(5) *Evidence to the Royal Commission on the Depressed Conditions of the Agricultural Interest, 1881*. Evidence of Andrew Allan, tenant of Munnoch, Dalry, Ayrshire –*see over*

(a) Qs. 37,667–37,669

. . . Have you any suggestion to offer with a view to making the farmer's occupation a more profitable one?—No, only moderate rents. That is a thing which we cannot complain of, at least as far as I am concerned. I had the satisfaction of making my own terms on this lease, and if I am wrong it is my own fault. I am under the Earl of Eglinton, and he has never changed any tenants; I was born on the estate and brought up on it. But I know that there is a great deal of land that comes into the market that is very high rented.

Is there great competition for land?—There is.

Can you give me any other reason for men offering more than the fair rent for the farms?—There are many farmers' sons wanting to get land, and if it comes into the market one outbids the other, and if the landlord is inclined to take the highest bidder, he generally lets too dear.

(b) Qs. 37,729–37,739

I think you said that your lease had lately come to an end?—I have just entered upon a new lease.

And then you added afterwards that there was great competition for land in Scotland?—Where it comes to the public market there is, but in estates such as I am on it never has in any time been in the market: the farms were always valued by the factors.

Have you no similar experience in Scotland to what we have very largely in England, that is to say, that there are a number of farms that the proprietor cannot let?—No, not in Ayrshire at all events. I am only speaking of my own district, but that is not known in our district.

Would not the inference be that the agricultural depression is much less in Scotland, or at least in your district, than it is in England?—One would say so. The land is different too. I do not think that a Scotch farmer is a judge of English land, because I went up with a friend who took a farm in England, and I thought it was cheap, but it has turned out otherwise.

I am not asking you to give an opinion about English land, but I am asking you whether, there being a great difficulty in letting farms in England, the same thing happens in Scotland?—It is quite different in Scotland I assure you.

Then, do you consider your prosperity here to be comparatively less affected than the English prosperity?—I think it must be. We are near good markets for butter and cheese.

And meat is a good price?—Mutton is, but warm milk and butter sell at an extremely good price in the west of Scotland, and that keeps up dairy land very much.

Do you conceive that you have been at all affected by the competition of American meat?—I think that cheese would have been at a little higher in price, and I think that meat would have been higher too, a good deal, but for the American competition.

But still the price of meat in Scotland is remunerative at present? —Well, it is fair. Land is too high rented, and it will not pay for feeding cattle. I do not feed cattle, I only grow stock.

But still in taking leases generally are not farmers apprehensive of the growth of foreign competition?—There is no doubt that all arable land that is mostly ploughed is very much affected thereby, and they are afraid of what might come; and the price of wheat and grain that we have must affect the class of land very much; but in the west, where we are dairy farmers, it is different altogether from the east country Lothian farmers, who depend almost altogether upon cropping.

Should you say that there was a difference between the competition for farms in your district where they do not sow wheat and grow meat which are affected by the American competition, and other parts of Scotland where those adverse forces are at work?— I think that there is less competition and less change in the rent in dairy farms than in any other farms in my district.

(6) *Evidence to the Royal Commission on the Depressed Conditions of the Agricultural Interest, 1881.* Evidence of John C. Shepherd, tenant of Glenhornie, North Berwick –

Qs. 36,494-36,503

Do you consider that the importation from abroad of grain and stock has seriously interfered with successful farming in your district?— Decidedly; there is no doubt about it; it keeps the price of grain at the minimum, grain looks as though it would never get beyond the minimum price, because the importations are overwhelming.

In what market does the foreign grain meet the grain which you grow in East Lothian?—This very day I have sold my wheat for

Penrith, and I find that the foreign grain is everywhere. The foreign grain comes to Leith. The east coast used to be the European side, and the west coast used to be the American side, but now the shipments are coming round the whole coast.

Is the American grain landed at Leith or is it landed at Glasgow and then brought across?—I have a son in the corn trade, and he tells me that they had several cargoes in Newcastle the other day, they go round and land there.

Do you keep stock upon your farm?—I do moderately; but chiefly cattle; more cattle than sheep.

Do you breed cattle, or do you purchase them?—I buy them all.

And you feed them off, I suppose?—Yes.

And then send them to market?—Yes, sometimes, but I generally sell them at home, the buyers come round and buy them. My feeding stock at present is about 80 cattle.

Is that your average number for the winter?—My average number would be about 70.

Have you found that the importation of American cattle has interfered with the prices of your cattle that you have been feeding? —That is the great question just now, we cannot complain much as yet, but this importation of American beef is a new thing, it has not been more than two or three years in existence, but if you give it the same time as the grain has had, I have no doubt it will have the same effect and bring things down.

Do you think that the British farmer will be able to compete with the American farmer in future?—No, I think he will have a very poor life of it.

(7) *Evidence to the Royal Commission on Agricultural Depression, 1896*. Evidence of James Drew, factor to the Earl of Galloway – Qs. 53,695 to 53,729

You have been factor on the Galloway estates for the last 30 years?—I have.

What is the acreage of these estates?—80,000 acres.

Comprising what kind of land?—Various classes of land, embracing higher lying sheep walks, and sharp turnip land, with a small quantity of wheat-growing land, and a limited portion devoted to dairying.

What is the present rental?—About 28,000 *l*.

Has that fallen to any considerable extent?—Yes, about 20 per cent.

For the last 16 years you have felt the depression more or less severely?—We have.

To what do you ascribe it?—At first to bad seasons, but gradually to foreign competition. The tendency of prices must be downward while the world's productions continue to exceed the world's requirements.

Have you studied the question of over-production, or are you assuming it?—We see it. This country, which has a vast population compared with its area, is a large purchasing country.

Do you consider that the over-production of the ordinary staples of consumption, such as wheat, is still going on?—I do.

What class of farm has suffered most?—The wheat-growing farms.

The fall in the value of wheat having been greater than in other products?—Yes, it is down practically to zero, and it is now impossible to grow wheat at a profit at present prices.

What other factor has contributed to the depression?—Dull trade, and I think strikes have also affected it. In our part of the country we find that when trade is brisk on the Clyde and in the large manufacturing centres we have an assurance of better prices than when trade is dull.

Because there is an increased power of spending among the artisans?—The power of spending has been seriously crippled by strikes. The last strike in the coal trade in Scotland, which paralysed the coal and iron industries, had a very serious effect on our cheese industries.

Have you any further causes of the depression to point to?—A short time ago we had a very serious fall in the price of sheep and cattle, which we attributed to the inability of the Englishmen to come forward and buy because of the great drought that had taken place, but this year we are very well satisfied with the prices to which stock have risen.

Are they still showing a tendency to rise, or are they stationary?—The tendency is to rise.

Do you attribute that to the decrease of foreign imports?—Partly. The imports of cattle have gone down, and the price of beef has increased, while the price of mutton is everything that could be desired, if it is maintained.

Do ocean freights still keep a low level?—Yes; but I hope that in time the shipowners of the country will not be so thoroughly disinterested as to carry on their trade at a loss. The home producer has also had to incur greater expense in sending his produce to market in the great centres of consumption.

Has that element of cost increased of late years?—I do not think so; but it has been increased in comparison with the cost of ocean freights.

Have the dairy farmers stood the strain comparatively well?—Yes, till this year, when the prospects are not so bright as they have been.

What is the cause of that?—It is owing to the enormous imports of both cheese and butter.

Have they reduced the price of the home-made articles?—Most seriously.

Can your farmers not compete successfully with the foreigners in regard to the quality of the butter?—We make the very best butter. We have the largest creameries in the country, but the fall in butter has been so great that the price of the raw material at the creameries has been reduced almost to vanishing point.

What price do you get for the best butter, as compared with the price of Danish?—I cannot give you the relative prices, but I should think this year the price will be down at least 30 per cent. for the best butter. All that our creameries are offering for milk is 4d per gallon, and it has also to bear the cost of transport.

Have the creameries been a great advantage to the farmer?—They were a considerable advantage at first, but with the enormous fall that has taken place in the price of the raw material the people are beginning to change their views on the subject.

Are they selling more milk?—Our ports being closed to foreign cattle, we are going in more for breeding.

Your farmers are opposed to the introduction of live cattle from abroad?—All our farmers are opposed to it.

Is the breeding of cattle largely on the increase?—Yes.

And with good results?—With very satisfactory results.

Particularly during the present time?—Yes, I speak of the present time.

What has been the fall in rents generally in your part of the country?—I put it at 20 per cent, all over, varying according to the different classes of land.

At the reduction, can farms be easily let?—I have had no difficulty in letting farms.

Is there more land laid down to grass than used to be the case?—We have had no appreciable change in the management, but I am one of those in favour of increasing the area laid down to permanent pasture.

The First World War provided a respite from foreign competition. Afterwards it was anticipated that government support would maintain its prosperity. When prices collapsed suddenly in 1921, and support was needed seriously for the first time, the Agricultural Act of 1920, which had provided its statutory basis, was repealed. Agriculture was once more at the mercy of world food prices until a variety of schemes of aid, most notably in the creation of marketing boards, appeared in the 1930s. After the Second World War a more comprehensive system of subsidy and support was devised chiefly in the Agriculture Act of 1947 and the Agriculture (Scotland) Act, 1948.

C. HIGHLANDS

Rapidly increasing population gave rise to a particularly urgent need for improvement in the Highlands; but lack of natural resources, together with a unique social structure, made the problem almost insoluble. Landowners, especially after 1745, no longer wished their estates to support large numbers of armed men, preferring increased wealth from rising rentals. The role of the tacksman was crucial. Before 1745 his income came from sub-letting at a higher rent land which he himself held on lease (tack) from the chief (usually a close relation), for whom he was also obliged to provide military support. After 1745 he and his function were redundant, and the clansmen were exposed to the direct exploitation of chiefs with new, expensive tastes. By the 1770s, emigration was common.

(1) S. Johnson, *Journey to the Western Islands of Scotland in 1773*. (Oxford Standard Authors edn., pp. 78-79; 85-90) –

(pp. 78-79.) Next in dignity to the Laird is the Tacksman; a large taker or lease-holder of land, of which he keeps part, as a domain, in his own hand, and lets part to under tenants. The Tacksman is necessarily a man capable of securing to the Laird the whole rent, and is commonly a collateral relation. These *tacks*, or subordinate possessions, were long considered as hereditary, and the occupant was distinguished by the name of the place at which he resided. He held a middle station, by which the highest and the lowest orders were connected. He paid rent and reverence to the Laird, and received them from the tenants. This tenure still subsists, with its original operation, but not with the primitive stability. Since the islanders, no longer content to live, have learned the desire of growing rich, an ancient dependent is in danger of giving way to a higher bidder, at the expense of domestick dignity and hereditary power . . .

I have found in the hither parts of *Scotland*, men not defective in judgment or general experience, who consider the Tacksman as a useless burden of the ground, as a drone who lives upon the product of an estate, without the right of property, or the merit of labour, and who impoverishes at once the landlord and the tenant. The land, say they, is let to the Tacksman at sixpence an acre, and by him to the tenant at tenpence. Let the owner be the immediate landlord to all the tenants; if he sets the ground at eight-pence, he will increase his revenue by a fourth part, and the tenant's burthen will be diminished by a fifth.

Those who pursue this train of reasoning, seem not sufficiently to inquire whither it will lead them, not to know that it will equally show the propriety of suppressing all wholesale trade, of shutting up the shops of every man who sells what he does not make, and of extruding all whose agency and profit intervene between the manufacturer and the consumer . . .

To banish the Tacksman is easy, to make a country plentiful by diminishing the people, is an expeditious mode of husbandry; but that abundance, which there is nobody to enjoy, contributes little to human happiness . . .

(pp. 85-90.) The Chiefs, divested of their prerogatives, necessarily turned their thoughts to the improvement of their revenues, and expect more rent, as they have less homage. The tenant, who is far from perceiving that his condition is made better in the same proportion, as that of his landlord is made worse, does not immediately see why his industry is to be taxed more heavily than before. He refuses to pay the demand, and is ejected; the ground is then let to a stranger, who perhaps brings a larger stock, but who, taking the land at its full price, treats with the Laird upon equal terms, and considers him not as a Chief, but as a trafficker in land. Thus the estate perhaps is improved, but the clan is broken.

It seems to be the general opinion, that the rents have been raised with too much eagerness. Some regard must be paid to prejudice. Those who have hitherto paid but little, will not suddenly be persuaded to pay much, though they can afford it. As ground is gradually improved, and the value of money decreases, the rent may be raised without any diminution of the farmer's profits: yet it is necessary in these countries, where the ejection of a tenant is a greater evil, than in more populous places, to consider not merely what the land will produce, but with what ability the inhabitant can cultivate it. A certain stock can allow but a certain payment; for if the land be doubled, and the stock remains the same, the tenant becomes no richer. The proprietors of the Highlands might perhaps often increase their income, by subdividing the farms, and allotting to every occupier only so many acres as he can profitably employ, but that they want people . . .

That causes very different from want of room may produce a general disposition to seek another country is apparent from the present conduct of the Highlanders, who are in some places ready to threaten a total secession. The numbers which have already gone, though like other numbers they may be magnified, are very great, and such as if they had gone together and agreed upon any certain settlement, might have founded an independent government in the depths of the western continent. Nor are they only the lowest and most indigent, many men of considerable wealth have taken with them their train of labourers and dependents; and if they continue the feudal scheme of polity, may establish new clans in the other hemisphere.

That the immediate motives of their desertion must be imputed to their landlords, may be reasonably concluded, because some Lairds of more prudence and less rapacity have kept their vassals undiminished. From *Rassa* only one man had been seduced, and at *Col* there was no wish to go away.

The traveller who comes hither from more opulent countries, to speculate upon the remains of pastoral life, will not much wonder that a common Highlander has no strong adherence to his native soil; for of animal enjoyments, of physical good, he leaves nothing that he may not find again wheresoever he may be thrown.

Social tensions made improvements difficult, and a continued rise in population increased the pressure to emigrate. The introduction of sheep, though defensible economically, reduced the land available for cultivation, causing eviction and resentment. Patrick Sellar was a sheep-farmer, as a tenant in Sutherland and as a landlord in Morvern. His activities, especially in Sutherland, have been severely criticised, but he felt Sutherland gained by his action. In 1820 he explained his views to James Loch, who published his *Account of the Improvements on the Estates of the Marquess of Stafford* in that year.

(2) Thomas Sellar, *The Sutherland Evictions of 1814* (1883). Extract of letter by Patrick Sellar to James Loch, 1st May 1850 –

You desire an account of my own particular progress, and to that I shall confine myself; but I cannot help mentioning a circumstance, which you will scarcely believe of a man who now farms a good many thousand sheep feeding in districts lately occupied by inhabitants; and that is, that I came to their country full of the belief that the growth of wool and sheep in the highlands of Scotland was one of the most abominable and detestable things possible to be imagined. The report of the Highland clergyman, in Sir John Sinclair's Book of Statistics, the essays written in the periodical publications, and the general assertion of every Highland gentleman whom one met with in the low country, and of every low-country man who had ever been in the Highlands, convinced my mind, as it did that of others who possessed similar means of forming their judgement, that the inroads then making on the ancient habits and manners of the children of the Gael were cruel and impolitic in the extreme.

Before I had been one or two years in Sutherland I explored the interior of the country. I found it to consist of extensive tracts of great bog,—broken into mountains, and rocks, and wild scenery, and interspersed here and there with patches of land, under imperfect tillage, near the river banks. Each patch, or haugh, or field, was surrounded by a country of bog, the exhalations raised by the sun from which were condensed during the night on the crops attempted to be grown, which during four years out of six, were mildewed and destroyed. I found an infinity of fine Alpine pasturage, which, by reasons of the softness of the bog or the inaccessible nature of the ground, the cattle of the Highlanders never cropped. I found that, while the cotton grass was in spring flowering with great luxuriance and fading untouched, the cattle were dying by scores. One gentleman, Captain Matthieson of Shiness lost two hundred, I think, in one spring, and Colonel Sutherland of Culmaily buried, the first year I came to Sutherland, eighteen milk cows and a bull in one hole or ravine.

Moreover, the inhabitants of the hills were fed every second or third year with meal imported by the proprietors from other countries, and all this misery was endured, in contending, in a country so situated, against nature. Countless myriads of herrings, cod, ling, etc., at the same time were swimming around the coast, and in every creek and bay of it, untouched. Why? Because the people in the interior remained in misery there, preventing it from being possible to apply its pasturage to any useful purpose; and those on the shores were sub-tenants of gentlemen whose style of education and pursuits through life made them quite indifferent to the treasures spread out before them.

On inspecting the grounds possessed by Atkinson and Marshall, the new stock-farmers, and comparing the condition of these with that of the ground, pared for turf, etc., in the occupation of the inhabitants; and on viewing the condition of the plants, trees and living creatures on the former farm, and contrasting it with the filth of the native huts, and the lean and miserable condition of every horse, cow, and sheep possessed by them, I was at once a convert to the principle now almost universally acted on in the Highlands of Scotland—viz., that the people should be employed in securing the natural riches of the sea-coast; that the mildew of the interior should be allowed to fall upon grass, and not upon corn; and that several hundred miles of Alpine plants, flourishing in these districts in curious succession at all seasons, and out of the reach of anything but sheep, should be converted into wool and mutton for the English manufacturer.

Let any person, I don't care who he be, or what his prejudices are, view the inside of the new fishermen's stone cots in Loth—the man and his wife and young children weaving their nets around the winter fire—let him contrast it with the sloth, and poverty, and filth, and sheep of an unremoved tenant's turf hut in the interior. Let him inspect the people, stock, cattle, horses, trees, and plants, in a stock-farmers' possession, and compare them with the pared bottom from which turf in all ages had been taken—with the closely cropped roots of grass, and bushes, and miserable 'lazy-bed' culture that surround a Highlander's cabin,—with the starved kyloes, and scabbed ponies and sheep that stagger about his place, picking up half an existence; and let him believe, if he can, that men are injured by civilization, and that during the last ten years, a most important benefit has not been conferred on this country.

There was no easy solution to the problem of rising population in an area of limited natural endowments. Some thought emigration could be avoided (3); others favoured it (4); others doubted the gravity of the problem (5).

(3) Thomas Telford, *Survey and Reports of the Coasts and Central Highlands of Scotland in Autumn of 1802*, pp. 15-17, In *Reports of the Select Committee on the Survey of the Central Highlands of Scotland*, Parliamentary Papers, 1802-3, IV –

That Emigrations have already taken place from various Parts of the Highlands, is a Fact upon which there does not remain room to doubt; from the best Information I have been able to procure, about Three Thousand Persons went away in the Course of last Year, and, if I am rightly informed, Three Times that Number are preparing to leave the Country in the present Year.

I shall not encroach upon Your Lordships' Time by investigating all the remote or unimportant collateral Causes of Emigration, but shall proceed to that which I consider to be the most powerful in its present Operation; and that is, converting large Districts of the Country into extensive Sheepwalks. This not only requires much fewer People to manage the same Track of Country, but in general an entirely new People, who have been accustomed to this Mode of Life, are brought from the Southern Parts of Scotland.

The Difference of Rents to the Landlords between Sheep and Black Cattle is, I understand, at least Three to One, and yet on Account of the extraordinary Rise in the Prices of Sheep and Wool, the Sheep Farmers have of late Years been acquiring Wealth. As the introducing Sheep Farms over Countries heretofore stocked with Black Cattle, creates an extensive Demand for the young Sheep from the established Farms, it is possible that the high Prices may continue until a considerable Portion of the Country is fully stocked; after this takes place, the Quantities of Sheep produced will bear a very great Proportion to the Demand, and then it is possible the Prices may fall below the average Value; in this Case it is probable the Farms will be subdivided, and a Proportion of Black Cattle and Cultivation be introduced in the lower Grounds in the Vallies, while the upper Parts of the Hills continue to be pastured with

Sheep. This I consider as the most improved State of Highland Farming, and is consistent with a very considerable Population; a beautiful Instance of this is to be seen along the North Side of Loch Tay. But improved Communications, by means of Roads and Bridges, are necessary for this State of Society, and for this Reason I have said, that if these Conveniences had been sooner introduced into the Highlands, it is possible this Emigration might not have taken place, at least to the present Extent.

The very high Price of Black Cattle has also facilitated the Means of Emigration, as it has furnished the old Farmers with a Portion of Capital which enabled them to transport their Families beyond the Atlantic.

In some Cases a greater Population than the Land can support in any Shape, has been the Cause of Emigration; such was the Island of Tiree.

Some have, no doubt, been deluded by Accounts sent back from others gone before them; and many deceived by artful Persons, who hesitate not to sacrifice these poor ignorant People to selfish Ends.

A very principal Reason must also be, that the People, when turned out of their Black Cattle Farms to make way for the Sheep Farmers, see no Mode of Employment whereby they can earn a Subsistence in their own Country, and sooner than seek it in the Low Lands of Scotland, or in England, they will believe what is told them may be done in the Farming Line in America.

What I have here mentioned appear to me to be the immediate Causes of the present Emigrations from the North Western Parts of Scotland. To point out the Means of preventing Emigrations in future, is a Part of my Duty, upon which I enter with no small Degree of Hesitation. As the Evil at present seems to arise chiefly from the Conduct of Landowners, in changing the Economy of their Estates, it may be questioned whether Government can with Justice interfere, or whether any essential Benefits are likely to arise from this Interference.

In one point of View it may be stated, that, taking the mountainous Parts of Scotland as a District of the British Empire, it is the Interest of the Empire that this District be made to produce as much human Food as it is capable of doing at the least possible Expence; that this may be done by stocking it chiefly with Sheep; that it is the Interest of the Empire the Food so produced, should not be consumed by Persons residing amongst the Mountains totally unemployed, but rather in some other Parts of the Country, where their Labour can be made productive either in the Business of Agriculture, Fisheries or Manufactures; and that by suffering every person to pursue what appears to them to be their own Interest, that although some temporary Inconveniences may arise, yet, upon the Whole, that Matters will in the End adjust themselves into the Forms most suitable for the Place.

In another point of View it may be stated, that it is a great Hardship, if not a great Injustice, that the Inhabitants of an extensive District should all at once be driven from their native Country, to make way for sheep Farming, which is likely to be carried to an imprudent Extent; that, in a few Years, this Excess will be evident; that before it is discovered, the Country will be depopulated, and that Race of People which has of late years maintained so honourable a Share in the Operations of our Armies and Navies will then be no more; that in a Case where such a numerous Body of the People are deeply interested, it is the Duty of Government to consider it as an extraordinary Case, and one of those Occasions which justifies them in departing a little from the Maxims of general Policy; that for this Purpose Regulations should be made to prevent Landowners from lessening the Population upon their Estates below a given Proportion, and that some Regulation of this Sort would in the End be in favour of the Landowners, as it would preserve the Population best suited to the most improved Mode of Highland Farming, such as is practised at Breadalbane, and to the Establishment of Fishing Villages, on the Principle laid down and practised so successfully by Mr. Hugh Stevenson of Oban, at Arnisdale on Loch Hourn.

In whatever Light the foregoing Statements may be viewed, there is another on which there can, I think, be no Difference of Opinion. This is, that if there are any public Works to be executed, which, when completed, will prove generally beneficial to the Country, it is advisable these Works should be undertaken at the present Time. This would furnish Employment for the industrious and valuable Part of the People in their own Country, they would by this Means be accustomed to Labour, they would acquire some Capital, and the Foundations would be laid for future Employments. If, as I have been credibly informed, the Inhabitants are strongly attached to their native Country, they would greedily embrace this Opportunity of being enabled to remain in it, with the Prospect of bettering their Condition, because, before the Works were completed, it must be evident to every one that the whole Face of the Country would be changed.

The Caledonian Canal, and the Bridges and Roads before mentioned, are of the Description here alluded to, they will not only furnish present Employment, but promise to accomplish all the leading Objects which can reasonably be looked forward to for the Improvement and future Welfare of the Country, whether we regard its Agriculture, Fisheries, or Manufactures.

(4) 5th Earl of Selkirk, *Observations of the present state of the Highlands of Scotland with a view of the causes and probable consequences of emigration* (1805) pp. 39-50 –

In consequence of the extensive distribution of landed possessions arising from the feudal manners, combined with the small progess that has been made in the arts of life and division of labour, the people of the Highlands are not separated into distinct classes of farmers, labourers, and mechanics: they are all more or less engaged in agriculture. There are no markets where provisions can be purchased, so that every man must be a farmer, at least so far as to raise provisions for his own family. Whatever additional employment a man may follow, he must occupy a small spot of land; and any one who cannot procure such a possession, cannot live in the country.

The farms occupied by the common tenantry, are hamlets or petty townships, held by six or eight partners, sometimes by many more. The shares appear to have been originally equal; but by the subdivision of some, and the accumulation, in other cases, of several in the same hand, it is now frequently found that one man has a third or a fourth part of a farm, while his neighbour has but a fifteenth or a twentieth part.

These farms consist, in general, of a portion of a valley, to which is annexed a tract of mountain pasture, often stretching to the distance of many miles. The habitations are collected in a little village, in the midst of the richest and best of the arable lands, which are used as *crofts* in constant tillage. The less fertile of the arable lands on the outskirts, termed *outfield* are only occasionally cultivated, and every part of them is in its turn left in grass. The lands in tillage, are sometimes cultivated in common, but are more usually distributed among the tenants in proportion to their shares: seldom, however, in a permanent manner, but from year to year. The produce of the tillage land rarely affords a superfluity beyond the maintenance of the tenants and their families. Their riches consist of cattle, chiefly breeding cows, and the young stock produced from them, which are maintained on the farm till of a proper age for the market; and by the sale of these the tenants are enabled to pay their rent. The number which each farm or *toun* is capable of maintaining, is ascertained by ancient usage, and may be, in general, from thirty to eighty cows, besides other cattle. The total amount is divided among the occupiers according to their respective shares, no one being allowed to keep more than his regulated proportion.

The joint occupiers of such farms are termed *small tenants*, to distinguish them from the *tacksmen*, who hold entire farms, and who are in general of the rank of gentry, each of them tracing himself to some ancient proprietor of the estate, who has allotted the farm as a provision for a cadet of his family.

Upon the farms of the tacksmen, are a number of subtenants or *cotters*, under which general term may be included various denominations of *crofters*, *mailers*, etc. etc. These people hold their possessions under various conditions: sometimes they differ from the tenants in little else than the diminutive scale of their possessions; but in general they have a greater or less amount of labour to perform as a part of their rent. Frequently they are absolute servants to their immediate superior, having the command only of a small share of their own time to cultivate the land allowed them for maintaining their families. Sometimes the tacksman allows a portion of his own tillage field for his cotter; sometimes a small separate croft is laid off for him; and he is likewise allowed, in general, to pasture a cow, or perhaps two, along with the cattle of the farm.

Cotters are not confined to the farms of the tacksmen—they are also intermixed with the small tenants. Two or three are generally employed on every farm, as servants of the whole partnership, for herding their cattle, or preventing the trespasses of others. There are also a few people who exercise the trades of black-smiths, weavers, taylors, shoemakers, etc. and who bargain with one or other of the tenants for a portion of his land. Sometimes persons who have been dispossessed of their own farms, and are unable to procure a share of one elsewhere, will secure a temporary residence in the country by taking *subsets* of this kind: sometimes individuals, connected by relationship with the tenants of a farm, and who have no other resource, are permitted, from mere charity, to occupy some corner of waste land, where, by raising crops of potatoes, they contrive to work out a miserable subsistence.

It may be easily conceived, that the line between these two classes, the small tenants and the cotters, is not always very accurately defined; some of the more opulent of the cotters being as well provided as the lowest of the tenants. Upon the whole, however, there is a great difference in the amount of their property, and in the views they may entertain, when, by the progress of sheep-farming, they are dispossessed of their tenements. Among the more opulent, it is not uncommon for one man to have twelve, fifteen, or even twenty cows; but in general the small tenant, according to his share of the farm, may have from three to four, to six or eight cows, and always with a proportionate number of young cattle. He has also horses, a few small sheep, implements of agriculture, and various household articles to dispose of; and, from the sale of all these he is enabled to embark in undertakings which cannot be thought of by the cotter, and which are not within the reach of the peasantry even in the more improved and richer parts of the kingdom.

There the labouring poor, though earning very considerable wages, are seldom possessed of much permanent property. Their daily or weekly wages are expended in the market as fast as they arise, for the immediate supply of their families. In the Highlands, there are few of the lower class who have the means of living nearly so well as an English labourer, but many who have property of much greater value. In the Agricultural Survey of the Northern Counties, details are given of the œconomy of a farmer of about 30 acres of arable land, whose diet and habitation appear to be of the lowest kind, the total value of his buildings not exceeding 10 *l.*, and the annual consumption of provisions for his own family and three *servants* amounting to about 15 *l.*; yet his capital is estimated at 116 *l.*; and by the advance in the price of cattle since the date of that publication, it must now be considerably more.

Of this description of people it has often happened that 30 or 40 families have been dispossessed all at once, to make way for a great sheep-farm:—and those who have attended to the preceding details will easily understand the dilemma to which everyone of these people must be reduced. The country affords no means of living without a possession of land, and how is that to be procured? The farms that are not already in the hands of the graziers, are all full of inhabitants, themselves perhaps in dread of the same fate, and at any rate too crowded to make room for him. Should he, in spite of every difficulty, resolve to earn his bread as a labourer, he can expect no employment in a neighbourhood, where every spot is occupied by many more people than are necessary for its own work; and if any casual opportunity of employment occur, it is too uncertain to be depended upon. Let his industrious dispositions be ever so great, he must, in the total want of manufacturing employment in his own neighbourhood, quit his native spot; and, if he do not leave the kingdom altogether, must resort to some of those situations where the increasing demand for labour affords a prospect of employment.

When a great number are dispossessed at once, and the land is to be applied to purposes that afford little or no employment, as in a sheep-walk, the conclusion is so evident as to require no illustration: but the case is not essentially altered when these people are dismissed in a gradual and continued progress one after another. In this way, indeed, the circumstance does not excite so much attention; but the effects on the state of the country are the same: and to the individual who is dispossessed, it makes no other difference than that he has fewer companions to share his misfortune. It is equally impossible for him to find resources in his native spot, and he is equally under the necessity of removing to a different situation.

Sheep-farming, though it is the most prominent occasion, is not the radical cause of the difficulties to which the peasantry of the Highlands are reduced: the disposition to extend farms by throwing several possessions into one, in the manner that has already been alluded to, must produce the same effect, in whatever mode the land is afterwards to be managed.

To the dispossessed tenantry, as well as to the cotters, who by the same progress of things are deprived of their situation and livelihood, two different resources present themselves. They know that in the Low Country of Scotland, and particularly in the manufacturing towns, labour will procure them good wages: they know likewise that in America the wages of labour are still higher, and that from the moderate price of land they may expect to obtain not only the possession of a farm, but an absolute property.

Of these alternatives, every one who is acquainted with the country must admit that Emigration is by far the most likely to suit the inclination and habits of the Highlanders. It requires a great momentary effort; but holds out a speedy prospect of a situation and mode of life similar to that in which they have been educated. Accustomed to possess land, to derive from it all the comforts they enjoy, they naturally consider it as indispensable, and can form no ideas of happiness without such a possession. No prospect of an accommodation of this kind can enter into the views of any one who seeks for employment as a day labourer, still less of those who resort to a manufacturing town.

The manners of a town, the practise of sedentary labour under the roof of a manufactory, present to the Highlander a most irksome contrast to his former life. The independence and irregularity to which he is accustomed, approach to that of the savage: his activity is occasionally called forth to the utmost stretch in conducting his boat through boisterous waves, or in traversing the wildest mountains amidst the storms of winter. But these efforts are succeeded by intervals of indolence equally extreme. He is accustomed to occasional exertions of agricultural labour, but without any habits of regular and steady industry; and he has not the least experience of sedentary employments, for which, most frequently, the prejudices of his infancy have taught him to entertain a contempt.

To a person of such habits, the business of a manufactory can have no attraction except in a case of necessity; it can never be his choice, when any resources can be found more congenial to his native habits and disposition. The occupations of an agricultural labourer, though very different, would not be so great a contrast to his former life; but the limited demand for labour leaves him little prospect of employment in this line. Both in this, and in manufacturing establishments, every desirable situation is pre-occupied by men of such greater skill than the untutored Highlander. He has therefore little chance of finding employment but in works of the lowest drudgery.

To this it is to be added, that the situation of a mere day-labourer, is one which must appear degrading to a person who has been accustomed to consider himself as in the rank of a farmer, and has been the possessor even of a small portion of land. In America, on the contrary, he has a prospect of superior rank; of holding his land on a permanent tenure, instead of a temporary, precarious, and dependent possession. It is not to be forgotten, that every motive of this nature has a peculiar degree of force on the minds of the Highland Peasantry. The pride, which formerly pervaded even the lowest classes, has always been a prominent feature of their national character: and this feeling is deeply wounded by the distant behaviour they now experience from their chieftains—a mortifying contrast to the cordiality that subsisted in the feudal times.

(5) R. Heron, *Observations made in a Journey through the Western Counties of Scotland (1792)* (1799), vol. i, pp. 246-252 –

Black cattle form still perhaps too considerable a part of the live-stock kept by the farmers in this neighbourhood. They are sold off, at certain ages to drovers from the Low Country of Scotland and from England; or perhaps driven to the cattle markets in Scotland and England by dealers from the country where they are bred. The prices vary with age, size, shape, season, and various other circumstances.

Managers of sheep from Clydesdale, and other southern countries, have, within these last ten or twelve years, begun to resort eagerly to the Highlands. They have obtained, in many places, long leases from the proprietors of the lands, in these parts . . . at rents much higher than were before paid for the same farms, . . . such as no Highlandman could pay, by the old practise of farming, . . . yet, such as these alien shepherds have, by their modes of managing livestock, been enabled to pay, and at the same time, to enrich themselves. Stocking their farms with sheep, instead of black cattle, smearing, feeding, and changing their flocks of sheep, in a manner peculiar to themselves, and unknown to the old Highland farmers; and selling them off at the best markets: They have thus been enabled to make seemingly unimproveable heaths and hills, afford a much greater proportion of subsistence for human life, than was before obtained from them. These improvers, however, and the landlords whose grounds they have rented, have become on this score unpopular in the Highlands. The prejudices of clanship have almost died away: Yet the Highlanders think it hard that a Highland Gentleman should let his lands to a stranger, in preference to one of themselves, even when tempted by the offer of higher rent. When excluded too from this, the only species of industry of which he is capable, a Highlandman has no other shift to follow, but to leave the country. He cannot prevail with himself to imitate in the management of his farm the practice of strangers. He cannot live upon it, if he manages it no better than formerly. There is no trade or manufacture to which the old farmer can turn himself. He leaves the place. And his friends who remain, complain, that the country is depopulated by the avarice of the landholders, and the intrusion of strangers.

By insensible degrees, however, the Highland farmers learn to imitate the practices of those strangers whom they see acquire opulence where they themselves can barely subsist. They find the same management which enriches strangers, succeed with themselves. The proprietors of the lands retain still so much of the old clanish spirit, that when a Highlander will pay the same rent for a farm as a Lowlander, the Highlander is always preferred. Nay at the expiration of a Lowlander's lease, if the landlord can possibly find a Highlander to manage the farm upon the same principles, and pay nearly the same rent; the Lowlander is sure to be dismissed. So that, the lower Highlanders have little reason to complain of any unreasonable partiality in their landlords for stranger tenants. Nay, a farmer from the Low Country is apt, not without cause, to think himself extremely ill used, when, after having taught the Highlanders the art of enriching themselves, he is immediately dismissed with contempt.

One ground of complaint, however, still remains. It is asserted that many fewer families are maintained upon those farms in the Highlands which have been turned into sheep-walks, than they afforded subsistence to, in their former more cultivated state. This idea has gone out through the whole kingdom: and I have met with many otherwise intelligent and enlightened men who were, in this view, unfriendly to such a mode of improving the Highlands.

Yet none surely but superficial thinkers, can sit down in the belief, that any species of management which renders a country more productive, can be, in the whole, injurious to it.

It may have been hastily alledged, but has never been proved, or even coolly asserted, that the population of the whole island is diminished with the population of the Highlands of Scotland. The contrary is the true fact. Our population has increased in other parts of the kingdom, in a much larger proportion than that in which it may be pretended to have here declined. The nation has been, as it were, contracting its relaxed forces, with an energetic effort, into the centre; from which it will soon expand them with new vigour. In places peculiarly favourable to trade, to manufacturers and agriculture, and enjoying, at the same time perhaps some accidental advantages, not reaching to these regions,—population has rapidly increased within the present century. The prosperity of those places, will, by degrees, raise the price of labour and of provisions, and diminish their industry, and impair their healthiness,—so as to give such parts of the kingdom which are now, in some sort, deserted and neglected, comparative advantages that will attract to them no scanty share of the population and opulence which they must till then want.—Thus have population, wealth, and industry been always spread, gradually over every country. Berwickshire was the first seat of improved agriculture in Scotland: Had not the tillage and crops of Berwickshire been eagerly adopted in several of the other more improveable counties in Scotland, it might have by degrees attracted as great a crowd of the husbandmen of Scotland, as it could well contain. The silk-manufacture originally established in Spittalfields, came at length to be tried also at Paisley, Halifax, and other places through Britain. The cotton-manufacture came from England to Scotland; and from those manufacturing towns in Scotland, in which it was first tried, is fast finding its way over the whole country. Only introduce trade and industry into a country: cherish them where they have first fixed themselves, without adding to the natural disadvantages of other places: They will, by degrees, diffuse themselves, more or less, over the country. Nor will their progress leave them less energy in their primary feats. The richest districts of a kingdom will ever attract population, to the disadvantage of the rest: But the heaped up fluid soon returns to its level.

Meanwhile, it is unreasonable to complain of the present depopulation of the Highlands of Scotland. It is much more inconsiderable than has been said. Those who are induced to leave the Highlands, find employment elsewhere, without being obliged to forsake their country. By those modes of managing the lands, which are complained of as depopulating, maintenance is obtained from them for a much greater number of mankind, than they could before maintain. And, all this maintenance is either consumed within the kingdom, or at least exchanged for commodities equally necessary, which are consumed within it. The natural course of human affairs, and the exertions of individuals, and of associated bodies, directed to this particular purpose will shortly be seen to restore to the Highlands, that population which they may seem to have lost.

Perhaps the major problem in the highlands was that additional means of subsistence had to be found for the growing population, especially when they were cleared from their traditional holdings, inadequate as they were. The expansion of the fisheries was a solution frequently advocated.

(6) John Knox, *Observations on the Northern Fisheries* (1786), pp. 149-150 –

Between the north point of Arran and the Firth of Dornoch, there are, upon the coast of the main-land and the islands, above two hundred lakes, bays, and openings, all of which are fishing grounds, and where ships may safely ride.

To put these extensive and valuable shores in a situation for prosecuting the fisheries effectually, and at all seasons of the year, FORTY fishing stations, or small towns, will be necessary, *in the first instance*: being only one station for every twenty-five thousand people, who reside on that coast, besides those who inhabit the interior country, the younger part of whom could soon become regular fishers.

For facilitating the growth of towns, accommodating the great body of the people with materials for the fisheries, and instructing others in the mechanical arts, a house will be required for each of the following professions, viz.—A boat-builder, cooper, net-maker, tanner, blacksmith, mason, house-carpenter, weaver, taylor, shoemaker, and tallow-chandler.

Also for a general dealer in meal, grain, fishing materials and stores, salt, timber, staves, hoops, pitch, tar, oil, and a great variety of other articles, which the fishers and the country people have at present no means of procuring, upon easy terms or when immediately wanted.

A public house or small inn, accommodated with beds for the conveniency of strangers, who may come thither to buy and sell, will be particularly necessary; and we hope, likewise, that a house will be deemed requisite for a school-master, and for an apothecary or surgeon.

The whole number will comprise sixteen houses, which, excepting those for the trader and inn-keeper, may be built upon one scale or plan of architecture, with stone, lime and slate; each house having two apartments on the ground, with stone-flooring; and two apartments above. The houses for the trader and inn-keeper should be more capacious, and accommodated with back-rooms for holding bulky articles. But, upon the whole, these sixteen buildings may be raised, in a country where materials (timber excepted) are plentiful, and where wages are low, at 80 *l.* each, of 1,280 *l.* for the whole.

As all the lakes and bays of the Highlands are more or less the receptacles of white fish, shell-fish, salmon, mackerel, and occasionally visited by the migrating shoals of herring, there ought to be a number of stationary, practical fishers in each town, at their first establishment, for whose accommodation twenty small houses should be built, with two apartments on the ground, at about 25 *l.* each: in all 500 *l.*

GENERAL ACCOUNT, VIZ.

Sixteen dwelling-houses to each town.	£80	1280
Twenty " "	25	500
A public well, paving, and other incidental expences		220
Expenditure on each town of 36 houses		2000
Number of towns		40
Total expence for building 40 towns, containing 640 houses, at 80 *l.* each; and 800 do. at 25 *l.* in all 1440 houses.		£80,000

The British Fisheries Society was incorporated in 1786 to build fishing stations in the Highlands and Islands. Little permanent success attended its efforts except at Pultneytown, now part of Wick.

(7) 26 Geo. III, c. 106 (1786). An Act for incorporating certain Persons therein named, by the Name and Stile of *The British Society for extending the Fisheries, and improving the Sea Coasts of this Kingdom*; and to enable them, when incorporated, to subscribe a Joint Stock, and therewith to purchase lands, and build thereon Free Towns, Villages, and Fishing Stations in the Highlands and Islands in that Part of *Great Britain called Scotland* . . . –

Whereas the building of Free Towns, Villages, Harbours, Quays, Piers, and Fishing Stations, in the Highlands and Islands of *North Britain*, will greatly contribute to the Improvement of Fisheries, Agriculture, Manufactures, and other useful Objects of Industry in that Part of the Kingdom, in which the dispersed Situations of the Inhabitants hath hitherto proved a great Impediment to their active Exertions; and their being collected into Fishing Towns and Villages would be the Means of forming a Nursery of hardy Seamen for his Majesty's Navy, and the Defence of the Kingdom: And whereas the finding immediate Employment at Home for great Numbers of People, would be the means of putting a Stop to the dangerous Spirit of Emigration now prevailing, and likely to prevail in a great Degree, to the Depopulation of that Part of his Majesty's Dominions, and Loss to the Kingdom of many of his Majesty's useful Subjects; And whereas an Undertaking for those laudable Purposes cannot be so conveniently or effectually carried on unless a considerable Joint Stock be raised for the Purpose: And whereas several Persons have already formed themselves into a Society, and subscribed considerable Sums for carrying the Purpose above mentioned into Execution, but are apprehensive that Difficulties may arise, as well in recovering Debts which may grow due to the Joint Stock, as in defending Suits or Actions which may be commenced or brought against the Subscribers for any Matter or Thing relative to the Joint Society, as by Law all the several Subscribers and Proprietors in the Joint Society must, in such Cases, both sue and be sued, implead and be impleaded, by their several distinct Names and Descriptions, and to prevent the several Subscribers from becoming liable to the Payment of any Sum or Sums beyond their respective Shares in such Capital Joint Stock; therefore, for the more easily carrying into Execution the several Undertakings herein before mentioned, and for avoiding the Difficulties aforesaid, the said Society are desirous of being incorporated, and having a Common Seal and Name, by which they may sue and be sued, implead and be impleaded.

The uncertainties of fishing made it an insecure source of supplementary cash income. The expectations of the late eighteenth century (8) were not fulfilled fifty years later. Traditional markets collapsed and a long struggle to obtain new and stable markets began (9).

(8) P. White, *Observations upon the Present State of the Scotch Fisheries* (1791), pp. 46–54 –

We now proceed to state . . . the present posture of the Fishery for herrings upon the coasts of the West Highlands; . . . It appears that the inhabitants of the town of Stornoway in the Island of Lewis (a property of the Seaforth family) have, with great industry and perseverance, followed the fishing ever since the union of the two kingdoms, and with exemplary success. Their ancestors followed this business from very early times, of which there are sufficient monuments remaining: but it was after the Union that the merchants in Stornoway had full scope for their laudable pursuits: then it was, that the herrings which they caught, might lawfully be sent to the British West-India Islands, and be exported thither, and to all other lawful places, attended with the encouragement of a bounty: from that time, the people of Stornoway have been gradually advancing. Some twenty-five or thirty years ago, all the fish they caught were carried for them to their port of destination by hired vessels. Now they can show in their harbour, in the fishing time, upwards of thirty sail of stout handsome vessels, from twenty to seventy tons burden, all their own property. Their town is a pattern of neatness and cleanliness; and when a stranger enters their convenient mansions, he will have set before him a piece of well-dressed Highland mutton, some choice fish and a bottle of port, the produce of the hospitable landlord's industry. To the everlasting credit of these industrious fishers and merchants, it falls to be recorded, that they have made their pleasant hamlet rise into view, and display upwards of a hundred slated houses, besides inferior ones, from their gain from the sea . . . Thus Stornoway stood alone for a long period, as the only fishing station upon that part of the coast: But in the year 1776, certain merchants from Liverpool and the Isle of Man, began to erect houses at the Isle Martin in Lochbroom, in the county of Ross, and at Loch-Inver in the county of Sutherland, for curing herrings after the Yarmouth way; that is, smoking them into red herrings: At the same time, a customhouse with proper officers, was established at Ullapool, two miles from the first mentioned place. Five or six years afterwards, some merchants at Inverness erected houses for the like purpose at Gairloch in Ross-shire, and also shedes [sheds], and other convenient houses for curing cod, which are caught in great numbers upon a bank which begins at the mouth of that loch; and five years ago, a merchant in Stornoway, with some partners in London, erected considerable buildings upon the Island Tavrera, a small holm upon the coast of the Cromarty estate in Wester Ross, about eight miles from the new village of Ullapool . . . The most considerable fishing upon all the coasts of Britain, for cod and ling, is in the neighbourhood of these islands, viz. upon that ground called the Mother Bank. This Bank runs between the Island of Mull on the east, and Barra and South Uist on the west. The best fishing is off Barra-head, whither a number of vessels resort every season. The merchants of Peterhead, and some people at Aberdeen, have made considerable profit of this fishing. The people in Cambeltown and Rothsay, and in the Clyde, rather prefer fishing for herrings than for cod, etc; whereas on the East coast they prefer the white fishing. The reason for the conduct of each are plain, viz. in the Clyde and other places in the west, the demand for herrings, owing to their West India trade, is brisker than for white fish; while, upon the East coast, where there is no American trade, it is *vice versa*. The salmon fishing upon the West coast is of no great consequence: this is owing to the short run of their rivers. There may be some of that fish caught in the river Nith, and in the Solway, and at Air; but they are no considerable object.

(9) J. Thomson, *The Value and Importance of the Scottish Fisheries* (1849), pp. 135-139 –

The prosperous condition of the herring fishery is undoubtedly impeded by the supply being greater than the demand . . . The first great change affecting the demand was undoubtedly the loss of the trade with our West India possessions. This most desirable and profitable outlet was shut against the fishery by the Act of slave emancipation in the year 1833. Although it is not likely that remonstrance would have been productive of relief, yet little or none was made at the time. This was the more remarkable, as the loss of consumption fell on a quality of fish not probably so easily otherwise disposed of. The West India market was supplied annually with about 60,000 barrels, principally made up of the quality of fish known by the 'spent' or 'shotten' herring, or more plainly described as the herring after it has spawned. The large blank thus occasioned still continues: and till within a year or two of the non-existence of the trade, twenty shillings per barrel on the spot was looked to as an average price, satisfactory to all parties.

The island of Jamaica had always been the chief mart, and several trials of the business continued to be made after the emancipation, but without that result which at the cost of production could be held as remunerative. The negroes have been inclined to lay out their wages on a better description of food. English hams have had the preference to salted fish. What of the latter is consumed is imported principally from their neighbours, the Americans. With the United

States there is a considerable traffic in barter between fish, sugar and molasses. This loss of demand has been a heavy drawback on the British curing interest. Breaking the chains of slavery must, however, be allowed to be in exact accordance with those principles of freedom, in carrying out which, Britain boasts, and justly so, of having taken the lead. In the next view of regretted change acting injuriously on demand, our sister island must be brought but too prominently on the canvas. Ireland has for years been unhappy in herself. Her rich resources have latterly become more and more paralyzed. It could not then be matter of surprise that her commercial relations with the coast of Scotland should by degrees suffer diminution.

It could not be expected that the food which the Irish formerly so largely took from us, and for which they liberally paid, should meet the fate of other articles of commerce. The trade in salted herrings has been much lessened, both in its amount of import and in the money value which the mass of the population could afford to pay. Ireland was wont to be freely a customer for 100,000 barrels, and quotations from her markets ruled from 23s. to 25s. per barrel; a value at which a remunerative trade to Scotland could be carried on. This is now altogether altered. The disease which has devastated vast tracts of potato culture has pressed severely on the consumption of salted fish; and the Indian corn which, on its first introduction into Ireland was not much relished, has latterly become by use more agreeable to the appetite. This circumstance may continue to work unfavourably on the eating of salted provisions.

Notwithstanding the signal failure of these two great supports of Scottish industry, our herring fishery, in the gross quantity taken, has been on the increase. This increase has been taken off by home consumption; and this in by far the greater part in the quality of ungutted herrings. These are with a small exception manufactured into red . . . On this trade there has probably been a profit, indeed the support of the fishery must have sprung from the consumption in Britain; had it not been that from this source some return for labour and capital had been experienced, it is impossible that the increase of supply could have gone on. Our foreign trade with Northern Germany has advanced: but the question is, has it done so profitably for this country? To this must be given a decided negative . . . Taking it for granted that the intrinsic value of a barrel of bung-packed full herrings, in proportion to that of other food, in the curer's yard ready for shipment is 18s. per barrel, it can be imagined that the trade is carried on at a discount greater than it can long bear, when it is stated that many of the returns made from Stettin, in the past season, have been from 13s., 14s. and 15s. per barrel. The loss on the foreign trade at stations from Peterhead to Wick both inclusive, must, in the past season of 1848, have been most severe on many. A gross sum of £20,000 loss is considerably under the mark. As to Ireland, so low have her markets been that 18s. per barrel ex store when landed, has been an average price, with freight and charges deducted, giving a nett return of 13s. and 14s. per barrel.

Only the introduction of the potato, with its high yield and easy cultivation, allowed the increasing population of the Highlands to eke out an existence. It was always precarious.

(10) Scottish Record Office. Seaforth Manuscripts. Letter from W. McGregor to J. M. Stewart Mackenzie, 28th February 1832 –

I am sorry to say, when I examined their Houses that I find the one half of the people from Caroloway to Eoropie are ill for want of Blankets as the few I mentioned in the List, so that it is impossible to supply their wants. In the most of their houses, there is nothing in the shape of bedding to be seen excepting one old Blanket and an old Covering, and 5 or 6 of a Family lying under that in one Bed, and some of them have none at all, but the generality of them might have been better off if they had an inclination to be so; they were ever careless regarding any sort of Cleanliness, so that it is to be feared if the Cholera comes among us that it will make a sad sweeping on this Coast, so far from Medical aid or any other assistance, but the Lord is merciful and may show his kindness to the poor people here and not visit them with such an awful Visitation.

We had some meetings in the Parish for the purpose of promoting Cleanliness among the people. We got them all to build partitions between themselves and the Cattle.

When the potato crops failed in the 1840s, there was widespread destitution. Emigration was inevitable.

(11) Letter from the Rev. N. McKinnon to Rev. Dr. Norman Mcleod. Reprinted in *Extracts from Letters to the Rev. Dr. Mcleod, Glasgow, regarding the famine and destitution in the Highlands and Islands of Scotland (1847)*, pp. 7-9 – *see over*

Bracadale Manse, 29th December, 1846

My Dear Sir,

Yours of the 19th I this moment received. It is unnecessary to state that the condition of the poor people all over the Highlands is fearful. Nothing of the kind that ever happened to them before can give the least idea of their present state: we frequently had bad *springs*, but this is a Winter of Starvation after one of the 'bad Springs'. Formerly, if they had anything, it was in Winter; always a good fire and plenty of potatoes, if nothing better. My only fear at present is, that relief will come too late. They are now in actual want of every thing in the shape of food; some of them days past told me they had not eaten anything for two days but a salt herring, which they said 'kept them in the heart': but even this much, only those who had a few shillings at the time could buy them from the other end of the country. Where they have been favoured with a good fishing—but comparatively of little value, from the want of potatoes—they get no price for them; but even this much the poor people of Bracadale had not got, but when they could get a few shillings they went to buy them, as being the cheapest thing in the way of food they could buy. I can scarcely find time, in writing you by return of post, to consider what the prospects of Spring are. The present evil is the worst; and, before another week ends, I would be afraid to conjecture the most favourable results under present circumstances. I have attended already death-beds that, though they actually did not die of want, may be said to have died of starvation, their disease having been evidently from want of proper food. In many cases I have seen some, who were said to be dying of some sickness, for which I found a little nourishing food an effectual one: but with what can I feed? I have already involved myself: and all my efforts would not give them one bit each. Too much cannot be said of the exertions of Mr. McAskill of Tallisker, who has in a great measure supplied the country with meal; and I should say, to a ruinous extent given it to poor people who can never pay him. This day, a great number came to my house, who said they had not a bite, and the meal store was run out; a Government store ship having come into the loch, on her way to Portree, they thought I could get them to land some of it; but this could not be done. Oh! send us something immediately, whatever may be done again. In this parish no works of any kind have commenced, and perhaps this very time is the worst that can be. Send it: whither from Establishment or Free

Church. I may say that nothing has been done in this parish, in a general way, for a starving population. The extensive farmers are trying to create some work for some of the people; but it is impossible for them to support the expenditure for any time . . .

I do believe there is no part of the Highlands in a more wretched state than Bracadale; the majority of the people being cotters, that had no cow or anything to calculate on when the potato failed. I implore your sympathies in behalf of your native land, as they are, from not having a herring fishing, and other circumstances, worse off, if possible, than any other parish I know. If you can send but a few pounds at present, let it come, for many are dying, I may say, of starvation.

In haste, Yours truly,
N. McKinnon.

The late nineteenth century found the problem of the Highlands equally intractable. The landlords who had cleared their estates for sheep and then later, when the price of wool fell, for deer and game, were subjected to severe criticism. One native of Morvern recalled what had happened there.

(12) Letter to the Editor on 'Land Allocation in Morven', *Oban Times*, 3 March 1883 –

Between forty and fifty years ago the population of this parish [Morvern] was 2000; at the last census it stood at 828, being a decrease of over 50 per cent of the whole population. In this district there never was what may be termed a crofter population. It consisted chiefly of well-to-do small farmers, and the land was principally held on what is known as the club-farm system. Within the memory of a few old people yet living in the district, there were at Gleann Geal (White Glen), that is, from the bridge of Acharn to Clonlaid, 60 families, which would amount, giving an average of five persons to every family, to 300 souls. On the farm of Achana-gamhna, 6 well-to-do tenants, each holding a stock of eight cows and followers with 100 sheep. At Aoinebeag and Aoinemor there were between 20 and 30 families equally well-to-do. Perhaps they were not possessed of much 'hard cash,' but they had plenty to eat and drink. They were a contented and hospitable people, and the stranger or wanderer was never turned away from their door. At this time the sum of £11 sterling per annum from the collection at the church-door was sufficient for the support of all the poor people within the bounds of the parish, and now with a population of about 800 the rates amount to between six and seven hundred pounds a year. At the time the people were cleared off the land by that ruthless evictor Sellar they owed not a single penny of rent. The land held by so many families is now inhabited by three or four shepherds. The greater part of the estate has lately been turned into a deer forest by the proprietor T. V. Smith, of Ardtornish. The overplus of stock sold off each year by these tenants, combined with what was sold off the adjoining farms of Ternaid, Eignaig, and Ardtornish, at that time in the hands of Sheriff Gregerson, could not have been under 1000 sheep and from 200 to 300 cattle. But today it is of no use to any one unless that it affords a few months sport to Mr. Smith and *his party* during the shooting season. Mr. Smith does not let the shootings so that he receives no revenue whatever from the greater part of his estate. Will any sane man assert that this sort of policy has been productive of good to the people of the State? when good land (better there is not in the district) has been laid waste for the pleasure of one single individual, and those whom he may delight to honour . . .

Let me now refer to what was done in another part of the parish, on the estate of the late Lady Gordon, of Drimnin, there was about 30 years ago in the crofts of Aulisten and Carrick 10 families, each having a stock of three or four cows, and a number of sheep. When the sheep farming craze took a hold on so many people, the factor on the estate took the hill grazing from the crofters, and annexed it to his own large farm. The people were still left on their crofts, but when the hill pasture was taken from them they were no longer able to make both ends meet. Some got disheartened and left the place of their own accord. Others rather than leave their native place, took an offer then given them, of going to live on an island on the Lochsunart side of the estate. This same island was about as unlikely a place for any person to think of being able to live on as possible, as it was mostly rocks and heather, with some patches of bog. The people, however, went to work with a will, and in a few years had all that was possible to reclaim under cultivation. In full expectation that their tenure was secure they latterly built good houses, each costing from £50 to £60. About this time the adjoining sheep farmer coveted the holdings held by the people, offered to give more rent, and as a matter of course the interests of the people were sacrificed. They had to leave this place, which, by their industry, they had redeemed from a state of nature, without a farthing of compensation for land reclaimed or houses built. There was in connection with this eviction, which took place only 14 years, circumstances of peculiar cruelty and hardship . . . There was about the same time another eviction which took place in the district. When the late Mrs Campbell Paterson came into possession of the estate of Lochaline there was between the burn of Savary and the Bridge of Achaforsa, 38 families in possession of moderate sized crofts, with hill grazing. The proprietrix took it into her head that it would be an improvement to have the people removed, and turn the whole property into an extensive sheep farm. This was immediately effected, although the late Dr. John MacLeod, to his honour be it said, did all in his power to prevent it. The summonses of removal came, and at the Whitsunday term the crobar and faggot made short work of the crofters' dwellings. To me it is a never-to-be-forgotten scene. The burning cottages, the roofs falling in, and the sods which formed the covering of the roof under the thatch continued to smoulder for days. The faithful collie still lingering about the smouldering ruins of his former master's dwelling, howling pitifully, and would not for a time be comforted—and be it remembered this happened only 15 years ago. Some of the people here referred to were huddled together in the village of Lochaline. The young and the able-bodied scattered to all parts, some went to the cities of the south, some went abroad. The old people were left behind in this miserable village to become a burden to the parish, which they soon did. And now the Parochial Board, composed of proprietors and sheep farmers of course, refuse to give relief to some poor widows, which their own or their predecessors' misdeeds have rendered destitute. The poor people's natural protectors (their sons and daughters) were driven away, and scattered, and now they are deprived of the poor pittance the law of the land allows to such as have no other means of living—

"Verily the tender mercies of the wicked are cruel." . . .

A Royal Commission (the Napier Commission) reported in 1884. It was exceptionally difficult to produce a satisfactory solution because of some unique aspects of the Highlands situation. As the cross examination of the nephew of Mrs. Paterson, who had cleared Lochaline, shows, full weight was not always given to the dilemma which faced many Highland landlords in the nineteenth century.

(13) *Evidence to the Royal Commission on the condition of the Crofters and Cotters in the Highlands and Islands of Scotland, 1884,* Qs. 2306 f. Evidence of William Henderson Hardie, managing trustee of Lochaline estate –

... what was the object of this wholesale clearance of the people? —So far as I can understand it was a disadvantage to a sheep farm to have little bits of corn exposed where the sheep were all going round.

Did it ever suggest itself to the minds of the managers or proprietors at that time that a fence might have been put up?—It might have been, but the buildings themselves were of so little value—none of those crofters' buildings were valued above £8 or £10.

The reason of their removal was that their presence was inconvenient to the neighbouring sheep farmer?—Not only that, but they were not employing themselves in any occupation, such as fishing or that, to bring them in a livelihood.

They were removed from their little farms in order that they might obtain profitable employment for themselves?—Those were not little farms, but crofts.

As I understand your statement, the people were removed for the benefit of the sheep farm, and you may say for the benefit of the estate?—And for the benefit of themselves.

But the people were not made the judges of their own benefit?—They were not asked in the first place.

What I want to arrive at is this, the people were virtually and substantially removed for the benefit of the estate, in order that this sheep farm, or some other part of the estate, might be more profitably administered and held; in removing the people, did the proprietor, in consideration of their number and poverty, and the difficulty of obtaining other places, make them any allowance or gratuity?—Not to my knowledge.

Do you know what became of them at all?—Some of them removed to Glasgow and other centres of industry, and some of them removed to the village here.

You say that the people were partly removed for their own benefit, in order that they might become more industrious, or have a profitable employment in the future, did the proprietor pursue these people with any care in order to assist them in their future amelioration?—I am not aware ...

You have given us a full and frank statement about the estate so far as you know it; have you ever heard the statement made with regard to property, 'I can do what I like with my own'?—Yes, but I don't believe that.

Have you heard the other statement that property has its duties as well as its rights?—Yes.

And which of these do you go upon?—Property has its duties as well as its rights.

I may take it for granted in this case that the rights of property were exercised when these people were put away?—Yes.

Take the alternative now; what in the nature of duty was done by the estate for those people?—I tell you I can give no information about it further than I have done.

Is there any use in beating about the bush; is it not the fact that these people were removed solely and entirely because they were in the way of sheep?—Certainly not.

If not, what other reason was there?—It would have entailed very considerable expenditure upon the proprietor to have built houses and put up fencing to have carried out any system of farming.

That is what I say, the people were in the way. The proprietrix did not choose to spend that money, and therefore they must go and make room for the sheep; is that not so?—I have given you all the facts I can.

The dilemma facing Highland landlords was that a higher standard of living for a few was often possible only by ensuring a reduction of the population, or at least some rearrangement of the holdings. But the Highlander has always resented interference with his land, whatever the legal position.

(14) *Evidence to the Royal Commission on the condition of the Crofters and Cotters in the Highlands and Islands of Scotland, 1884.* Evidence of Rev. James Cumming, Free Church Minister, Melness –

Have you been elected a delegate by the people of Melness?—I have . . . Would you be so good as to make a verbal statement to begin with?—I have to state on behalf of the people that they complain of the smallness of their lots, the uncertainty of tenure, and that they are subject to annoyances if they happen to offend any official . . . They also complain of lack of harbour accommodation, which shuts up the district from intercourse with other parts of the empire. That is true of the whole coast as well as to the district of Melness. The people are so located that in the greater number of cases their lots cannot be extended unless two-thirds, or at least one-third of them were removed so as to make room for the remainder to be somewhat comfortable. They are also subject to fines, not by the Sheriff or according to the laws of the empire, but according to estate laws. If a man receives a lodger into his house—his son-in-law or his daughter-in-law—he is subject to a fine, and that fine in some instances, if not in all, gradually finds its way into his rent, and becomes an increase of rent . . . The fact is, that there is such a spirit of dissatisfaction, and such a sense of insecurity gone abroad, that it may become dangerous on the part of the Government, if they don't do something to ameliorate the conditions of the people. The people feel that they have no country; that they have no right. If they are known to have a gun, or if they are known to transgress any of what are called the byelaws of the estate, there are a dozen ways which cannot be formulated, in which their condition is made intolerable, and it is tantamount to punishment to them. There is not a bit of ground which a countryman can call his own, or build a bothy on, from the top of Kilbreck down to the sands of Naver. And that is a very unhappy condition for the whole people to be in. There are, so far as I can make out, between 7,000 and 8,000 people in the Reay country—that is the country of Lord Reay or the Mackay country—and all that population . . . have only somewhere about one-thirteenth part of the Reay country allowed to them . . . and the rest is under sheep, under deer, under hares, under rabbits, and under grouse, and other unprofitable occupants of the soil. I think it is true, on account of all these things, for some higher power to interfere. We are, in fact, under an absolute despotism. It is quite true that the House of Dunrobin, in intention at least, is a benevolent house. As a rule their crofters are not rack-rented; but then the agents of his Grace are his hands, his eyes, his ears, and his feet, and in their dealings with people they are constantly like a wall of ice between his Grace and his Grace's people. And this is not the case in a single instance, or with respect to one individual, but it has been the case for the last fifty or sixty years. There may be in a locality here and there, and in the case of one individual now and again, an exception, but what I have said describes the district as a whole.

Following the Napier Commission an Act of 1886 gave perpetual tenancy with the Land Court fixing rents if necessary. It set up the Crofters Commission with power to enlarge buildings and later with power to create new ones. A series of subsequent acts, in 1897, 1911 and 1955, tried to tackle the problem.

CHAPTER III

Industry

A. TEXTILES: LINEN

The first major industrial success in modern Scotland was the linen industry. Though its origins were ancient, it was only gradually transformed in the eighteenth century into an industry with many full-time workers and with an export trade. Towards the end of the century it made an important contribution to the growth of the cotton industry.

The linen industry's growth owed much to assistance given by the Board of Trustees for Fisheries and Manufactures in Scotland, a semi-official agency constituted in 1727 to administer funds provided by the Treaty of Union and by various statutes encouraging economic projects.

(1) 13 Geo. II, c. 30 (1726). An Act for encouraging and promoting Fisheries, and other Manufactures and Improvements in that Part of *Great Britain* called *Scotland* –

Whereas by the fifteenth Article of the Treaty of *Union* it is provided, that two thousand Pounds *per Annum*, for the Space of Seven Years, should be applied towards encouraging and promoting the Manufacture of course Wool within those Shires of *Scotland*, which produce the Wool, and that the first two thousand Pounds should be paid at *Martinmass* then next, and so yearly at *Martinmass*, during the Time aforesaid: And whereas by an Act . . . 5 Geo. I, c. 20 . . . It is amongst other Things provided. That yearly and every Year, reckoning the first Year to begin from the Feast of the Nativity of St. *John Baptist* one thousand seven hundred and nineteen, the full Sum of two thousand Pounds of lawful Money of *Great Britain* should be one yearly Fund, payable at the four most usual Feasts of the Year, . . . to be charged upon and paid out of the Monies arisen and to arise, from Time to Time, of or for any of the Customs, Duties, Excises or Revenues that are or shall be under the Management of the Commissioners of the Customs, and Commissioners of the Excise in *Scotland*, after the Payments therein directed to be made, and . . . to be wholly applied towards the encouraging and promoting the Fisheries, and such other Manufactures and Improvements in *Scotland*, as may most conduce to the general Good of the united Kingdom, according to the Tenor and true Meaning of the said fifteenth Article of the said Treaty of *Union*, and to no other Use, Intent or Purpose whatsoever; which said Annuity hath not hitherto been paid or applied to the Purposes for which the same was intended: 'And whereas by an Act . . . 12 Geo. I, c. 4 . . . it is amongst other Things provided, That if the Rate of three Pence *per* Bushel, charged upon Malt to be made in *Scotland*, should produce a greater Sum than the Sum of twenty thousand Pounds, clear of all Charges of Management, the Surplusage so produced, over and above the said Sum of twenty thousand Pounds, should be wholly applied towards the encouraging and promoting the Fisheries, and such other Manufactures and Improvements in *Scotland*, as may most conduce to the general Good of the united Kingdom, and to no other Use, Intent, or Purpose whatsoever, in such Manner as should thereafter be settled and directed by Parliament:' To the End therefore that these several Funds and Sums of Money, and any other Fund or Sum of Money, that may arise, grow due, or be provided and become payable for the Advancement and Improvement of Fisheries and Manufactures in that Part of *Great Britain* called *Scotland*, may be regularly applied for the said Purposes; Be it enacted . . . That it shall and may be lawful to and for his Majesty, his Heirs and Successors, by Letters Patents under the Great Seal appointed by the Treaty of *Union* to be kept in *Scotland* in Place of the Great Seal thereof, to lay down, settle and establish a particular Plan or Method, and to fix and direct proper Rules and Regulations, whereby the several Funds and Sums of Money aforesaid, already provided and grown due, or which hereafter shall be provided and grown due, for the Improvement and Encouragement of Fishery and Manufactures in that Part of *Great Britain* called *Scotland*, shall be wholly applied, laid out and distributed, according to the Tenor and true Meaning of the said fifteenth Article of the Treaty of *Union*, and for the Improvement of Fisheries, and such other Manufactures in *Scotland* as may most conduce to the general Good of the united Kingdom, and to no other Use, Intent or Purpose whatsoever; . . . And be it further enacted by the Authority aforesaid, That it shall and may be lawful to and for his Majesty, his Heirs and Successors, by Letters Patents under the Seal aforesaid, to appoint, name and authorize any Number of Persons resiant in that Part of *Great*

Britain called *Scotland*, not exceeding the Number of twenty-one, to be Trustees and Commissioners for managing and directing the Application of the said Sums, according to the Plan or Method that shall be settled and established as aforesaid, and for executing the several Powers and Authorities which by the said Letters Patents shall to them be committed by his Majesty, his heirs or Successors.

A number of defects in the linen industry had to be removed. At first the Board of Trustees concentrated its limited resources on encouraging better foreign techniques either by introducing skilled foreign labour into Scotland or by sending Scots to learn abroad. The distribution of expenditure for one year (November 1737 to November 1738) shows the direction of the Board's activities.

(2) Scottish Record Office. Records of the Board of Trustees for Fisheries and Manufactures. States of the Annual Progress of the Linen Manufacture, 1727-1754, pp. 54-56 –

The Sum expended this year for promoting the Linen Manufacture was as underviz.

For premiums for sowing Lintseed .	£93 - -	
For instructing young men in the art of raising flax and dressing it by the mill	50 - -	
For salary to a foreign flax raiser and for the maintenance of young men while instructing with him . .	60 - -	
For salaries to twelve flax raisers stationed in different parts of the Country	90 - -	
For a salary to an officer for surveying and examining the flax raisers .	60 - -	
		£353 - -
For supporting two Heckleries .	£40 - -	
For instructing young men in the Art of Heckling	16 - -	
For Heckles given to these young men, when instructed . .	26 - -	
		82 - -

For supporting three spinning Schools and for Prizes on yarn		67 – –
For a salary to a dutch Reedmaker		30 – –
For models of instruments for improving the manufacture		25 10 –
To dutch master weavers for instructing Journeymen Weavers in use of the dutch Loom . . .	180 – –	
For dutch Looms and other utensils given to journeymen perfected by these dutch weavers, for enabling them to set up and carry on their Trades	213 15 –	
		393 15 –
For prizes on the best Webs of Linen Cloth		210 – –
For salary to an officer for instructing the Weavers in the best method of washing, sorting, slaying and weaving of their yarn		97 10 –
For a salary to the warehouse keeper of the Cambricks	100 – –	
Towards further supporting the Cambrick Manufacture . .	100 – –	
		200 – –
For enabling Andrew and William Grays to enlarge and compleat their Bleachingfield at Grays green near Glasgow	£1,000 – –	
To two other master Bleachers towards indemnifying them of part of the expense of filling up the bleachfields	350 – –	
To the said Andrew and William Grays of Salary for instructing the undertakers of the other Bleaching or Whitening fields and for propagating the Whitening of low priced Cloth	200 – –	
		1,550 – –

For salaries to fifty five Stamp masters	550 – –
For salaries to two General Riding Officers	250 – –
In whole	£3,808 15 –

The Board's activities were limited by financial stringency. Even obvious improvements could not then be introduced. Private ventures suffered from the same problem.

(3) Scottish Record Office. Clerk of Penicuik Manuscripts. Letter from Alexander Mackenzie to Sir George Clerk, 8th November 1751 –

Dear Sir,

My Earnest Concern for you and family obliges me to offer you this trouble begging of you to let me hear from you. I have the pleasure to tell you that my Spinning Undertaking goes on Successfully notwithstanding of the many Dissappointments Rubs and Crosses I meet with from the Ill will of those who do not at all favour any such Attempt in this Countrey but I am determined with patience and Assiduity to proceed expecting Encouragement and approbation from the Trustees who were so good as to send me Wheels and Reels to encourage my Spinners which I have distributed as I was directed but confess it gives me pleasure to see Contentions among the poor people for preference to the Wheels. The great difficulty with me is the manner how I can get these Wheels occupy'd which will occasion an Expence I am not able to bear without assistance. I have written to Mr. Flint and to the Trustees upon this Subject and I hope you will patronize my Pretensions to their Encouragement. Among my Difficultys this occurrs that tho' I get Credit from the Brittish Linnen Company for the Flax yet the Advance of ready money to pay for spinning etc. bears very hard upon me. It is therefore very necessary for me if I could go Credit on the Bank for such an Advance of Money. I am Confident 200 Libs Credit would perfectly answer and put the Bussiness on a certain good footing but then I do not know how far a Tailzied Estate will be an Objection to that Credit even tho' the Bussiness itself is security sufficient to obviate all Risque. I can find no Disposition in the people of this Countrey to join with me in so good a

Work and I am bashfull to propose it to my friends in the South. This Dr. Sir is a point of Delicacy in which I would need your Advice. I am very unwilling to drop an Undertaking of such Consequence to my Countrey and so Creditable to myself. Yet without more ready Money than I can spare my Undertaking must Languish that is to say it must be Creeping not Walking—I am extremely oblig'd to the Good Offices of Lord Deskfoord who Corresponds with me and does me great honour tho' I never had the happiness of seeing his Lordship.

Alex[r] Mackenzie.

Coul 8th Nov[r] 1751

In spite of the barriers to improvement, there was soon a marked improvement in the quality of linen, so that it was more readily exported.

(4) *Scots Magazine*, 1739, p. 361. Letter to the Editor from an Englishman, Westminster, 9th July 1739 –

The increase and *improvement* ... lately made in the Linen manufacture of *Scotland*, has afforded the most solid satisfaction to every friend of the interest of Great Britain. And the quantities of *fine* cloth that have been sent hither of late, hath very much altered the judgment of people here; who, from the large parcels of *slight goods* you have hitherto sent us, were apt to conclude you incapable of furnishing linen of any considerable fineness; but there is room to conceive hope of seeing you match the productions of your *rivals of Ireland*.

Yet there were flaws in the achievements. Even late in the century, when the industry was much improved, it was possible for a critic to point out its continued deficiencies. David Loch was prejudiced, because he was anxious to see the woollen industry encouraged instead, but his arguments had force.

(5) David Loch, *Essay on the Trade, Commerce, and Manufactures of Scotland* (1775), pp. 28-32 –

The thing that is called FLAX, of the growth of this country, does not deserve the name, nor will be considered as such, by any person who has been in a country where real flax grows . . . I would fain flatter myself with the hope, that the Board of Trustees, being once convinced, that this country is no ways adapted for the raising of flax, would desist from offering any more premiums for the culture of that exotic, as I am fully persuaded it is so far from answering any good purpose, that it has an effect entirely the reverse, and tends only to make the farmer, for the honour and the regard of the premium, which, by the bye, will do little more than indemnify him for his labour and expence, neglect his sowing so many acres with corn, which might have afforded cheap bread to our labouring poor . . .

It was never my intention to dissuade those who are already engaged in the Linen Manufacture, to give up that branch altogether; but to get out of it slowly, and apply more to the Woollen. Linens for our own consumption, ought certainly to be made at home, and even some for our neighbours the English; but these should be of a course quality, and from foreign flax. The Scots manufacturer cannot make daily bread by working fine linen, and selling it in the English market; neither need we imagine to make linen that will bring a proper profit, by exportation to any country abroad, or to our own plantations.

This would be a very absurd idea, while Germany, and the Eastern countries, continue our rivals in that branch; for they are, and will probably ever be, able to undersell us, both as to price and quality, 30 per cent. It is not then to be supposed, that the Americans, or West Indians, will purchase from us, when they can be supplied with German linens, at the Dutch and Danish freeports in the West Indies, upon much better terms. No restriction that can be laid on trade, by our laws, will prevent this; indeed, the temptation is too great to be withstood.

Experience ought to have convinced us, long before this time, that the Linen Manufacture, instead of being a lucrative, was in many instances a losing trade, especially the finer sorts of it, which we have been in use of sending to the London and foreign markets. I dare venture to say, that the manufacturers of fine linen, thus exported, have, upon an average, been losers by the trade, at the rate of 4d per yard; so that the mere hundred thousand yards which have been made and sent abroad, as the staple of the country, have been at the loss of an equal number of fourpences, besides the price of materials paid to foreigners. Surely such a trade, if it was meant to give employment to our poor, was the very worst which could possibly be thought of; for, while the masters were losers by the business, it was not to be expected they should be able to afford such wages to their journeymen, as to make them live with any degree of decency; but, on the contrary, it is well known, these poor people's pittance has been so truly scanty, for a number of years back, that it has required the most parsimonous œconomy to preserve them from starving altogether.

The British Linen Company made the trial of this branch, and with the best appearance of success. That Company had the greatest support which ever was afforded to any undertaking attempted in this country. Their directors were composed of gentlemen the most sensible and knowing. Their servants honest, and some of them very alert, witness Mr. W. T - - d; yet all would not do. I had the honour to be acquainted with some of the gentlemen who were in the direction some years ago. I have furnished the company with ships for several seasons to bring home their flax. My poor opinion has often been asked by some gentlemen, largely concerned in this trade. I was always uniform and explicit, that it could not support itself.—The money that has gone out of this country, (and it is all cash) in my time, to pay flax, and flax-seed, to Holland and Russia, is so immense, that it is almost beyond credibility. I know, very nearly, the sum that has been remitted, for these twenty years past, to Amsterdam, Rotterdam, and Hamburgh, for these articles; but it is so very large, that I do not chuse to mention it, as it would stagger the belief of the most credulous. The sum paid for pot, pearl, weed ashes, etc. has likewise been far from being inconsiderate. This trade, I am persuaded, has carried more money out of Scotland in my time, than all our foreign trade put together; for the French and Spaniards take our goods in exchange for their commodities; but those who supply us with flax, flax-seed, etc. take nothing but ready money. It is to this cause, therefore, that I must attribute the great scarcity of cash, and of the London and Dutch exchange being so much against us. As there have been less of these articles, however, imported within these two years past, the exchange has become more moderate, which is an evident proof of my assertion being well founded. That I am equally so, with regard to the advantages that must attend a less vigorous exertion in favours of the Linen, and a proper application being made to that of the Woollen manufacture, I shall endeavour to make evident in its proper place.

B. TEXTILES: COTTON

The new methods of spinning applied in the cotton industry from the late eighteenth century led to new forms of industrial organisation in the west of Scotland. The linen industry, which had all the necessary skills, was soon displaced by a buoyant cotton industry, except in the east, where it retained a hold in Fife and in Dundee, and was transformed into the jute industry.

Buildings were converted (not always cheaply) to the new activities (1); the traditional textile areas expanded and, most striking of all, some new settlements appeared (2).

(1) Scottish Record Office. Hamilton of Pinmore Manuscripts. Letter from John Dunlop to Hugh Hamilton, 15th December 1790 –

Dear Sir,

I rec'd your letter of the 12th, which would have been answered in course according to your desire, but I could not obtain the necessary information till today, and indeed it is only such as can inable us to form a rough grip of the matter—

The Sugar House is a very proper length & width, but it would require the windows to be enlarged and perhaps new placed—The first floor with perhaps a trifling addition of a Shed, would do for Carding Roving & Slubbing, and would be filled as follows—

5 Carding Machines	£20 each	£100		
5 Roving "	£16 "	£ 80		
5 Slubbing "	£40 "	£200		
			£380	
The 2nd 3rd 4th 5th & 7th Stories would hold 12 Jeanies each— 60 @ £43			2,580	
			£2,960	

The 6th Story might do for Cotton Wool, Lumber etc, but is thought too low for the best sort of Jeanies which require 6½ feet—

Each Jeany of the Medium size would work 156 Spindles which multiplied by 60, the number of Jeanies, gives 9360, a work far larger than it would be provident to undertake at first; the whole number of people needed might be about 200—and the money necessary might be about £4,000 besides the price of the Houses—You can easily get information what a house of such dimensions would cost with you, and you can also enquire what it would take to repair the Sugar House giving it a large New Window for every Jeany & Machine; you will also consider that the Dwelling House is worth something—

When you get this information, and know the price Mr. Findlay puts upon the Sugar House you will be able to form a pretty accurate Notion, whether or not it is to be got a pennyworth, for unless it were to be sold very cheap, in my opinion we ought to have nothing to do with it, as I think it is too large for your purpose, and wants the advantage of water which would incure a considerable expence—

5000 Spindles would be a *very* capital beginning, and the buildings might be enlarged as we found it prudent and convenient—30 Jeanies is reckoned a very handsome establishment and I am informed there is no work about Manchester that exceeds 40—

I shall be glad to hear from you, and shall give you any further information in my power— . . .

Since writing, I have got a note of the people necessary which is as follows—

60 Spinners Men
60 Piecers Boys & Girls
5 Rovers Men
5 Winders Boys & Girls
Besides Manager, Clerks, labourers etc.
12 Carders & Drawers—2 of them Men,
the rest about 14 to 15 years old
28 Pickers and for other purposes, Women
—
170

(2) *Old Statistical Account*, vol. 16, pp. 116-117 – (Parish of Killearn.)

Trade—Every encouragement is given the farmer by having a profitable and ready market in *Balfrone*, to which he has an easy access. The late rapid [increase in] population of that newly erected village, has greatly improved the adjacent country. This pleasing alteration arises wholly from a variety of manufactures, recently introduced into the neighbourhood, chiefly by Robert Dunmore of Ballindalloch, Esq. This public-spirited gentleman, inspired with the ambition of doing good to mankind by employing them in useful industry, began his improvements in the year 1788, by establishing a muslin manufactory at Balfrone. This village, which is in the immediate neighbourhood of Killearn, and which formerly contained no more than six or seven families, was at that time laid out according to a regular plan, and now contains no fewer than 220 families. The houses, many of which are 2 stories high, are in general covered with slate. The *Ballikinrain* cotton-mill was erected by Mr. Dunmore in 1792. It is constructed for spinning woollen as well as cotton; the former for the carpet, the latter for the muslin manufacture. This work, at present carried on under the management of Mr. Robert Macmorran from Douglass, employs about 100 persons, most of whom reside in the neighbourhood of the mill. The greatest manufacturing work in the parish is *Enrick printfield*, which was begun in 1792. The operative part of the business is carried on by Mr. J. F. Moriar, a Swiss, under the firm of Messrs. Monteith, Warren, and Company, Glasgow. The buildings are constructed to contain 16 printing presses, to go by water, and 72 tables for block-printing, besides boiling-houses, dye-houses, etc, for executing business on a very extensive scale. Every part of the apparatus is new, and of the most approved construction, especially the washing wheels, which are not surpassed by any in Europe. One of the bleaching-fields, consisting of a plain of 15 acres, is secured from the inundations of Enrick by an artificial bank, the raising of which cost a considerable sum of money. Business was begun here in the month of June 1793. But unfortunately an entire stop was almost put to the work by the present stagnation of trade, which has communicated its baneful influence through all this country. The whole work at present (Sept. 1793) employs no more than 250 persons, the most of whom reside in Balfrone.

By the end of the Napoleonic Wars the Scottish cotton industry was well established; in the boom of the mid-1820s much of its weaving became mechanised; but by the 1830s the industry was beginning to suffer from foreign competition. Its leading figure at that time was Kirkman Finlay, who, in evidence to a parliamentary inquiry in 1833, complained that the cotton trade was hardly profitable any longer and described how the change had come about (3). Another leading cotton manufacturer, Henry Houldsworth, indicated that the Scottish manufacturers' technical backwardness was perhaps to blame for their failure to be able to meet competition (4).

(3) *Evidence to the Select Committee on Manufactures, Commerce and Shipping*, 1833, Qs. 648-662. Evidence of Kirkman Finlay –

You stated that you thought the rate of profit in the cotton trade has declined; can you state the period at which that decline commenced, and what has been its progress?—I have seen when the profit in the cotton manufacture upon a piece of goods to the manufacturer was as much as the price of the goods altogether is at present.

What was the highest state of profit?—The best time that I ever knew in the spinning was about 1802; it was, however, even better before that.

Has it materially altered since the war?—Yes, very much.

Does not the rate of profit in spinning depend in a great measure upon the introduction of improvements, and vary in different establishments, according as any individual may obtain a priority of the use of improvements?—It would always depend upon that; unless the individual lays hold of an improvement as soon as possible, his loss will be augmented by that, by his neglect; but it has not always been very profitable; even where a considerable improvement has been introduced, other circumstances may have tended to depress the rate of profit.

At what period did you begin to feel the competition of foreign manufacturers in the foreign markets in the cotton manufacture?—When I first knew the cotton manufacture in this country, which was in the year 1787, and when I first entered into business extensively, which was in 1792, there was no manufacture of cotton of any importance in any part out of Great Britain. There were, perhaps, some domestic cotton manufactures carried on abroad, but there were no finer fabrics of any kind. I believe my house was amongst the first that ever exported cotton manufactures of fine fabrics generally to the continent of Europe, to Germany, to Italy, to France and to Switzerland. In those times there was no cotton manufacture in France at all; none in Switzerland worth speaking of; none in any part of Germany. Then the practice came to export cotton twist; and I think it was about the year 1794 or 1795 when we first began to export a good deal of cotton twist. At that time there was no cotton twist spun in any part of Germany. Now there is not a single country in which there is not a great manufacture of cotton carried on. There is a very extensive spinning carried on in Switzerland; there is a very extensive spinning carried on in Austria, and a large cotton manufacture carried on there. By the recent accounts it appears that the Government has relaxed a little the prohibition against cotton twist, and that it may be introduced in future on the payment of a moderate duty. Their manufacture has, in my recollection, entirely grown up. The French manufacture, which did not exist at all at the period I first spoke of, in 1792, and which was very inconsiderable at the conclusion of the peace in 1814, when I was in France and saw it, has become of late very formidable; and by the means that are taken, as I understand, by the regulation of the drawback, by which the manufacturer receives more amount of drawback than he pays of duty, there is a very formidable advantage given to the French manufacturer by that fiscal regulation.

You have stated that the French competition has grown up since 1814; what was the state of the other countries after the period of 1814?—In the United States there was no manufacture in 1814 worth speaking of.

Was there any in Austria and Switzerland?—It was beginning.

Then the principal foreign competition has grown up since the peace of 1815?—Yes, I think so.

Do you think that that competition is on the increase?—I think it is, decidedly.

And has been steadily on the increase since 1815, growing every three or four years greater and greater?—Yes, I think every year.

Can you state what advantages are particularly possessed by any foreign country in the cotton manufacture?—In the first place, in some countries, particularly in France, and Switzerland, and Flanders, they have a body of workmen well trained to the other manufactures; to linen, for instance, which was the great manufacture in Flanders, and by that means they were prepared for engaging in the cotton manufacture.

Are there any other natural advantages that they possess?—The low price of labour.

Do the improvements in machinery, which are made originally in this country, pass very readily and promptly into those other countries?—They can easily get the improvement; but it is not very easy for them to work it with equal advantage.

Do you know what facilities they possess of obtaining command of borrowed capital and the discount of bills, in the French market, for instance?—I do not know.

Do you know the disadvantages of manufacturing in Scotland as compared with this country?—I think that there would not be such a tact in carrying on every operation of the work in Scotland for a time, at any rate, as there is at Manchester and in Glasgow, in a particular kind of goods that are made in each. We find, in practice, that it is impossible, with all the knowledge and the opportunities that we have at Glasgow, to transfer from Manchester to Glasgow the manufacture of a particular article. Now at Manchester, again efforts have been made to manufacture particular articles that they make at Glasgow and Paisley, and it is found impossible to do them with the same advantage, and therefore unless there are very great advantages in those other parts, I think it would be a very long time before they could do it just as well as it is done at Manchester and Glasgow, in all the variety of the manufacture; but then they may seize some particular kind of goods, and make that equally well, or perhaps better.

(4) *Evidence to Select Committee on Manufactures. Commerce and Shipping*, 1833, Qs. 5209-5230. Evidence of Henry Houldsworth –

Have the wages paid to the mechanics fallen of late?—No; mechanics' wages have risen much very recently; machine-makers' have risen 10 per cent. within these six months.

From what cause?—From the increase in demand for machinery, and in part from emigration; a great many have gone to America, the number of hands are reduced; and there is another cause, which is, that they have commenced a union, by which they have been able to control their masters, and get up the wages.

Then in part you ascribe the recent rise of wages to the new formation of this union?—In part, I certainly do.

Has there been, in addition to that, an increased demand for machines which those men have been employed in making?—There has been an increased demand for machinery: for instance, cotton-mills were so exceedingly reduced in their profits, that they were obliged to lay out additional capital, in order to accomplish the object of bringing the manufacture into the market cheaper, which they could only do by improved machinery.

Do you consider that before the manufacturers adopted those new improvements, the cotton machinery at Glasgow was rather inferior to the average of the cotton machinery in other parts of the kingdom?—I have no doubt that Manchester is the leading place for machinery; there have been great improvements going on in Manchester for two or three years past, which have been only slowly adopted by the Scotch, till they saw the necessity of adopting them in consequence of being undersold in the market by the Manchester people, and they have been obliged in consequence to adopt the new system of machinery; the improvements have not been confined to new cotton-mills, but also in additions of new machinery to old mills.

At what percentage do you estimate the advantage of the manufacturer by substituting the new machinery for the old?—I am not aware of the percentage, but even one per cent. is a great matter in our profits; if it is one per cent. it is worth while to lay out additional capital for it.

Do you conceive that the ingenuity of inventing machinery, and the spirit of enterprize in laying out money upon it, is greater at Manchester than it is at Glasgow?—The scale of ingenuity must always be in proportion to the extent of the business; and it follows that in Manchester the business being more extensive, the improvements more generally take place there than at Glasgow: but there are some exceptions to the contrary.

You think they are generally ahead of you in Manchester?—Yes.

What are the improvements you speak of?—It is difficult to say; some years ago there was nothing but can-frames in Scotland; now those are changed for bobbin and fly-frames.

How long is it since that improvement was adopted in Scotland?—It was not begun to be adopted generally more than six or seven years ago; there might be some few 10 or 12 years ago; there are some that keep a few can-frames still, but very few indeed, and they are throwing them out as fast as they can get the new ones made.

Has the low state of profits compelled the manufacturers to adopt this change?—That is my belief.

Are there any other improvements that have taken place?—Those bobbin and fly-frames have been thrown out in many mills, and substituted by another machine, an American invention, called the tube frame, which does more work in the same time than the bobbin and fly-frame.

So that even before the bobbin and fly-frame has come into general use, it has been superseded in some measure by a new machine?—Yes.

Is there anything else that is superseding the tube-frames?—I have no doubt that before many years the tube-frame will be superseded by some new inventions; there is something of that sort going on at Manchester, by an improvement of the bobbin and fly-frame.

Have those alterations been adopted for all descriptions of spinning, both fine and coarse?—It is chiefly the coarse descriptions that are made at Glasgow; there is very little fine; the tube-frame is only applicable with any advantage to number 36, and below.

Can you state how much cheaper per pound you can produce this yarn now with the tube-frame than with the can-frame?—Perhaps it does not amount to more than a fraction of a penny per pound; but it does more work in the same room with the same hands.

Would all the improvements you have mentioned give a saving of 1d. a pound?—I should think not; but these improvements have enabled us to spin inferior cotton into equal yarn.

You say that in Glasgow they spin chiefly the coarse numbers; from what number downwards?—From number 50 downwards.

Do you consider that trade generally has been prosperous in Glasgow during the last seven or eight years?—Profits have been diminishing; but the workpeople have been well employed, and have been prospering, partly because new power-loom factories have been increasing to a great extent; cotton-mills have not increased to the same extent, but the people have been employed.

Do you consider that the present profits of trade are so considerable and so solid as to induce you to recommend a friend of competent knowledge and industry and prudence to embark his capital in trade in Glasgow?—I could scarcely answer that question, because I believe that the circumstance of cotton spinning being depressed in point of profits is not an exception to every other branch of business; I think that all trade is depressed in profit to a serious extent.

Would you recommend a man that could afford to live out of trade to go into trade with a view to bettering his condition?—Certainly not.

During former periods, have you not known times in which you would have recommended a man of property to embark his capital in trade?—Certainly.

The power loom, invented in the 1780s, was extensively adopted only after the Napoleonic Wars, and especially in the boom of 1825. Many handloom weavers, who had prospered when earlier innovations in spinning increased the demand for their services, found that they were redundant. Their plight was worsened by the continuous entry of Irish into the trade, even as demand continued to fall. By the middle of the nineteenth century the handloom weavers who remained suffered severe privation.

(5) *Evidence to the Children's Employment Commission.* Parliamentary Papers, 1864, XXII, p. 227. Evidence of George Boyd, May Boyd, Jane Boyd –

George Boyd, Great Eastern Road, hand-loom weaver.—I have worked in or been through all the hand-loom weaving districts in the south of Scotland, e.g. Ayrshire, Lanark, Girvan, Kilmarnock, Maybole, Kilsyth, etc., and places where all kinds of materials were worked up or made, e.g. wool, cotton, silk, grass, gauze figured and plain etc. At all, the hours and mode of work are just about the same on the whole, there being however no fixed limit, but each individual working just as circumstances impel. What we call a regular weaver's day in small work places is from 6 a.m. till 10 p.m., but if a man has a large family and is industrious he will work much longer, and I have known men who have wrought till 1 a.m. before getting any supper. It is very prevalent to work till 12 and 1, and I have done so myself; indeed in the winter time 12 is more regular for many than any other hour. But it is cruel work, and any one would tell you so. I believe that I am not off three quarters of an hour all day: a quarter of an hour or 20 minutes is the outside that I get for any meal I take. This is not general, but a married man with a family to provide for cannot get an hour for a meal, and does not look for it.

You may say that from 10 to 12 is the age for putting children on a loom, choosing a light web for them. It is too soon. They ought to be at school, that is the plain of it. For six months they are more loss than profit; you have to dress their web and help them so much that it would be better to want them. But it is the practice which they get and the hope of earning something soon which causes it. I put on one of my girls at 9 years old, and it may have been putting her ower young which has made her bad now. I should be putting on my boy there, now 10 years old, but there is so little work now that men do not put their sons to it. It is not worth it. If any children are put on it is most commonly girls, or boys merely till they are put out to public works and other things. But just within the last two or three years I scarcely know a wean learning here. I could count nearly 100 small shops altered into dwellings in this part of the town within the last three or four years, and this is the general way. I had my own looms and shop, but I now have to rent a loom out for 1s. a week for tear and wear, and the man finding me work.

About a year ago I was on a committee for forwarding an emigration scheme for hand-loom weavers, and collecting information which was published. We took the average wages of 150 men just as we met them, scattered in different parts of the city and engaged on all kinds of fabrics, and found them to be from 7s. to 8s., to be safe, say 8s. a week. Two or three were as high as 12s., and some on white work were as low as 4s. 3d.

In town a room and kitchen above and a four-loom shop below is the most universal system, sometimes a six-loom shop, but in country districts "a but and a ben," i.e. a room with part divided off for a loom or two, is very common. Some of the shops are so damp that a fire has no effect upon them; I have seen some quite wet. But there is not one in ten of the small shops now in Glasgow that there were. The system now is getting all for factories with a large number of hand-looms, say 300 or more. One has 500 and no power-looms; in some there are both power and hand-looms. All large factories, whether they have power or not, work the same (i.e. factory) hours. As I am informed, some who have laid out money on power-looms say that if they had known the result they never would have done it. They have the expense of the machinery, and heavy wages to pay, and the fabric, it is thought, cannot be made so correct, and sells for less, so that, as I understand, the hand-loom is considered nearly as remunerative, except that orders can be executed quicker by steam.

I have eight children living, some grown up, and have had nine. Only two of them have ever been at school, and neither of these for a year. All that any know beyond this I have taught them myself, but I shall be content if the younger can only read. I might have got them free education, but only at the parish school, by humbling myself as a pauper. That will never do. Though I never applied, I believe that I must plead poverty, and get a line signed by the minister and elder. It is a poor thing for a man to demean himself and plead for that which is a natural right. Education is a natural right. If the mind is not fed how can it grow? The state should educate, and see that a child gets its due. I would let people say what they liked about interfering with our independence. There has never been so much murders as till within the last two years, and these all come from want of proper bringing up.

May Boyd, wife of last witness.—Weavers get their winding done by their own families if it is not o'er muckle; if it is they have to pay some one else. None employ persons by the day in their house, but some take in a girl to wind, and give her 1s. a week and her meat. Children dinna ken how to handle it before 8 years old, but begin from about that age to 9.

It is a wearisome job, far waur than the weaving. You're never up. It's a paining thing,—sair, sair,—and you're weary and sair as night comes on. It's no for nae young body to sit at, and makes one grow aside. That is why I took my Colin off it, when about 9; he was like waning awa and wasting. I have known people grow up aside from winding.

Jane Boyd, age 20, daughter of above.—Have been six years winding at home. For me, I have to begin in summer at 6 a.m. and stop at it till dark, but in the winter I was up at 4 a.m. and worked till 10 p.m. regular. Sometimes I have an ache in the side, and when I sit constant at it I get a pain in my breast, maist just in front. Have been off two hours in a day altogether.

A sister, about 16, weaves but cannot sit long; she has been in bad health this three years. Geordie was 9 years old when he commenced, but he gave it up after a twelvemonth. ("Your cant confine a wean so close when he's 9 years old," remarked the mother.) Most weavers are very regular from Monday to Saturday, working from about 6 a.m. till dark in summer, and from 7 a.m. till 11 p.m. in winter.

C. THE HEAVY INDUSTRIES

The growth of the heavy industries began with the foundation of Carron Company in 1759. Carron dominated the industry for the next three-quarters of a century because of its size and because it pioneered modern methods of production. A rough report of the plan of operation of the works for 1762 shows the initial scale of its development.

(1) Scottish Record Office. Carron Company Manuscripts. Letter to A. Fairholm, London, 20th November, 1761 –

Total Charge of Carron Works for 1762.

Blast Furnaces	£5200
Air Furnaces	988
Boring Mill	100
Sand Iron Handles & Grinding	700
Slitt Mill	2000
Forge	4224. 10. –
Nail Trade	819
Building & Oncost expenses	1560
Craigforth—Hawkins—Clerks Wages &c	420
	16011. 10. –

Besides we have not reckoned upon the Balance of Mr. Downing, Thomas Bourne & John Hassals Acco[t.] which are yet unsettled.

The Produce of these Works will probably be

B. Furnaces	2	tons Loam	£15	£30	£82 a week each
	1½	" Flash		18	Suppose it £80
	1	" Open Sand		10	
	4	" Pigs		24	
				£82	

	Tons			
Cylinders, Pipes, Cannon, Sugar Roles, Cockles, Boilers, Garden Rollers, Screws, Stoves, Press Plates, Ovens, Aquafortes, Pots &c.	200	@	15/–	£3000
Stove Backs, Sand Pans, Ovens, Grates, Girdles &c.	150	"	12/–	£1800
Open sand Plates & other sand work	100	"	10/–	£1000
Pig Iron	400	"	6/–	£2400
Tons	850			£8200
2 weeks produce omitted 34 tons				£320
884 tons Iron value				£8520

Boring Cylinders, Pipes, Cannon &c		
Turning Sugar Roles, Pistons &c	may be	250
Air Furnaces Sad Irons 100 tons Value £20		£2000
Pots, Kettles, Ballisters, Skellets in Flask	150 tons 12/–	£1800
Bushes, Weights, Bars	100 „ open sand 10/–	£1000
		£4800
from which deduct 420 ton Pig Iron & old Metal used @ 6/–		£2520
		£2280
Slitt Mill 100 ton Hoops 21/– & Value of Slitting 200 ton		2300
Forge 300 ton Bar Iron @ 16/–		4800
Nails may sell at		920
		£19,070

We apprehend there will probably be sold in N. Britain to the value of £3000 in Cast Iron annually of which we may be in Cash £1500 within the year. Slitt Mill—the sale for Hoops in Scotland may be 50 ton a year at £22 a ton £1100. Perhaps we may receive of this within the year £600 Mail Iron—The sale of Britain including our own consumption in Rod & Handle Iron we expect will be near 200 ton a year at £20 a ton. Of this we may receive within the year near £5000.

N.B. The principal plans of sale are Leith, Glasgow, Bannockburn, Stirling, Rutherglen, Northumberland. As long as we can sell Rod Iron at £20 money our Forge never can be better employed than in making Mill Iron. The Profit is good & it is the best way that we can convert our Iron into that useful commodity Cash. We presume there will be no great difficulty in disposing of the Nails either in Glasgow or London. But we find Crowley's people are used to give long credit on this article. If it is found that the quantity of Castings we are likely to make from the B. & Air Furnaces is more than can readily be sold in London, Newcastle & North Britain in this case we must either think of extending our Sales into foreign markets or of lessening our quantities. When you have occasion to write to Hamburgh we beg you may get yourself particularly informed about the state of the Cast-Iron Trade. We would be glad of an order or two to begin with there. We do not think Dantsig or Copenhagen unlikely places for sale of Cast Iron. In the state of affairs for next year Kinnaird is not mentioned. We apprehend that we cannot entirely desist there without Bruce's permission. Even as affairs now are we have a disagreeable jarring with him. He complains loudly of our having broke the Contract with him. We shall always be glad to be favoured with your best advice which you may depend will be duly regarded.

Total People employed by the Carron Co$^{y.}$

Blast Furnaces				63
Air Furnaces	22	Warehouse	4	26
Handle Makers	6	Grinders	14	20
Slitt Mill	16	Forge	6	22
Nailers	11	Women & Children	9	20
Ironstone	20	Wood Cutters & Colliers	10	40
Carpenters, Sawyers, Blacksmiths, Masons Bricklayers, Labourers, Carters &c employed about the Forge.				124
Joiners & Blacksmiths about the Works				9
Kinnaird Bricklayers, Labourers, Blacksmiths & Carters.				26
Kinnaird Coal				4
Quarole Coal				140
Callander Coal 68, Brightons, Shieldhill & Croftandy 34				102
Waggons employed about the railway 6 Farm 4				10
McLeish, Hawkins & Carron Harbour				9
				615

N.B. Easton, Moir & Ogilvie & the men employed by them in finishing the Houses between Carron & Quarole, about 30 men, are not in this acco$^{t.}$ Secondly there is about 12 Carts employed in driving Coal from Callander to Carron & Salt Pool not in this acco$^{t.}$ There is constantly employed 6 small Vessels drawing Ironstone, Lime & Limestone, carry 3 men each is 18 not reckoned. In summer the carts employed in driving Ironstone & Charcoal will not be less than twenty. The people employed in pulling & carrying Bark in summer will exceed 100 for May, June & July. When things are reduced to their narrowest compass the necessary people employed by the Carron Company will never be under 500. If ever it shall be thought their interest to issue Notes of hand the circulation within themselves will be more extensive than any other society in N. Britain.

Carron Company was a specialist producer. A new age of mass production dates from the patenting by J. B. Neilson in 1828 of the use of hot instead of cold air in blowing blast furnaces (the hot-blast). Only then was the full exploitation of the country's rich resources of coal and ironstone possible. The fortunes of individual ironworks were transformed when the hot-blast was adopted.

(2) Scottish Record Office. Shotts Iron Company Manuscripts. Sederunt Book 2 (1831-37) pp. 234-235. Report of the Annual General Meeting held in Royal Exchange Coffee House, Edinburgh, on 10th September 1834 –

The Manager having reported to the Directors, that after due enquiry, he was satisfied that the recent invention of smelting Iron by means of a hot blast, was a great improvement in the manufacture, they authorised Mr. Baird to make the necessary erections for blowing the Company's furnaces with heated air. Accordingly a License was obtained from the Patentees, authorising the Company to use their invention, upon payment of 1/– for every ton of Iron melted by means of it, with power to the Company to relinquish the use of it at any time they may see proper. The heated air apparatus was completed & set going on 12th August, and the directors are happy to report, that the advantages of it have not only realized, but greatly exceeded their expectations. The produce of Iron made from 12th August to 7th September 1834 inclusive, amounted to 280 tons. The iron made from No. 1 Furnace, in the corresponding period last year, was only 180 tons, being a difference of 100 tons in favour of the heated blast. The Manager however considers that twelve months must elapse before the advantages of hot over cold blast can be accurately and definitely known.

The industry which appeared after about 1830 was not concerned to any considerable extent with the further processing of pig iron. By the

1840s the disparate rate of growth of subsequent processes of iron manufacture was a marked feature of the industry, but attempts to encourage malleable iron production at that time proved unsuccessful.

(3) *The Mining Journal*, 20th December, 1845 –

The Scotch Iron Trade

There is a singular feature in the Scotch iron trade not generally known, but which must be rectified before the trade be put upon a secure basis. We allude to the fact that, although the rails now universally used are made of malleable iron, there are in Scotland only sufficient malleable works to convert the produce of fifteen furnaces to that description of iron. The Scotch ironmasters are also shut out from the benefit of the numerous English malleable iron-works, which may be said to be supplied with pig-iron of their own manufacture. The total quantity of Scotch pig-iron taken to England, and manufactured there, is so trifling that it is not equal to the produce of more than a very few of our blast-furnaces. The late high prices, we fear, will be found to have had a most injurious effect upon the trade, both by stimulating the production to an enormous extent, and by cutting off the export of pig-iron; for, under the new duties imposed by the Zollverein, foreigners cannot afford to take out pig-iron except at low prices. And when it is remembered that in 1842 (the last year in which the continental exports were considerable), the amount of pig-iron exported from Glasgow alone was 70,000 tons, it will be seen how important it is to cultivate this branch of the trade. And this can only be effected by keeping prices moderate. It is a painful fact that since 1842 the exportation of pig-iron has all but ceased.

Under these circumstances, we are at a loss to conceive how the surplus pig-iron is to be disposed of. Should the prices fall, of course part will be exported; but until there have been erected as many malleable iron works as there are pig-iron works, the trade, we fear, will suffer great depression in consequence of the constant accumulation of stock. On account of the many railways in course of formation or projection there must be a great demand for malleable iron. We are therefore surprised that this branch of the trade has hitherto escaped the attention of our capitalists.

In the later 1860s the industry began to experience competition in its own field of the production of pig iron from the industry of the north east of England around Middlesbrough. The year 1872 was a turning point. A high level of prosperity was then reached and never again surpassed.

(4) *Iron*, 18th January 1873 –

The Scotch Iron Trade of 1872

The year just closed was the most remarkable which the history of the iron trade has probably seen. The phenomena, whether as regards price, stocks, demand and production, and the misunderstandings and disputes of masters and workmen, are alike novel and unprecedented, and have, moreover, attained such an appearance of performance as to justify the deepest possible interest as to the future . . . The following are the comparative production, consumption, exports, and stocks of Scotch pig iron, as at the 25th of December, the last three years:-

	1872 (*tons*)	1871 (*tons*)	1870 (*tons*)
PRODUCTION			
From return of makers	1,100,000	1,160,000	1,206,000
CONSUMPTION			
In foundries	300,000	275,000	298,000
In malleable works	160,000	190,000	208,000
	460,000	465,000	506,000
EXPORTS			
Foreign	633,810	512,479	388,842
Coastwise	224,190	303,494	230,984
By rail to England, about	52,000	54,027	35,174
	910,000	870,000	655,000
STOCKS			
In Connal's Stores	109,000	359,180	394,520
In Forth and Clyde Canal Co's Stores	none	12,865	16,185
At makers' works, by their returns	120,000	117,275	254,295
	229,000	490,000 (sic)	665,000

During all these three years the production of pig iron has been steadily and annually diminishing in Scotland; and this diminution has been going on in the face not only of greatly increasing demand, but of constantly rising prices, and of prices in their culmination this year, quite unprecedented in amount, and destructively reactive on all the springs of industry and manufacture by their very existence. The average price of Scotch pig iron in 1870 was 54s. 4d. per ton, when the production was 1,206,000 tons; in 1871 the average price was 58s. 11d., and yet the production sank to 1,160,000 tons; and this year the average price has been 101s. 6d; when the productions have been only 1,100,000 tons! There is certainly no branch of production in this country that has ever exhibited such results as these; and we may be prepared to find some cause counteracting and over-ruling the natural laws that ordinarily govern the relations of demand and supply and of price and production, which cause either may be— . . . (1) some exhaustion of the physical materials of production, coal and iron-stone; or (2) some increasing difficulty of bringing these essential physical materials into practical co-operative conjunction; or (3) some chronic misunderstanding between iron and coal masters and their workpeople, by which they have been rendered quite unable to command the labour necessary to supply the demand for their products under the most favourable conditions otherwise ever known; or (4) some inherent stupidity on the part of working miners and their families alone, and the labouring class generally, that has rendered all the best and most profitable situations of the masters fruitless; or (5), which is the least conceivable hypothesis of all, that there is something wrong in the mere marketing of pig iron, whereby the profits of increasing and exorbitant prices go wholly into the pockets of merchants and speculators, and consequently exercise no economic action over iron and coal owners at all. With apparently the most rigorous intentions to meet both foreign and domestic demand, the Scotch ironmasters have altogether failed to do it. At the end of last year the number of furnaces reported as "existing and nearly ready" was 154. At the end of 1870 they were over 160. But the average number of furnaces actually in blast, which had been 130 in 1870, sank to 127 in 1871, and during the present year have further fallen to 123. But in striking an average for a year one must be cautious, for the furnaces in blast this year have been diminished by a dozen or two within the last few days. What can all this mean under the growing demand and high price given for "Scotch pig"? Has a great blight fallen suddenly on the once famous mining enterprise and energy of Scotland? Have the coal and ironmasters and Mr. Alex. McDonald and the working miners in their furious struggles against each other for years fallen into a trance of mutual masculation, and become all unconscious that the sceptre is departing—if it has not already quite departed—from them? The great world, in its demand for iron, will certainly not be long stopped in its progress by a market which discovers no elasticity, and shrinks year after year in dimensions when it has every motive and inducement to enlarge.

D. INDUSTRIAL DEPRESSION BETWEEN THE WARS

The success of the heavy industries was the cause of so much of Scotland's prosperity before 1914. Their collapse after the war led to widespread depression. There were several examples of the transformation. Shipbuilding was notable. It had a record output in 1913 and its prosperity had wide repercussions in other industries, especially steelmaking. Few industries suffered as severely from international competition.

(1) Scottish Economic Committee, *Scotland's Industrial Future*, (1939), pp. 65-69 –

Shipbuilding needs no advertisement as Scotland's most famous industry. It occupies a key position, both in itself, and through the considerable dependence on its prosperity of the steel industry, and of a great variety of ancillary industries covering equipment of every kind, down to the furniture needed for passenger vessels.

As the demand for mercantile tonnage depends on the state of international trade, any contraction in such trade has a depressing effect not only on Scottish shipbuilding as such, but on the whole group of industries associated with it. A further difficulty arises owing to subsidised competition from foreign shipbuilding industries.

The position is illustrated by the fact that, whereas the merchant navy of the U.K. was reduced by 1,712,825 gross tons between 1914 and 1937 (from 19,256,766 gross tons to 17,543,941 gross tons), foreign shipping increased by 21,500,000 gross tons in the same period. The United Kingdom's share of world output fell from an average of about 61% in the five pre-war years to approximately 34% in 1937. The Scottish share of world output declined from 21.5% to rather less than 15% during this period, but Scottish production expressed as a percentage of the United Kingdom's output rose from 35% to about 40% over the period.

With periodic fluctuations British shipbuilding output rose from the 1890's to a peak in the immediately pre-war period, and was again very active immediately after the Great War. A short recovery from the ensuing depression occurred in 1924, and in the years 1927 to 1930 the shipyards were again fairly busy. The world depression of the early 1930's, however, was catastrophic in its effects, and virtually brought the Clyde shipbuilding industry to a standstill. In 1932 and 1933 practically 70% of the shipyard workers were unemployed, while on the North-East Coast of England this proportion was actually exceeded in both years. The slow recovery, which reached its height in 1937, failed to restore merchant shipbuilding activity to anything approaching the level of ten years earlier, and fell far short of that of 1913, largely due to the lack of foreign orders.

Naval construction has long been an important factor in the prosperity of the Clyde, and the industry was hard hit by the Washington and London treaties. In 1929 British warship construction was less than one-seventh of the average for the three pre-war years, and the minimum naval output unfortunately coincided with the worst years of the depression. It was not until 1936 that naval orders were again placed on a really substantial scale. The result was to bring total United Kingdom construction in 1937 (including both mercantile and naval tonnage) up to about the level of 1929 (about 1,500,000 tons), although there was a great change in its composition. Whereas in 1929 there was comparatively little naval construction, the 1937 total included approximately 500,000 tons in this category.

The contraction of the industry and the severe depressions to which it has been subject, have naturally tended to diminish the numbers employed. Between 1924 and 1937 the number of insured workers in the industry in Scotland fell by 20,000 from 65,000 to 45,000, and half this decrease occurred between 1929 and 1937. In March, 1938, there were some 7,000 fewer shipyard workers in employment in Scotland than in March, 1929, although the unemployment percentage was actually lower at the later date.

The coincidence of rearmament and commercial recovery has brought about a very serious rise in shipbuilding costs during the last two and a half years, particularly during 1937. This circumstance, combined with the increasing prevalence of the movement towards economic nationalism abroad, has operated to produce a drastic curtailment of orders for new mercantile construction, threatening to merge into a practical cessation of such orders—our prices remaining at a figure at which it is almost impossible to cope with foreign (subsidised) competition. Tonnage under construction in British shipyards reached a peak (since the depression) in the June quarter of 1937, and has since been declining. Vessels commenced in Great Britain and Ireland during the first half of 1938 aggregated 330,000 tons, as compared with 621,000 tons in the first half of 1937, a decline of 46.9%, whilst the tonnage of vessels commenced abroad fell by only 8% during the same period. In the third quarter of 1938 the Clyde, which formerly provided one-fifth of the world's ships, received only the following mercantile orders: July and September —nil; August—two tugs. Meantime the "Economist" index of freight rates (1898-1913 = 100; 1913 = 116.3), which had risen from 83.9 in the third quarter of 1935 to 162.0 in the third quarter of 1937, declined again to 111.7 in the same quarter of 1938 (113.0 in September, 1938).

Serious features have been the decrease in foreign orders for British built ships and the increase in British shipbuilding contracts placed abroad, due partly to the need for recovering credits which, owing to foreign currency restrictions, could not be transferred in cash, but only in kind, and partly to the cheapness of foreign subsidised competition and the lower costs, in some measure thus accounted for, of our competitors. In the present year, for the first time on record, the tonnage ordered abroad by Great Britain is in excess of British tonnage built on foreign account.

It should, however, be borne in mind that some 65% of the British mercantile fleet is over ten years of age, and that substantial replacements must be effected in due course, seeing that modern ship construction has evolved a technique enabling a far higher degree of economy in transport power for a given weight of cargo to be effected than was formerly the case, and modern vessels constructed on the most recent principles must infallibly replace less economic types of shipping. Further, the rise in the percentage of Inter-Imperial trade has been of substantial benefit to British shipping, and can reasonably be expected to import a certain stable element into our carrying trade and therefore into our mercantile construction so far as it is increasingly dependent on the demands of that trade. It 1913 the British Empire provided 24.9% of British imports and received 37% of British exports. In 1937 these proportions had risen to 39.4% of British imports and 48.3% of British exports, while in the first half of 1938, more than one half of the total export trade of Great

Britain was with the Empire. It is relevant to point out that most of the products of Inter-Imperial trade are carried by British vessels. Thus, in the case of imports into the United Kingdom from the British Empire (to quote the figure for 1936) 93.4% of the total trade involved is so carried, and in the case of British exports to the Empire, 98.5%. These figures may be contrasted with those illustrating British trade with foreign countries. In the case of that trade, only 51.6% of British imports, and 62.8% of British exports were carried in British bottoms. It should be added that Inter-Imperial trade, involving on the average longer voyages, is of special value to British shipping interests, and that the Empire is now the most considerable source of overseas orders to the British mercantile shipbuilding industry.

Imperial trade, however, is only a part, though an increasingly substantial part, of our world trade, and the prospect of any considerable increase in foreign orders is in present circumstances, for the reasons already suggested, extremely remote. Again, naval construction, even on a considerable programme, gives work to only a proportion of our shipyards, and the prosperity of the industry as a whole must ultimately depend on the flow of orders for mercantile vessels.

It may be hoped that the recent European crisis, the immediate dangers of which have been overcome, may be the prelude to a wider basis of co-operation between the nations, not only in the political but in the economic sphere. If, in consequence, existing barriers to the natural current of international trade could be, in part at any rate, removed, our shipbuilding industry should have a reasonable chance of enlarging its markets through the admitted excellence of its products. This would depend upon economic appeasement between nations, a wide question which cannot be fully developed in a brief note such as the present one. Meanwhile it may be said that if subsidised foreign competition should be continued, and if the recent high level of costs throughout the supplying industries catering for the British shipbuilding industry persists, it may well prove to be the case that, in the interests of a great home industry, the question of meeting foreign subsidies may require urgent Government consideration.

Opinion on the future of the traditional heavy industries underwent a change in emphasis roughly between the 1920s and the 1930s. At the beginning of the period some thought the earlier competitive position of the old industrial structure could be regained, though only if costs were reduced (2). In the 1930s it was more commonly believed that there was a permanent surplus of unemployed labour in the old industries and that it could be re-employed only by the successful prosecution of a policy of diversification of industry (3). Both views are illustrated by Sir James Lithgow, perhaps the most influential Scottish industrialist of the inter-war years.

(2) James Lithgow, '*Shipyard Prospects*', in *The Glasgow Herald Trade Review* (1921), p. 36 –

Efficient conditions of employment, by which might be understood the use of the individual's skill, the work-shop space, and the costly machinery up to the maximum of their capacity, are well-nigh hopeless when employers are called upon to consult a trade union delegate before an individual workman will agree to work half an hour after the usual stopping time to finish some small but essential job, and so enable a ship worth perhaps £500,000 to sail by the evening tide; and where the shift system is surrounded by so many stipulations as to make it so costly as to preclude the intensive working of the plant. Similarly, skilled men are required, to waste their skill on work that a reasonable craftsman would consider unworthy of his brains, but his latent and unwanted skill has to be paid for.

Why are these absurd and obvious obstacles to economy not swept away? The answer is two fold. In the first place, labour clings with extraordinary tenacity to these archaic privileges which it has managed to establish in the past, and does not seem to realise that in the aggregate these reduce to a great extent the real value of labour. In the second place, these matters seldom affect all employers in the same manner at the same time, and it is, therefore, not unreasonable that they should adopt the alternative method of all-round reductions of wages, which affect all to a similar and easily calculated extent. To those who blame employers for this attitude, I would say that it is up to those who suffer from this method to adopt the other alternative, which they get ample opportunities of doing.

When labour leaders instruct their members to welcome changes designed to reduce total costs, and to work up to the reasonable capacity of their skill, realising that the laws of supply and demand in a democratically governed country are an ample safeguard against exploitation, there will be some real hope of maintaining weekly wages at a higher level. Under present conditions suggestions that our prosperity as a shipbuilding country can be regained at anything like the present level of wages, are the purest humbug, and those who make them are doing our men an ill service in fostering hopes which the hard logic of events is bound to blast.

(3) Sir James Lithgow, 'Scotland's Industrial Future' in *The Glasgow Herald Trade Review* (1932), p. 29 –

Our problem in Scotland is how to organise our older industries so as to recover such portion of our export trade as the changed world conditions may leave open to us, and also to take advantage of the present favourable circumstances to stimulate the pursuit of our more domestic industries, so that we may provide our fair share of the needs of these islands . . .

The general facts of the coal trade, iron and steel and shipbuilding and engineering are fairly well known . . . Each industry is faced with the same two main problems. The first is the question of wages costs, which, however efficient the industry itself may be, must ultimately be the limiting factor in competition with other countries, since these other countries have now had ample opportunity to share our technical discoveries. The solution of this problem can hardly be laid upon those in control of industry.

The general public has set a standard in its conditions for public servants and sheltered industries which is already in excess of what the export industries have been able to agree with their employees, and until the public, through their elected representatives, take steps to rectify this injustice, it is unreasonable to expect the exporters to economise much further.

The second, a problem within the power of industry itself to deal with, is that of equating productive capacity to probable demand, by concentrating production in the most effective units.

In the coal trade, in spite of, or because of, Acts of Parliament the individualistic outlook characteristic of the Scot still prevails, but users of coal can feel satisfied that the technical standard of coal mining in Scotland is high, and that any losses which are arising through excessive productive capacity are not being borne by the consumer.

The situation in the manufacture of steel is rather otherwise. It is an undoubted fact that failure to achieve co-operative control of the several Scottish works is keeping in operation an unnecessary number of plants each inadequately supplied with orders, and it is fair to assume that in this way economies are being lost which would benefit producer and consumer. Both in technical development and in administrative coordination much progress has been made. With a unified steel trade, Scotland will compare both in quality and in price with any district in England, and, subject to the effect of public policy on wage and taxation costs, we will be able to hold our own with the best productive plants in the world.

The British shipbuilding industry has taken very definite steps to reduce a capacity which obviously could never be called for owing to the permanent loss of some of our customers, both merchant and naval. There can be no doubt that trade revival will find Scottish shipbuilders in a better position to compete for foreign work as a result of these co-operative efforts. We can still claim superiority in technical ability and in economic design . . .

A personal survey of the industrial field in Scotland leads me to the conclusion that we must look forward to a smaller percentage of our population being employed in what have hitherto been regarded as our heavy basic industries, but that without exception those engaged in these industries do appreciate that by determined effort on their part they may still maintain a highly efficient industry in Scotland, perhaps on a reduced scale. It is equally apparent that the balance of the population must seek an outlet for their activities in the lighter and more specialised industries associated with articles of domestic consumption, ranging from tinned tomatoes to electric fires.

The policy of industrial diversification was encouraged in the 1930s by the Commissioner for the Special Areas in Scotland and by the work of the independent Scottish Economic Committee. The most notable achievement was the industrial estate at Hillington. Major difficulties limited the success. A pessimistic outlook on the future of the old industrial structure may have led to a neglect of the need for innovation and growth in the traditional fields (4), or, more generally, though understood only later, the policies may have aimed at removing unemployment rather than at promoting economic growth (5).

(4) *An Industrial Survey of the South West of Scotland, 1932.* (Prepared for the Board of Trade by the University of Glasgow), para. 543 –

The estimates of male employment in 1934 provide for estimated normal developments in each industry. They do not take account of new industries. It has been shown that there has been no failure of the inventive powers of the people, and enterprise is active ... Therefore it seems reasonable to expect that, once it is realised that recovery in the basic industries will probably be slow, industry will broaden out and many new types of manufacture will be started .. We have to consider the employing capacity of such possible new developments apart from the influence of a tariff. In recent months there have been several significant signs of new developments ... There are numerous indications that enterprise and invention are both getting ready to move forward, and by 1934 the aggregate addition to employment will be very considerable. It would be hazardous to make a definite estimate, but, allowing for this factor, it may be concluded that in 1934 the surplus male labour in the Survey Area ... would be about 100,000. It is clear that if this figure is to be reduced, there must be more movement from the district or more new industries in it or both together.

(5) The Scottish Council (Development and Industry), *Report of the Committee on Local Development in Scotland* (1952), paras. 69 and 70 –

The emphasis of present location policy has been on the needs of the Development Areas, which have been put, so to speak, in the shop-window, while other parts of the country have been given less prominence. The attention of industrialists has been directed first towards the Development Areas, and most of those who have been attracted to Scotland from elsewhere have been moved largely by the advantages offered to firms going to those areas. For the many firms that did not contemplate a location outside an established industrial area, a move to the Scottish Development Area seemed natural, since the two main parts of it included nearly all the older industrial centres. This fact, and the emphasis that was laid on the rehabilitation of those older centres, meant that there was little disposition to change the boundaries of the Development Area once they were scheduled. That static feature of the Development Area contrasts with the dynamic character of industrial development which may involve the growth of new centres of industry in order to exploit the possibilities of technological advances and new materials. Development Area policy, therefore, has tended to put undue emphasis on the difficulties and dangers in the older areas—notably unemployment or the threat of unemployment—and given too little encouragement to the industrial growth in other parts of the country.

The priority that has been enjoyed by the Development Areas has usually been justified in terms of the unemployment figures for those areas. Unemployment, however, cannot be the sole criterion of policy. Apart from the over-riding need to promote the growth of new industries in suitable locations, there may be a greater volume of concealed unemployment in other areas; or the danger to the community fabric may be in greater jeopardy in areas where unemployment is not at present high but where a steady drift of population has already set in.

It is not surprising that even in 1937, the best year of the 1930s, it was felt that industrial diversification would not remove the need for labour to move to jobs elsewhere.

(6) *Report of the Commissioners for the Special Areas in Scotland, 7th July, 1936, to 31st August 1937*, Cmd. 5604, para 174 –

The problem of the Scottish Special Areas is essentially different from those of either the English or the Welsh Areas. Transference from the Areas is more difficult because there is in Scotland no busy expanding industrial centre like the Midlands or South of England and the time has not yet come when transference to England will become a normal outlet for Scottish youths. It is not entirely clear whether such a development is wholly desirable but I have noted with interest the extent to which young men are finding their way to employment in England via the Training Centres of the Ministry of Labour and it may be that such a movement may continue to be necessary for some years. It is certain at any rate that transference out will not conflict with efforts to bring fresh industry to the Areas, until much greater progress in both directions has been made than has so far proved practicable.

CHAPTER IV

Trade and Finance

A. THE UNION AND TRADE

The terms of the Treaty of Union brought Scotland into an Anglo-Scottish common market and within the provenance of the Navigation Acts. To compensate for the inevitable equalisation of taxation in the two countries, Scotland was given a payment of £398,085 10s., known as the Equivalent, and promised a further proportion of the increased revenue which it was anticipated would accrue in Scotland when duty was charged at the higher United Kingdom rate.

After 1707 anti-unionists felt their forebodings were fulfilled. The imposition of the malt tax was a particular source of grievance (1). Such complaints were ill-founded. Remittances to London from the main sources of revenues did not increase conspicuously after 1707 (2). Much of the criticism arose because some Scots had unduly inflated expectations of the benefits they expected from the Union; others, probably Wodrow among them, would never have been convinced of its benefits whatever the outcome. A more moderate judgement could see a number of changes after the Union, but insufficient to give rise to any major economic change in the short-run (3).

(1) R. Wodrow, *Analecta* (Maitland Club edn.), vol. iii, pp. 280-281 -

23rd March 1726.

In the end of this moneth, we hear that the Malt-tax Bill is passed, and three pence [a] bushell continuoed on Scotland, with a declaration, that the excrescencys above twenty thousand pound should be applyed to Scotland. Mr. Grant, from Aberdeenshire, moved that it should be reduced to three half pence a bushell, this being all Scotland could bear, and what would amount to twenty thousand pound. Mr. Dundas backed him, and fully draucht [inferred, proved] that three half pence would not only defray the twenty thousand pound demanded, but all the charges in gathering it. That the excrescencys being apply[ed] to Scots manufactorys, was but a blind to make the tax go doun, which would be an [in]tollerable burden, and this would be of no use at all to the country, but enrich particular persons. No body wer with Mr. Dundass, save Mr. Grant and Brigadeer Steuart. We are at a lou pass, when ther are none but three of forty-five to appear in a matter that so nearly concerns Scotland, and as to which most part of the shires and the burrous have addressed. But we nou see under what influence our Members of Parliament are, and that they must be reimbursed in the charges they are at in their elections and attendance in Parliament; and it's much to be feared, the most part are influenced either by pensions or hopes; and, let matters that be of never so great importance for Scotland come in, they all, almost, act by direction at London, without any regard to their country's true interests.

They add, that in the Committy it came to be considered in whose hands the managment of the excressency above the twenty thousand pounds for Scots trade and manufacters should be. The Royall Burghs wer spoke [of], but an English member said, it might as well be put in the hands [of] the toun of Edinburgh; others proposed the Lords of Session and Barrons of Exchequer, who wer yearly to given ther accounts in to the Treasury of Great Brittain. But this matter is not yet determined.

Great things are expected by one side from what is in dependance as to our trade and manufacters; and as litle by the other side, since they expect the managment of this affair will fall into the hands of such as will enrich themselves, and consume it in servants and clerks. Whatever be in this, ther is a vaster fund than ever Scotland had for publick encouragment in trade and manufacters, forteen thousand pounds of the remains of the Equivalent money, with the interest since 1712, which makes it twenty-six thousand pounds, and two thousand pounds a year by act of Parliament, and this yearly excressency of the malt-tax. But, alace! we have no faithfull hands to intrust so much to, who will mind the publick interests!

(2) Scottish Record Office. Records of the Scottish Exchequer and Customs Board –

Remittances to London

Year	*Excise*	*Land tax*	*Year*	*Excise*	*Land tax*
1707–08	24,000	47,854	39–40	15,350	47,890
08–09	33,856	47,854	40–41	7,150	47,846
09–10	21,562	47,854	41–42	17,950	47,898
10–11	3,723	47,954	42–43	17,300	47,526
11–12	—	47,954	43–44	21,150	47,899
12–13	18,804	23,977	44–45	17,700	47,931
13–14	41,805	23,977	45–46	13,600	47,832
14–15	3,906	23,977	46–47	20,000	47,831
15–16	15,968	41,674	47–48	21,000	47,918
16–17	2,376	35,759	48–49	31,600	47,921
17–18	—	35,965	49–50	24,400	35,920
18–19	—	35,965	50–51	20,000	35,910
19–20	—	35,965	51–52	21,600	35,915
20–21	—	35,965	52–53	26,800	23,907
21–22	—	23,977	53–54	28,300	23,856
22–23	—	23,977	54–55	22,200	23,889
23–24	—	23,975	55–56	18,500	47,829
24–25	—	23,974	56–57	12,009	47,698
25–26	23,805	23,946	57–58	11,000	47,797
26–27	20,008	47,917	58–59	16,812	47,851
27–28	20,000	35,931	59–60	21,000	47,819
28–29	20,000	35,941	60–61	31,000	47,805
29–30	20,000	23,956	61–62	42,491	47,847
30–31	20,000	23,946	62–63	42,200	47,943
31–32	20,000	11,964	63–64	47,000	47,921
32–33	—	11,959	64–65	53,300	47,901
33–34	20,000	23,945	65–66	36,400	47,916
34–35	20,000	23,939	66–67	45,550	47,923
35–36	21,000	23,960	67–68	40,200	35,926
36–37	20,000	23,944	68–69	55,200	35,925
37–38	20,000	23,977	69–70	56,600	35,911
38–39	18,000	23,928			

(3) Scottish Record Office. Clerk of Penicuik Manuscripts. Sir John Clerk, *Observations on the Present Circumstances of Scotland* (1730). Printed in Scottish History Society publication, vol. 2 (fourth series) pp. 195–201 –

As to our trade immediately after the Union it stood thus as it still does. The importatione of our black catle to England increased considerably, as did likeways their prices and by consequence the value of these lands which produced them; but the people of England found noe less their advantage in all this than we did, because it appeared that our black catle and even our sheep were aboundantly fed on the refuse of their pastures.

Our linnen manufactures were improven in proportion to the care that was taken of them. The justices of peace and other gentlemen in the several counties where these manufactures are most in use began to consider at last that it was their interest not to protect their tennants and coaters in the bad practises which formerly took place in the working and whitening our linen cloths. But what begins nou to give them the greatest credite is a late appointment by His Majesty of some Trustees who without fea or rewards, and with a regard only to the interest of their country, make it their business to put the several good laus we have in execution against all transgressors. 'Tis from the care of these gentlemen that we expect very great advantages in this trade, especially when it seems to be what the genius of our country people is most inclinable to promot. We begin nou to export considerable quantities of linen cloth, especially into England, and indeed it is happy for us that it is so, for without this trade and that aforementioned of our black catle we wou'd be in noe condition to live in this part of Britain, by reason of the vast sums which are drawn yearly out of this country for the support of our people who live in England, or for purchasing the commodities we want from that country.

As to our woolen manufactures, we are much in the same condition as at the time of the Union. Some cloaths are made here in several places, but it seems a standing rule amongst our country gentlemen that such who by the narouness of their fortunes ought most to make use of them are most averse to them, unless when it happens that they are sold for English cloaths or (to please them better) are sometimes actually sent into England and return'd again amongst other cloaths from that country. We manufacture likeways considerable parcels of serges, and these meet with some encouragement in our mercats because they generally make up a part of our habiliments which are least in vieu, otherways perhaps they wou'd be in the same discredit amongst us as with our broad cloaths. We manufacture likeways great quantities of stockings in the shire of Aberdeen but this trade is not so considerable as it formerly was. In the meantime, since we are so happy as not to export our wool, it is hoped that in time we may be induced to make better use of it than formerly. But I shall again have occasion to talk of this hereafter.

Other branches of our exportations are tobaco from the West Indies. This happened for some years after the Union to be a considerable branch of trade, particularly at Glasgow and some of our western parts, but some unfaire practises appearing, it fell under discouragements and continues so; houever, it is hoped that it may again revive in proportion to the honesty and dilligence with which it shall be managed, for provided the duties be faithfully ansuered to the Croun it must, by the nature of the Union of the two Kingdoms, meet with the same encouragement here as in any place of England. I have heard it given out that the complaints against the merchants of Glasgow on the head of their managements in the tobaco trade was occasioned by the jealousies of some of the people who trade from the western ports of England. This may be partly true, but it is certain that there were too good grounds for what was advanced.

Our salmon and herring fishings are much in the same state they were in at the time of the Union, yet there is this difference, that by the care of the Trustees for our fisheries and manufactories the credite of our herrings is somewhat better established, and it is hoped that by the assistance of England nou in a time of peace very considerable profits may be made. We are generally fondest of what is least in our pouer, and so through manifold dangers and difficulties force a trade to Africa and the Indies, but when our fishings come to be considered in that light which de Wit and other great men in Holland held them they will be found a greater treasure than any other place of the world did ever produce to Great Britain.

We export likeways considerable quantities of corn by reasone that since the Union our lands are more improven, but I wou'd fain hope that in time there will be such an increase of manufactories amongst us and by consequence such an increase of people that there will be noe occasion for such exportation.

As to those branches of our exportations . . . such as lead, coal etc., the first is vastly increased by neu discoveries of several mines and from the industrie of several persons, particularly those concerned in the York Building Company. We have reason to hope that considerable improvements may be made. We have nou several rich iron mines in vieu, and from some tryals that have been made of our Highland woods we have sufficient grounds to believe that as much timber of all kinds may be brought up on our barren mountains as may in time supply the want of timber from the Northern Kingdoms.

As to the exportation of coall, it lyes under some descouragements by reason of duties which effect it, but I am very well satisfied that a century or tuo will consume all that lyes near our sea coast and that there will scarce remain such a quantity in any part of this country as will be necessary for inland consumpt. Thus haveing mentioned the principal branches of our exportations I come nou to speak of our importations.

The chief of these are French wines and brandies, but here a very black and scandalous scene will appear from the following considerations.

Firstly, a good dale of these liquores imported are really run, by which means the King is not only defrauded of his duties but the faire traders are undersold and ruined.

These liquors have been imported into this poor country with an incredible disadvantage, for in regard the French take little or nothing from us by way of bartar. The species of our monie is carried out for purchasing these liquors, or which is the same thing, the price of our black catle, linnen cloath and other things is keept back and retained in London for paying the bills of our merchants at Burdeaux from whence these wines and brandies are generally brought. What the prime cost of such liquors are may be easily guess'd from the quantity imported, and I dare be positive that the real loss on the ballance of trade with France cannot be much under £30,000 yearly and consequently that in a tract of 22 years we have lost £660,000 of our monie. 'Tis to this cause only that we oue the scarcity of our monie or its not increasing in that proportion as it ought, for except a litle salmond I believe it will be difficult for our wine merchants to shoue that the French have for that time taken any of our commodities.

In the next place, this trade of French wines and brandies is founded on notorious perjury, for it is will knouen that since the Union when the high duties on these liquors took place the wines have been entered on the oaths of the importers as Spanish wines and have all payed the Spanish duties, and the brandies (as is before mentioned) were run without paying any duties at all . . .

Our other importations are for the most part as prejudicial to us as these of wines and brandies from France. I say for the most part only, because it must be acknouledged that some of them are for the benefit of our shiping or our manufactories. I shall here briefly enumerat the chief of both kinds. Our prejudicial importations are foreign spirits, linnen cloath, flanders laces, Indian and Persian commodities not imported by our own East Indian Company or discharged by law to be made use of, foreign soap, paper, starch, arms, Dutch ware, etc., with all other importations contrary to the form of the Act of the 12th King Charles entituled 'Act for encourageing Shipping and Navigation'. These and many more are burdened with high duties in order to preserve the ballance of the British trade with foreign countries and to encourage our own manufactories, yet our merchants are so fare from follouing the rules and regulations that are so just and necessary to us that they not only import such goods in great quantities but run most of them without payment of duties to the great damage of our manufactories, the oppressing and starveing the poor, and the ruine of the fair traders.

As to these importations which are necessary for our manufactories, such as lintseed, potashes, whale oile, etc., a litle of them goes a great way when these manufactories are under so much discouragement. We import likeways timber of all kinds, pitch and tarr, hemp and flax from Sweden, Denmark and the northern parts of Germany: such are fare from being useless importations as we are stated, but if our mountains were stored with woods and our valeys improven as they might be there wou'd be noe great occasion for them.

The protection of the Navigation Acts proved most fruitful to the tobacco trade of Glasgow, but the Glasgow merchants' success rested also on their own efficient methods of trading.

(4) John Gibson, *The History of Glasgow* (1777), pp. 205f. –

A spurt of commerce appears to have been raised among the inhabitants of Glasgow between the periods of 1660 and 1707, when the Union with England took place . . . Whatever their trade was, at this time, it could not be considerable; the ports to which they were obliged to trade lay all to the eastward; the circumnavigation of the island would therefore prove an almost unsurmountable bar to the commerce of Glasgow; the people upon the east coast, from their situation, would be in possession of almost the whole commerce of Scotland. The Union with England opened a field of trade, for which the situation of Glasgow was greatly to her advantage; the commerce of the east coast, since that period, has declined; that of the west has increased to an amazing degree.

So sensible were the people of Glasgow of the advantages which they had procured by the Union, that no sooner was this treaty signed, than they began immediately to prosecute the trade to Virginia and Maryland; they chartered vessels from Whitehaven; they sent out cargoes of goods, and brought back tobacco in return. The method in which they proceeded in this trade was certainly a very prudent one, a supercargo went out with every vessel, who bartered his goods for tobacco, until such time as he had either sold all his goods, or procured as much tobacco as was sufficient to load his vessel; he then returned immediately; and, if any of his goods remained unsold, he brought them home with him. Happy would it have been for Britain if she had always traded with America in this manner . . .

From the period of 1735 to the aera of 1750, the commerce of Glasgow advanced but slowly; soon after the year 1740 a new mode was adopted in carrying on the trade to America; in place of the prudent method of bartering, which I formerly took notice of, factors were established in the country, who received the goods, and remitted the tobacco; these goods they gave credit of to the planters, on condition that they should receive their crops of tobacco, when ready for the market; for several years this method succeeded extremely well, and the payments were generally made in a reasonable time; but the trade, after the period of 1750, being exceedingly increased, and factors established in every corner of the country, the interests of these gentlemen began to interfere with one another; ambition for who should be possessed of the largest share of the trade took possession of them; they lent to the planters large sums of money, in order to secure them for customers, they gave them unlimited credit; and thus, by their endeavours to get the better of one another, rendered the commerce with the people of America, rather a speculative, than a solid branch of business.

. . . Several cargoes [of imports] from North America and the West Indies, the property of Glasgow, are delivered in London; and . . . very great quantities of wheat are sent from North America to the southern parts of Europe, on account of the merchants of Glasgow; therefore the particular imports of the port of Glasgow must fall very far short of the real imports of the property of Glasgow; and . . . very large quantities of goods are exported annually from London, and other ports in England, for account of the people in Glasgow; consequently the particular exports of the port of Glasgow must fall very far short of the real exports made by the merchants of Glasgow.

When the American trade was interrupted after 1776 the West Indian trade helped to replace it.

(5) D. Macpherson, *Annals of Commerce* (1805), vol. iv, pp. 34-35 –

The merchants of Glasgow, when their American trade was interrupted by the war, extended the West-India branch of their commerce, and resumed, or enlarged, their trade with the continent of Europe, which their convenient situation for the trade with America had made them in some degree overlook for many years bypast. A considerable number of them withdrew their capitals from foreign trade and shipping, in order to employ them in manufactures, the improvements of which, and the establishment of new ones, were with good reason thought to afford a prospect of more permanent, as well as more solid, prosperity than foreign trade ... From about this time the quantity of manufactured goods, sent from Glasgow to London and other parts of England, was greatly increased; and ... besides supplying the shopkeepers of London and other places, great quantities of them are shipped by the merchants, and some of them to the same countries, to which the merchants of Glasgow used to send goods of the same species, manufactured in England or in India; such are the revolutions of trade! And hence the export trade of the west part of Scotland bears now a smaller proportion to the whole of the exports of Great Britain, than it formerly did, though the real amount of the capital employed in trade, and of the productive industry, in that part of the country has in fact been greatly increased.

The statistics of the official values of Scottish imports and exports from 1755, when they first become available again after the Union, until 1827, when the series ends, indicate the growth of external trade.

(6) *Scottish Imports and Exports 1755-1827.*

Sources: Public Record Office. Customs 14, vols. 1-39.

Scottish Record Office. Customs Ledgers (includes only the years 1762, 1775-81, 1783, 1786, 1788-95, 1801, 1806).

National Library of Scotland. Melville MS 60, gives only

summary figures for the years 1755-82, and does not distinguish exports and re-exports –

(Foreign includes colonial)

	Imports £	*Exports of British goods* £	*Re-exports of foreign goods* £
1755	465,412	284,701	250,876
1756	480,425	286,968	339,081
1757	619,836	353,867	472,709
1758	659,165	382,327	448,931
1759	605,888	412,888	530,917
1760	850,793	437,237	648,968
1761	748,640	424,387	741,335
1762	708,925	347,819	650,346
1763	903,891	1,091,435*	
1764	886,353	426,758	817,170
1765	922,401	400,928	779,950
1766	980,990	355,627	808,077
1767	1,023,197	452,298	793,192
1768	1,236,648	454,757	1,047,392
1769	1,225,529	1,563,053*	
1770	1,213,360	510,576	1,217,341
1771	1,386,329	503,473	1,353,861
1772	1,210,264	472,230	1,088,526
1773	1,115,802	442,973	1,169,205
1774	1,202,277	509,840	862,302
1775	1,267,300	352,404	771,514
1776	746,600	439,229	586,743
1777	802,254	555,464	282,178
1778	740,654	450,637	252,183
1779	774,772	533,835	303,438
1780	902,724	767,412	234,627
1781	803,871	580,338	182,772
1782	809,022	496,078	157,631
1783	1,007,591	613,599	216,225
1784	1,153,507	758,155	171,747
1785	1,379,476	659,546	348,089
1786	1,175,910	639,217	275,422
1787	1,468,928	744,724	370,410
1788	1,476,116	787,682	401,406
1789	1,413,063	809,928	360,149
1790	1,688,148	864,831	370,574
1791	1,941,631	914,207	382,328

	Imports £	*Exports of British goods* £	*Re-exports of foreign goods* £
1792	1,761,657	886,238	344,646
1793	1,430,943	775,081	249,661
1794	1,443,095	862,125	222,606
1795	1,268,520	848,462	128,530
1796	1,724,610	1,134,417	188,307
1797	1,490,084	1,037,677	179,444
1798	1,893,728	1,373,689	295,508
1799	2,353,591	1,618,755	297,876
1800	2,212,791	1,847,723	497,579
1801	2,579,844	2,449,185	395,331
1802	2,913,202	2,023,069	579,790
1803	2,497,733	1,722,135	341,087
1804	2,611,942	1,856,748	398,936
1805	3,010,978	2,138,207	368,921
1806	3,033,963	2,232,936	483,678
1807	2,989,158	2,228,288	508,420
1808	2,152,584	2,321,556	496,024
1809	—	—	—
1810	3,687,133	4,123,413	617,826
1811	2,447,578	3,155,211	740,404
1812	2,775,458	5,132,121	993,197
1813	3,182,223	6,748,024	1,081,971
1814	3,757,053	6,236,592	1,949,063
1815	3,447,354	7,441,889	1,546,890
1816	2,539,234	5,872,689	834,457
1817	3,426,754	7,329,746	426,278
1818	4,129,339	6,254,725	514,809
1819	3,240,348	5,328,777	542,622
1820	3,275,461	5,478,226	416,552
1821	4,086,029	5,747,896	365,458
1822	3,818,916	6,070,535	335,056
1823	3,927,430	5,474,734	236,635
1824	4,349,991	5,656,474	242,957
1825	4,994,304	5,654,521	187,578
1826	3,084,112	4,283,074	147,429
1827	3,948,234	5,932,852	126,651

* Missing in P.R.O. and S.R.O. series; supplied from Melville MS.

The trade with America and the West Indies encouraged the growth of a variety of industries in Glasgow.

(7) I. Lettice, *Letters on a Tour through various parts of Scotland, in the year 1792*, pp. 78-82 –

Glasgow, August 30th, 1792.

After having with much pleasure contemplated the various and abundant proofs of the flourishing state of this city, in the beauty, splendour and convenience of its streets, and its public and private buildings, I was anxious to take a view of the Clyde; the grand and original source of its prosperity. This river, which runs on the south side of the town, rises in Annandale, and taking a long north-westerly course through Clydesdale, and passing by Lanark, Hamilton and Glasgow, falls into the Firth of Clyde between Greenock and the Isle of Bute, and thence meeting the sea in the north channel of Ireland, communicates with the German Ocean and the Atlantic. The stream at Glasgow is of considerable breadth; its channel indeed being too wide for the quantity of water flowing through it. Its navigation too was formerly much incommoded by a number of shoals. The accessory waters, brought up even by the spring tides, do not add above three feet, nor those by the neap-tides above one, to the periodical depths of the stream. Great inconveniences were experienced from this shallowness of the river; and lighters in seasons of drought, were, many weeks together, detained at a distance from the quays of Glasgow. An able engineer some years ago undertook to deepen the channel at Broomylaw quay; so as to command seven feet of water, even at the neap-tides. The removal of some of the shoals was another object of this important undertaking; and vessels of seventy tons can, at present, approach the town . . .

In our walk from this bridge westward, betwixt the river and the town, we passed the great glass-works, the ropery, and others of those vast and numerous establishments of manufactures, which, by means of the Clyde, make their way into every part of the world, and are returned to the citizens of Glasgow in all the various forms of wealth. At no great distance from the water are situated their tanneries, their sadleries, and every sort of leather manufacture. These furnish great exports to America and the West Indies. Their sugar refineries, their potteries, which rival those of Staffordshire, their stone and iron manufacturies, not to mention their woollen looms, their fabrics of cotton, linen, lawn, and cambric, are distributed in various quarters of the lower town. The letter foundery, for printing types, deserves particular notice; a species of manufacture at Glasgow, allowed to be executed with superior neatness and intelligence.

The active inhabitants of Glasgow partake also in the fisheries of North Britain; but their concern in this branch is chiefly carried on at Port Glasgow, about twenty miles distant, at the head of the Firth of Clyde.

The first benefit, which this town derived from the union, was the large share it took, with England, in the Virginia tobacco trade. Since the American revolution, this article of commerce and manufacture has greatly declined throughout the whole kingdom; but I was informed, that, in the year 1772, out of ninety thousand hogheads of tobacco, imported from Virginia to Great Britain, the town of Glasgow alone, engrossed forty nine thousand. The vigorous spirit of trade, and manual craft, engaged in importing and working up so abundant a quantity of that article, has since been successfully turned to new objects of commerce; so that there is reason to believe, that, were an accidental failure to happen in any other branch, in the ordinary system of business at Glasgow, the ingenuity and industry of the inhabitants would soon supply the chasm.

B. BANKING: COMMERCIAL BANKS

The foundation of the Scottish banking system came with the incorporation of the Bank of Scotland by act of Parliament in 1695 (1). Its monopoly was broken when the Royal Bank of Scotland was incorporated by Royal Charter in 1727. Other banks were incorporated by Royal Charter, or later under the provisions of the Companies Acts. Until well into the nineteenth century many were unincorporated and in law remained partnerships. The structure of Scottish banking was marked by a number of important banks, which at times engaged in outright rivalry.

(1) Acts of the Parliaments of Scotland, IX, 494-495 (1695). Act for Erecting a Publick Bank –

Our Soveraign Lord considering how usefull a Publick Bank may be in this Kingdom according to the Custom of other Kingdoms and States and that the same can only be best sett up and managed by persons in Company with a Joynt Stock sufficiently indowed with these powers and authorities and liberties necessary and usual in such cases Hath therefore allowed and with the advice and consent of the Estates of Parliament allowes a joynt stock amounting to the soume of twelve hundred thousand pounds money to be raised by the Company hereby Established for the Carying on and the manageing of a publick Bank And farder Statutes and Ordains with advice forsaid that the persons under named . . . or any three of them And in case of the deceas of any of them the persons to be choisen by the survivers shall have power to appoynt a Book for Subscriptions of persons either Natives or Forraigners who shall be willing to Subscribe and pay in to the joynt stock Which Subscriptions the forsaids persons or their quorum are hereby Authorized to receave in the forsaid book which shall ly open every tuesday or ffriday from nine to twelve in the forenoon, and from three to six in the afternoon betuixt the first day of November next and the first day of January next following in the publick Hall or Chamber to be appoynted in the City of Edinburgh And therein all persons shall have liberty to Subscribe for such soumes of money as they shall think fitt to adventure in the said joynt stock one thousand pound Scots being the lowest soume and twenty thousand pound Scots the highest And the two third parts of the saids stocks belonging alwise to persons residing in Scotland Likeas each and every person at the time of his Subscribing shall pay in to the hands of the fornamed persons or any three of them Ten of the hundred of the sums sett doun in their respective Subscriptions towards the Carying on the Bank. And all and every the persons Subscribing and paying in to the said stock as aforsaid shall be and are hereby Declared to be one Body Corporat and Politique by the name of THE GOVERNOUR AND COMPANY OF THE BANK OF SCOTLAND under which Name they shall have perpetual Succession and shall have a Common Seal And their Successors by the name forsaid shall be able and capable to purchase and enjoy as also to give grant alienat and dispose of Lands tenements and all other heretage As likewise of all Sums of money and other moveable goods and gear whatsomever And farder to do and Execut all other things which any other Company or body Corporat can or may lawfully doe or Execut And that as amplie and fully as if the several matters and things were particularly sett doun in this Act.

The general principles governing Scottish banking in the eighteenth century were clearly stated by Adam Smith.

(2) A. Smith, *Wealth of Nations* (Cannan edn.), vol. i, pp. 280-299 –

An operation of this kind [the issue of paper money] has, within these five and twenty or thirty years, been performed in Scotland, by the erection of new banking companies in almost every considerable town, and even in some country villages . . . The business of the country is almost entirely carried on by means of the paper of those different banking companies, with which purchases and payments of all kinds are commonly made. Silver very seldom appears except in the change of a twenty shillings bank note, and gold still seldomer. But though the conduct of all those different companies has not been unexceptionable, and has accordingly required an act of parliament to regulate it; the country, notwithstanding, has evidently derived great benefit from their trade . . .

It is chiefly by discounting bills of exchange, that is, by advancing money upon them before they are due, that the greater part of banks and bankers issue their promissory notes. They deduct always, upon whatever sum they advance, the legal interest till the bill shall become due. The payment of the bill, when it becomes due, replaces to the bank the value of what had been advanced, together with a clear profit of the interest. The banker who advances to the merchant whose bill he discounts, not gold and silver, but his own promissory notes, has the advantage of being able to discount to a greater amount by the whole value of his promissory notes, which he finds by experience, are commonly in circulation. He is thereby enabled to make his clear gain of interest on so much a larger sum.

The commerce of Scotland, which at present is not very great, was still more inconsiderable when the two first banking companies were established; and those companies would have had but little trade, had they confined their business to the discounting of bills of exchange. They invented, therefore, another method of issuing their promissory notes; by granting, what they called, cash accounts, that is by giving credit to the extent of a certain sum (two or three thousand pounds, for example), to any individual who could procure two persons of undoubted credit and good landed estate to become surety for him, that whatever money should be advanced to him, within the sum for which the credit had been given, should be repaid upon demand, together with the legal interest. Credits of this kind are, I believe, commonly granted by banks and bankers in all different parts of the world. But the easy terms upon which the Scotch banking companies accept of re-payment are, so far as I know, peculiar to them, and have, perhaps, been the principal cause, both of the great trade of those companies, and of the benefit which the country has received from it.

Whoever has a credit of this kind with one of those companies, and borrows a thousand pounds upon it, for example, may repay this sum piece-meal, by twenty and thirty pounds at a time, the company discounting a proportionable part of the interest of the great sum from the day on which each of those small sums is paid in, till the whole be in this manner repaid. All merchants, therefore, and almost all men of business, find it convenient to keep such cash accounts with them, and are thereby interested to promote the trade of those companies, by readily receiving their notes in all payments, and by encouraging all those with whom they have any influence to do the same . . .

The facility of discounting bills of exchange, it may be thought indeed, gives the English merchants a conveniency equivalent to the cash accounts of the Scotch merchants. But the Scotch merchants, it must be remembered, can discount their bills of exchange as easily as the English merchants; and have, besides, the additional conveniency of their cash accounts . . .

By issuing too great a quantity of paper, of which the excess was continually returning, in order to be exchanged for gold and silver, the bank of England was for many years together obliged to coin gold to the extent of between eight hundred thousand pounds and a million a year; or at an average, about eight hundred and fifty thousand pounds . . .

The Scotch banks, in consequence of an excess of the same kind, were all obliged to employ constantly agents at London to collect money for them, at an expence which was seldom below one and a half or two per cent. This money was sent down by the waggon, and insured by the carriers at an additional expence of three quarters per cent. or fifteen shillings on the hundred pounds. Those agents were not always able to replenish the coffers of their employers so fast as they were emptied. In this case the resource of the banks was, to draw upon their correspondents in London bills of exchange to the extent of the sum which they wanted. When those correspondents afterwards drew upon them for the payment of this sum, together with the interest and a commission, some of those banks, from the distress into which their excessive circulation had thrown them, had sometimes no other means of satisfying this draught but by drawing a second set of bills either upon the same, or upon some other correspondents in London; and the same sum, or rather bills for the same sum, would in this manner make sometimes more than two or three journies: the debtor bank, paying always the interest and commission upon the whole accumulated sum. Even those Scotch banks which never distinguished themselves by their extreme imprudence, were sometimes obliged to employ this ruinous resource . . .

The Scotch banks, no doubt, paid all of them very dearly for their own imprudence and inattention. But the bank of England paid very dearly, not only for its own imprudence, but for the much greater imprudence of almost all the Scotch banks . . .

It is now more than five-and-twenty years since the paper money issued by the different banking companies of Scotland was fully equal, or rather was somewhat more than fully equal, to what the circulation of the country could easily absorb and employ. Those companies, therefore, had so long ago given all the assistance to the traders and other undertakers of Scotland which it is possible for banks and bankers consistently with their own interest, to give. They had even done somewhat more. They had over-traded a little, and had brought upon themselves that loss, or at least that diminution of profit, which in this particular business never fails to attend the smallest degree of over-trading. Those traders and other undertakers, having got so much assistance from banks and bankers, wished to get still more. The banks, they seem to have thought, could extend their credits to whatever sum might be wanted, without incurring any other expence besides that of a few reams of paper. They complained of the contracted views and dastardly spirit of the directors of those banks, which did not, they said, extend their credits in proportion to the extension of the trade of the country; meaning, no doubt, by the extension of that trade the extension of their own projects beyond what they could carry on, either with their own capital, or with what they had credit to borrow of private people in the usual way of bond or mortgage. The banks, they seem to have thought, were in honour bound to supply the deficiency, and to provide them with all the capital which they wanted to trade with. The banks, however, were of a different opinion, and upon their refusing to extend their credits, some of those traders had recourse to an expedient which, for a time, served their purpose, though at a much greater expence, yet as effectually as the utmost extension of bank credits could have done. This expedient was no other than the well-known shift of drawing and re-drawing; the shift to which unfortunate traders have sometimes recourse when they are upon the brink of bankruptcy. The practice of raising money in this manner had been long known in England, and during the course of the late war, when the high profits of trade afforded a great temptation to over-trading, is said to have been carried on to a very great extent. From England it was brought into Scotland, where, in proportion to the very limited commerce, and to the very moderate capital of the country, it was soon carried on to a much greater extent than it ever had been in England . . .

The difficulties . . . which the bank of England, which the principal bankers in London, and which even the more prudent Scotch banks began, after a certain time, and when all of them had already gone too far, to make about discounting, not only alarmed, but enraged in the highest degree those projectors. Their own distress, of which this prudent and necessary reserve of the banks was, no doubt, the immediate occasion, they called the distress of the country; and this distress of the country, they said was altogether owing to the ignorance, pusillanimity, and bad conduct of the banks, which did not give a sufficiently liberal aid to the spirited undertakings of those who exerted themselves in order to beautify, improve, and enrich the country . . .

In the midst of this clamour and distress, a new bank [Douglas, Heron and Company, popularly known as the Ayr Bank] was established in Scotland for the express purpose of relieving the distress of the country. The design was generous, but the execution was imprudent, and the nature and causes of the distress which it meant to relieve were not, perhaps, well understood. This bank was more liberal than any other had ever been, both in granting cash accounts, and in discounting bills of exchange. With regard to the latter, it seems to have made scarce any distinction between real and circulating bills, but to have discounted all equally. It was the avowed principle of this bank to advance, upon any reasonable security, the whole capital which was to be employed in those improvements of which the returns are the most slow and distant, such as the improvements of land. To promote such improvements was even said to be the chief of the public spirited purposes for which it was instituted. By its liberality in granting cash accounts, and in discounting bills of exchange, it, no doubt, issued great quantities of its bank notes. But those bank notes being, the greater part of them, over and above what the circulation of the country could easily absorb and employ, returned upon it, in order to be exchanged for gold and silver, as fast as they were issued. Its coffers were never well filled. The capital which had been subscribed to this bank at two different subscriptions, amounted to one hundred and sixty thousand pounds, of which eighty per cent. only was paid up. This sum ought to have been paid in at several different instalments. A great part of the proprietors, when they paid in their first instalment, opened a cash account with the bank; and the directors, thinking themselves obliged to treat their own proprietors with the same liberality with which they treated all other men, allowed many of them to borrow upon this cash account what they paid in upon all their subsequent instalments. Such payments, therefore, only put into one coffer, what had the moment before been taken out of another. But had the coffers of this bank been filled ever so well, its excessive circulation must have emptied them faster than they could have been replenished by any other expedient but the ruinous one of drawing upon London, and when the bill becomes due, paying it, together with interest and commission, by another draught upon the same place. Its coffers having been filled so very ill, it is said to have been driven to this resource within a very few months after it began to do business. The estates of the proprietors of this bank were worth several millions, and by their subscription to the original bond or contract of the bank, were really pledged for answering all its engagements. By means of the great credit which so great a pledge necessarily gave it, it was, notwithstanding its too liberal conduct, enabled to carry on business for more than two years. When it was obliged to stop, it had in the circulation about two hundred thousand pounds in bank notes. In order to support the circulation of those notes, which were continually returning upon it as fast as they were issued, it had been constantly in the practice of drawing bills of exchange upon London, of which the number and value were continually increasing, and, when it stopt, amounted to upwards of six hundred thousand pounds. This bank, therefore, had, in little more than the course of two years, advanced to different people upwards of eight hundred thousand pounds at five per cent. Upon the two hundred thousand pounds which it circulated in bank notes, this five per cent. might, perhaps, be considered as clear gain, without any other deduction besides the expence of management. But upon upwards of six hundred thousand pounds, for which it was continually drawing bills of exchange upon London, it was paying, in the way of interest and commission, upwards of eight per cent., and was consequently losing more than three per cent. upon more than three-fourths of all its dealings.

The operations of this bank seem to have produced effects quite opposite to those which were intended by the particular persons who planned and directed it. They seem to have intended to support the spirited undertakings, for as such they considered them, which were at that time carrying on in different parts of the country; and at the same time, by drawing the whole banking business to themselves, to supplant all the other Scotch banks; particularly those established at Edinburgh, whose backwardness in discounting bills of exchange had given some offence. This bank, no doubt, gave some temporary relief to those projectors, and enabled them to carry on their projects for about two years longer than they could otherwise have done. But it thereby only enabled them to get so much deeper into debt so that when ruin came, it fell so much the heavier both upon them and upon their creditors. The operations of this bank, therefore, instead of relieving, in reality aggravated in the long-run the distress which those projectors had brought both upon themselves and upon their country. It would have been much better for themselves, their creditors and their country, had the greater part of them been obliged to stop two years sooner than they actually did. The temporary relief, however, which this bank afforded to those projectors, proved a real and permanent relief to the other Scotch banks. All the dealers in circulating bills of exchange, which those other banks had become so backward in discounting, had recourse to this new bank, where they were received with open arms. Those other banks, therefore, were enabled to get very easily out of that fatal circle, from which they could not otherwise have disengaged themselves without incurring a considerable loss, and perhaps too even some degree of discredit.

In the long-run, therefore, the operations of this bank increased the real distress of the country, which it meant to relieve; and effectually relieved from a very great distress those rivals whom it meant to supplant.

The foundation of the Ayr Bank could be interpreted as a protest, however ill-conceived, against the conservative lending policies of the established banks. As a Whig politician, Henry Cockburn was probably biased in his judgement, but his views were echoed by others and lay behind the flotation of the Commercial Bank of Scotland and the Western Bank of Scotland in 1810 and 1832 respectively (3). The critics were often from the ranks of the rising industrialists. By contrast the merchants had readier access to funds. But the supply of credit was such that there was considerable integration of the various sectors of the economy, as was explained by the Chairman of the Glasgow Chamber of Commerce after the financial crisis of 1810 (4).

(3) Henry Cockburn, *Memorials of His Time* (1910 edn.), pp. 238-240 -

The rise of the Commercial Bank marks the growth of the public mind. It seems odd now that so slight an occurrence as the opening of a private association of money-changers could do so. But the principle on which this one was erected must be considered. No men were more devoid of public spirit, and even of the proper spirit of their trade, than our old Edinburgh bankers. Respectable men they were; but, without talent, general knowledge, or any liberal objects, they were the conspicuous sycophants of existing power. What else could they have been? All the Whig business of the country would not have kept them going for a week; and Government dealt out its patronage in the reception and transmission of the public money only to its friends. So they all combined banking with politics. Not that they would discount a bad bill for a Tory, or refuse to discount a good one for a Whig; but their favours and their graciousness were all reserved for the right side. A demand for a bank founded on more liberal principles was the natural result of this state of things, as soon as these principles had worked their way into any considerable portion of the community. Hence the origin of the Commercial, professing to be the bank of the citizens. It was not meant, and has never acted, as a political engine; nor were all even of its founders, and still less of its proprietors, of the popular party. But simply because it was understood to be erected on the principle of excluding politics from its trade, and tended consequently to emancipate the people, its announcement was a clap of thunder; and efforts, of which the virulence attested the necessity of the stablishment, were made to crush it. It prevailed over these unworthy attempts, and was at the time, and until the other banks were tamed, of incalculable benefit. Moderating the illiberality of the other establishments, by freeing the citizens from their absolute control, it deeply and silently improved the condition of our middle classes, on whose rise its effects have been far more real than apparent.

(4) *Journal of the House of Commons*, vol. 66 (1810-11), p. 657. Report from the Select Committee appointed to enquire into the state of Commercial Credit –

It appeared to Your Committee, that the principal part of the distress which was complained of, has arisen out of great and extensive Speculations, which commenced upon the opening of the South American markets in the Brazils and elsewhere . . .

Mr. Garden, the Chairman of the Chamber of Commerce and Manufacture at Glasgow, said—'That in Glasgow and the neighbourhood the distress began among the manufacturing body of people, and it has pressed more severely upon them hitherto, than on any other class.—That it began about the month of October or beginning of November last: The cause of it appeared to him to be this; That a set of Merchants in London, Liverpool and Glasgow, conceiving that the markets of South America would consume a vast quantity of our manufactures, entered into a project of very extensive Exports to those Countries and to the West India Islands, chiefly intended for the Spanish Colonies; these expeditions not meeting a ready market, those Exporters have not been able to pay the Manufacturers, when the bills became due; these bills were therefore returned upon the Manufacturers, which created a great deal of distress.—Many of those houses that were the original causes of the evil, are gone to bankruptcy long ago; but they have created this evil upon the manufacturers of whom they purchased the goods, that the manufacturers have their property locked up in bankrupts estates; that part of it will be lost no doubt, but yet that in the course of nine, twelve or fifteen months, a considerable part of the capital will return to the manufacturers; but while they are deprived of it, they go on with the greatest difficulty: many of the weaker have been broken down. That the manufacturers of goods who have capitals, still feel great distress from this cause; and it is that class of people that it would be desirable to relieve, because a little aid from Government would enable them to go on with their business, though on a limited scale; but still they would be enabled to retain a certain proportion of their work people or labourers; whereas, if they get no kind of relief they must be broken down also, and the labourers, with their families, must be left without means of subsistence. That this distress still presses very heavily upon them, the export Merchants not being able to pay the Manufacturers for the goods they have taken. That in the course of trade great quantities of goods from Scotland were sold by agents in London; those agents gave a temporary accommodation to the Manufacturer, but nothing more; when the Merchants could not pay those bills which they had given for goods, the bills went back upon the Manufacturers.

That there is this chain of connexion between the manufacturing body and the upper classes of Merchants, the Banks in Scotland having discounted or advanced money upon those bills of the Merchants for the Manufacturers; those bills having gone back, the Manufacturers are not able to take them up; the Capitals of the Banks are therefore taken up also, and they are not able to give the regular accommodation which they had been used to do to their customers.—In this situation of things too, a want of confidence arises in the Banks themselves; when they see people breaking down around them, they become timid and afraid of transacting any business; a want of confidence on the part of the Banks, naturally creates distress among the upper classes of merchants, who are thus deprived of the usual accommodation or means of negotiation; that therefore persons who are possessed of solid property have not the same means of obtaining credit that they usually have had, and very far from it—this want of confidence in the banks makes them distrustful of every body, and the merchants have felt great inconvenience in consequence: The witness said, He understands that some of the banks at Glasgow and in that neighbourhood, do little business, they will rather accumulate their capital and wait the result of the present situation of things; this want of confidence creates general distress among very respectable Merchants.

That the intercourse of credit among the Merchants themselves was much broken down by means of these circumstances, even where the Merchants are solvent.

That there is considerable injury to the Manufacturer; from being obliged to stop his work, his machinery gets out of order, his workmen get dispersed through the country, and he cannot collect them again, but at considerable trouble and expense: and when it is understood that his business is stopped, he loses his custom, and when he begins again, it is almost the same as beginning a new business. It is therefore extremely important that the Manufacturer should go on, though on a limited scale.

That in his opinion, the demand would in a great measure come round to them again: That the home trade, and some other markets, are still open to them: That he has always seen in his experience of thirty years, that a glut in a market is followed by a brisk demand; for no person will supply the markets, or adventure at all, when they are overstocked, hence the market becomes exhausted, and of course a very good demand arises afterwards. The markets of South America and the West India Islands are overstocked at present, but they will naturally come round, and the home trade always takes off a certain quantity; so that he had no doubt, in six or twelve months, this increased demand will do more than take off what is on hand now, or what will be manufactured in the mean time, which will be a very limited quantity indeed.

That if there was no particular glut in the market, from the time of shipping the goods till the payment could be commanded in this country, he should conceive would be twelve or fifteen months; it may in some instances be sooner, but, generally speaking, he should conceive about that time. In some instances payments have been much quicker, perhaps by the return of the same ship; and he mentioned, that there have even been instances of ships returning within four or five months.

The usual date of bills given by the Merchant to the Manufacturer is six or nine months, but in some cases it may be extended to twelve months; in cases where the goods are sold by an agent in London, that agent interposes his credit, and gives an accommodation to the Manufacturer sooner, if he requires it, taking his chance of payment from the Merchant.

That the distresses were immediately, and in the first instance, occasioned by the want of payment for those that were vended; but at the same time the want of a market is certainly a part of the cause. The markets of South America having been for a time overstocked, there is no great demand at present; and even though there were a demand, in the present situation of things, with the want of confidence and the want of credit, it would be difficult for the Manufacturers to know to whom to sell with safety; that is chiefly occasioned by the want of payment for the goods sold: that will in some measure come round in the course of twelve months, and then the Manufacturer will have his own capital again.

That there has been a very considerable supply of this sort of manufactures sent to the Peninsula, which was in a great measure with a view to their being sent to Spanish colonies; that the same failure of payment happened in some degree, in respect of those goods, as those sent to South America; that one considerable house in London connected with this trade, which stopped or made a pause within the last two or three weeks, has sent a great quantity to Cadiz; and they informed the witness, that the last account they had, was, that the goods would all be sold in this and the next month; by which means they should be able to make a handsome dividend to their creditors; but their bills having gone back on the Manufacturers, they are depressed in the mean time.

That there had been a great fall in the price of the manufacture; that when he left Glasgow, there were some articles of manufacture which had fallen perhaps 40 or 50 per cent; but he understands from communications since, that the fall is greater, because the distress is become more general.

With respect to the failures that had happened, there are several houses which will probably pay very large dividends; and indeed there are several of the houses in Glasgow that he alludes to, which stopped payment, have undertaken to pay their creditors in full in a certain time; one who had more than £.200,000. of bills out, has undertaken to pay his creditors in 3, 4, 8, 12 and 16 months, and probably he will do it, but in the mean time, the manufacturers cannot command a shilling of this money: That the failure of those houses, before he left Glasgow, had amounted to from one to two millions; one house (the same to which the witness alluded before) has failed since that time for £.519,000.; they have undertaken to pay in full.

That the failure of the export houses certainly arose from their having gone greatly beyond their capital, having exported goods to a far greater extent; but he understood many of those houses were not without capital, and some even had large capital, but being disappointed in the markets, it was found that they could not make their returns so quickly as their bills became due: there are houses of that description in Liverpool, and some in Glasgow.'

Being asked, As to the amount of failures on the present occasion, as compared with those in 1793? he said, 'The proportion of failures will be always something in proportion to the extent of the trade, (which has increased wonderfully since 1793;) and of course the failures now are to a much larger amount than they were at that period.'

A number of attempts were made to control banking by legislation. The note issue was subjected to the closest surveillance. The 'optional clause', which provided for the payment of a banknote on demand or (at the option of the issuer) after a period, was prohibited in 1766. In the 1820s an attempt to restrict the issue of £1 notes was stopped only after spirited opposition, especially from Sir Walter Scott (5.) Similar fears were expressed over proposed banking legislation in the 1840s (6). In 1845 an Act to regulate the issue of Bank Notes in Scotland became the statutory basis of the note issue and began a new era in Scottish banking by prohibiting new issuing banks (7). In the later nineteenth century determined opposition, aimed especially at their note issuing privileges, prevented much progress by Scottish banks when they opened branches in various parts of England.

(5) Malachi Malagrowther (Sir Walter Scott), *A Second Letter . . . on the Proposed Change of Currency* (1826), pp. 34-36 –

I am willing to explain in a general and popular manner the peculiar nature of the paper currency in Scotland, and especially the guards and protections by which it is secured against such evil consequences as have resulted in England from a system the same in name, but operating very differently in practice.

The people of Scotland are by no means, as a hasty view of their system of currency might infer, liable to be imposed upon, or to suffer loss, through the rash and crude speculations of any man, or association of men, who, without adequate capital and experience, might choose to enter into a Banking concern, and issue their own notes.

The Banking Companies of Scotland, who take on themselves the issuing of notes, are, no doubt, independent of each other so far as they severally contract with the public; but a certain course of correspondence and mutual understanding is indispensable among themselves, and, in that respect, the whole Banks and Banking Companies in Scotland may be said to form a republic, the watchful superintendence of the whole profession being extended to the strength or weakness of the general system at each particular point; or, in other words, to the management of each individual Company.

No new Banking institution can venture to issue notes to the public, till they have established a full understanding that these notes will be received as cash by the other Banks. Without this facility, an issue of notes would never take place, since, if issued, they could have no free or general currency. It is not the interest of the established Banks to raise rivals in their own profession, and it is directly contrary to that interest to accept of payment in the notes of a new Company, to whose responsibility there occurs any shadow of doubt. They, therefore, only agree to give currency to such new issues, where satisfactory information has been obtained of the safety of affording it. The public have, in this manner, the best possible guarantee against rash and ill-concocted speculations, from those who are not only best informed on the subject, but, being most interested in examining each new project of the kind, are least likely to be betrayed into a rash confidence, and have the power of preventing a doubtful undertaking at the very outset.

The circulation of a Scottish Banking Company, when once established, cannot maintain itself a week without redeeming its pledge to the Banks which receive its notes, by taking them up, and replacing the value either in the notes of such Banks reciprocally, or in specie. A check is thus imposed, which is continually in operation, and every Bank throughout Scotland is obliged to submit its circulation, twice a-week, in Edinburgh, to the inspection of this Argus-eyed tribunal. Satisfactory information that any distant Banking Companies were leaving the safe and moderate walk of commerce, and embarking their capital in precarious speculations, would very soon draw upon them the suspicion of the moneyed interest at large, and certainly put a period to their existence before it could injure the public.

This important species of check is unknown to the practice of England; nay, it is probably impossible to establish it there, since the metropolis, which is naturally the common point of union, is nearly inaccessible to the notes of private Banking Companies. In stating a circumstance, not perhaps generally known, I may perhaps remove some of the prejudice which has extended towards the Scottish system, as if exposed to the same inconvenience with that of the sister kingdom.

(6) Hugh Miller, *Words of Warning to the People of Scotland, on Sir R. Peel's Scotch Currency Scheme* (1844), pp. 50-52 –

In dwelling, as we have done, on the great degree of perfection at which our bank scheme of book-keeping has arrived, and on the singularly ingenious character of our Cash Credits, we wish to impress the reader with some idea of the amount of mind that has been expended on the system, which a rash intermeddling statesman would so ruthlessly consign to ruin. Its book-keeping and its Credits are but specimens of the whole. But even were this whole a much inferior thing to what it is, the fact of its having so interwoven itself for a century and a half with the entire business of the country, that scarce a step can be taken in any transaction save through its agency, should of itself be sufficient to deter the experimentalist from submitting it to the amputation-knife and the tourniquet. Men have fed upon even poison until it became death for them to want it. We have authority of the first men of the country for holding that our Cash Credits could not outlive the projected change of Sir Robert for a twelvemonth,—a fact which we believe capable of demonstration; and the question comes to be, not so much whether such Credits were originally good and well devised, as what now would be the effect of their entire withdrawal? Franklin refers in his will to the "two friends whose kind loans in money were the foundation of his fortune;" and the state of ruinous embarrassment, as narrated in his autobiography, out of which they relieved him, well exemplifies the condition into which the withdrawal of the Credit Accounts of Scotland would plunge the very numerous and interesting class which these accounts enable to trade both to their own advantage and to that of the community . . .

We have here described to us, we say, exactly the reverse process to which Sir Robert Peel is on the eve of subjecting so large a portion of the traders of Scotland, that the capital advanced to them, in sums varying mostly from fifteen hundred to fifty pounds, amounts to not less than seven millions sterling. But even were the annihilation of Credit Accounts possible without involving that vast amount of ruin which must of necessity follow in its train, we would, from other considerations, deem their extinction one of the greatest calamities that could befall the country. They at present furnish one of the ascending ladders through which men of sense and character rise, after the manner of Franklin, from the lower to the higher walks. They are connecting links between the condition of the steady, industrious working man, and that of the capitalist; and their existence, by giving hope to the humbler classes, gives security in a corresponding ratio to the upper. Let Sir Robert once succeed in extinguishing them, and our lower classes shall have less to hope, and our higher more to fear . . .

One man possesses capital without business talent,—another possesses business talent without capital; and through the arrangement of allowing a certain fixed per centage for the use of the capital, it is brought under the command of the business talent. Nor is it in the power of enactment to alter this state of things. It must exist of necessity in all commercial communities. Banks never yet created it,—*it*, on the contrary, has created banks. Now, in the opinion of Sir Robert Peel, and of not a few of his coadjutors, these institutions have the effect of rendering more perilous the operations of this borrowing and lending principle than it would be without them. We hold, however, that it would be by no means difficult to demonstrate that, when well conducted, as in Scotland, they have an entirely opposite effect. Instead of giving an undue impulse to the wheels of speculation, they constitute their proper drag; and it is only when great accumulations of capital, in forcing for themselves a market, lessen this restraining ability by lowering the rate of interest, that dangerous paroxysms take place in the world of trade. The power of the banks, for instance, is weak at present: capital has accumulated in the country,—the Three per Cents. have risen to par and a fraction above it,—and the rate of bank interest is correspondingly low. And hence our class of capital-lenders are looking anxiously out for a more advantageous market than that which our banks furnish them. But to the extent to which they furnish a market at all, is speculation checked. If disabled, however, from giving interest on deposits, they could no longer constitute markets to the lender, and would, in consequence, exist no longer as checks on rash speculation. And yet Sir Robert's plan of checking speculation is just to destroy the money-market to the lender which our banks at present supply. Never surely was there infatuation more extreme!

(7) 8 and 9 Vict., c. 38 (1845). An Act to regulate the Issue of Bank Notes in Scotland.

Whereas by an Act made and passed in the Eighth Year of the Reign of Her Majesty, intituled *An Act to regulate the Issue of Bank Notes, and for giving to the Governor and Company of the Bank of* England *certain Privileges for a limited Period*, it was enacted, that from and after the passing of that Act no Person, other than a Banker who on the Sixth Day of *May* One thousand eight hundred and forty-four was lawfully issuing his own Bank Notes, should make or issue Bank Notes in any Part of the United Kingdom: And whereas it is expedient to regulate the Issue of Bank Notes by such Bankers as are now by Law authorised to issue the same in *Scotland*: Be it therefore enacted . . . That every Banker claiming to be entitled to issue Bank Notes in *Scotland* shall, within One Month next after the passing of this Act, give Notice in Writing to the Commissioners of Stamps and Taxes, at their head Office in *London*, of such Claim, and of the Place and Name and Firm at and under which such Banker has issued such Notes in *Scotland* during the Year next preceding the First Day of *May* One thousand eight hundred and forty-five, . . . then the said Commissioners shall proceed to ascertain the average Amount of the Bank Notes of such Banker which were in Circulation during the said Period of One Year preceding the First Day of *May* One thousand eight hundred and forty-five, . . . and it shall be lawful for every such Banker to continue to issue his own Bank Notes after the Sixth Day of *December* One thousand eight hundred and forty-five, to the Extent of the Amount so certified, and of the Amount of Gold and Silver Coin held by such Banker . . . but not to any further Extent; and from and after the Sixth Day of *December* One thousand eight hundred and forty-five it shall not be lawful for any Banker to make or issue Bank Notes in *Scotland*, save and except only such Bankers as shall have obtained such Certificate from the Commissioners of Stamps and Taxes . . .

And be it enacted, That all Bank Notes to be issued or re-issued in *Scotland* shall be expressed to be for Payment of a Sum in Pounds Sterling, without any fractional Parts of a Pound; . . .

And be it enacted, That from and after the Sixth Day of *December* One thousand eight hundred and forty-five it shall not be lawful for any Banker in *Scotland* to have in Circulation, upon the Average of a Period of Four Weeks, to be ascertained as herein-after mentioned, a greater Amount of Notes than an Amount composed of the Sum certified by the Commissioners of Stamps and Taxes as aforesaid and the monthly average Amount of Gold and Silver Coin held by such Banker at the head Office or principal Place of Issue of such Banker during the same Period of Four Weeks, . . .

And be it enacted, That in taking Account of the Coin held by any such Banker as aforesaid, with respect to which Bank Notes to a further Extent than the Sum certified as aforesaid by the Commissioners of Stamps and Taxes may, under the Provisions of this Act, be made and issued, no Amount of Silver Coin exceeding One Fourth Part of the Gold Coin held by such Banker as aforesaid shall be taken into account, nor shall any Banker be authorized to make and issue Bank Notes in *Scotland* on any amount of Silver Coin held by such Banker exceeding the Proportion of One Fourth Part of the Gold Coin held by such Banker as aforesaid.

And whereas, in order to ensure the rendering of true and faithful Accounts of the Amount of Bank Notes in Circulation, and the Amount of Gold and Silver Coin held by each Banker, as directed by this Act, it is necessary that the Commissioners of Stamps and Taxes should be empowered to cause the Books of Bankers issuing such Notes, and the Gold and Silver Coin held by such Bankers as aforesaid, to be inspected as herein-after mentioned; be it therefore enacted, That all and every the Book and Books of any Banker who shall issue Bank Notes under the Provisions of this Act, . . . shall be open for the Inspection and Examination at all seasonable Times of any Officer of Stamp Duties authorized in that Behalf . . .

And be it enacted, That if the monthly average Circulation of Bank Notes of any Banker, taken in the Manner herein directed, shall at any Time exceed the Amount which such Banker is authorized to issue and to have in Circulation under the Provisions of this Act, such Banker shall in every such case forfeit a Sum equal to the Amount by which the average monthly Circulation, taken as aforesaid, shall have exceeded the Amount which such Banker was authorized to issue and to have in Circulation as aforesaid . . .

And be it enacted, That if any Body Politic or Corporate or Person or Persons shall, . . . publish, utter, or negotiate in *Scotland* any Promissory or other Note (not being the Bank Note of a Banker hereby authorized to continue to issue Bank Notes), or any Bill of Exchange, Draft, or Undertaking in Writing, being negotiable or transferable, for the Payment of Twenty Shillings, or above that Sum and less than Five Pounds, . . . every such Body Politic [etc.] . . . so publishing [etc.] . . . Promissory or other Note [etc.] . . . shall forfeit and pay the Sum of Twenty Pounds.

Provided always . . . That nothing herein contained shall extend to prohibit any Draft or Order drawn by any Person on his Banker, or on any Person acting as such Banker, for the Payment of Money held by such Banker or Person to the Use of the Person by whom such Draft or Order shall be drawn.

C. BANKING: SAVINGS BANKS

The first savings bank was founded in the Dumfriesshire parish of Ruthwell by the minister, Henry Duncan.

(1) *Evidence to the Committee on the Poor Laws*, 1819, pp. 15 f. Evidence of Rev. Henry Duncan –

We know how much the public are indebted to you on the subject of banks for savings, and we wish to know from your experience in the operation of them, whether it is your opinion that they are likely to be very efficient as the means of improving the condition of the poor?—I certainly conceive that they are. A very general interest has been excited among the lower classes in favour of these establishments; and desire, amounting sometimes to a painful anxiety, now exists among them, of laying up a portion of their earnings.

Among the lower orders?—Yes; and the upper classes of the community have greatly contributed by their judicious encouragement to foster this laudable spirit. These establishments have a manifest tendency to increase habits of industry, economy and sobriety.

How long is it since the parish bank of Ruthwell was established?—It was established in May 1810.

What is at present the amount of the fund?—I believe about £1,600 or £1,700.

Is that institution confined to that particular parish?—Not entirely; the inhabitants of the neighbouring parishes have it in their power to make deposits.

Have they done so?—Yes, several of them have taken advantage of this facility.

Are you sensible that the operation of this system has already produced any good effects?—I believe it has; in many instances the depositors have gratefully acknowledged, that they first thought of saving since the institution was established; and that they would not have possessed at this moment a single shilling, but on this account.

Are there any other means of a similar nature which you conceive to be useful, for giving the lower orders facilities in providing for their own support?—I conceive friendly societies, in some respects, even of superior advantage to the lower orders.

Detail, if you please, to the Committee, any interesting particulars with which you may be acquainted in the operation of these institutions, and state their present condition?—When I first was settled in the parish of Ruthwell, there was one friendly society in it; it was, however, going to decay; the reason of this was, that party spirit had got among the members and a struggle for superiority and for the management had commenced, which had induced several members to withdraw altogether. I was anxious to support the society, from a conviction of the usefulness of such institutions. I was made a member, and from the kind of influence which my station in society gave, I was enabled to counteract that party spirit which previously prevailed. The consequence was, that the institution increased immediately to a very considerable extent; so much so, that taking into account the female society which was afterwards established under my inspection, there are now no fewer than 300 members belonging to the parish, out of a population of 1,160. I state this to show the good effect likely to be produced on these institutions, by the higher classes taking a share in the management of them. I know, that the operation of this society has been extremely beneficial, particularly in cases of sickness; many persons have been relieved by this means, who would otherwise have become burthensome to the parish, on account of protracted illness. I conceive, therefore, that friendly societies are a most excellent means of supplying a desideratum in the management of the poor, to which banks for savings do not extend: that in fact the system by which the poor are enabled to provide for themselves, would not be complete without such institutions. The reasoning on which I found this observation is sufficiently obvious: considerable sums cannot be accumulated by the operation of banks for savings, except during a series of years. If a labourer who had become a depositor in a savings bank falls sick, before he has acquired a sufficient fund for his maintenance, it is evident that in a few weeks, or at most in a few months, all the funds which he has actually acquired will be expended, and he will again be thrown upon the world without a shilling. A friendly society operates in a different manner; it is in fact an insurance against sickness and infirmity, an insurance against incapacity for labour. When a poor person, who is a member of a friendly society, falls sick, he immediately receives an allowance, which enables him to subsist, if not comfortably, at least without having recourse to the parish, whilst the funds which he may have accumulated in his parish bank remain untouched. . .

I conceive, therefore, that the operation of these two institutions would complete the system, by which the poor would be enabled to provide for themselves; but that without both, the system would be incomplete. I beg leave to observe, however, that the allowances of a friendly society, during sickness, ought never to be so high as to operate as a bribe to idleness and should therefore be something less than a labourer could earn by his employment, otherwise it would be impossible to prevent applications on false pretences.

Have not the institutions nevertheless in many instances disappointed the hopes of their supporters?—They have; because they have very frequently been founded on erroneous principles; widows funds, which have been frequently attached to these institutions, have been particularly defective in their calculations. The allowances for funerals have also been very improvident . . .

Another reason why these societies have frequently disappointed the hopes of their founders, is, that they cannot rely on a constant succession of new members, which seems to be essential for their prosperity. The younger inhabitants of a parish have an ambition to found an institution for themselves. They desert the old societies therefore, and begin a new establishment, which in its turn, is likewise deserted when its members are becoming old; and thus those societies, the provisions of which are calculated on the expectation of a constant succession of new members, will necessarily be found insecure. The cabals which sometimes take place in friendly societies, and to which I have alluded in another part of my evidence, are another great disadvantage to these institutions. Another cause also is, that the funds of the institutions are liable to be dilapidated either by mismanagement or by fraud.

Do they combine for illicit purposes also?—Not in the district in which I live.

Savings banks were sometimes criticised for failing to attract the class of depositors for which they were chiefly intended.

(2) A. Alison, *The Principles of Population* (1840), vol. ii, pp. 157-159 –

In Scotland, the establishment of public banks, on secure foundations, which have long given interest on the smallest sums deposited, has been the great cause of the parsimonious habits, and unremitting industry of the people. It appeared from the evidence laid before the Parliamentary Committee, that upwards of *twenty millions* Sterling are deposited in the Scotch banks, chiefly *in sums under* L.50 *each*; and so great is the amount of the total savings of the nation in these establishments, that the operations of the Scotch bankers have always a great effect either in raising or depressing the government securities. To the fortunate establishment and secure foundation of these great depositories for the public savings, the unexampled prosperity of Scotland during the last half century is mainly to be ascribed; for the public funds are too remote to influence the labouring classes, and the ruinous system of entails has excluded them from the natural investment of their capital. If it be really true, as the Scotch bankers alleged, that the suppression of the circulation of small notes, would have compelled them to desist from giving interest on the sums placed in their hands, the measures lately pressed upon Government by the advocates for free trade would have been the most ruinous which philosophy ever recommended to practical men.

Much was expected at their first establishment from *savings banks*; but although they have in many instances been of great service, their success upon the whole has greatly fallen short of public expectation. In places where the wages of the lower orders are the highest, as in Manchester and Glasgow, they have almost totally failed in the manufacturing class, for whom they were principally intended. The sums deposited in the public funds in the name of these banks is indeed considerable; but the greater part of it belongs to domestic servants or small tradesmen, or persons in a higher condition than those for whom they were intended, and who, by means of entries in fictitious names or other devices, frequently hold larger sums in them than the regulations admit. And in Scotland it has been found by experience, that the lower orders prefer depositing their money in the public banks to placing it in establishments solely intended for their benefit; from a greater confidence in the stability of the former than the latter, and from an opinion which is probably not altogether unfounded, that banks where a large proportion of the national wealth is deposited, and in whose prosperity a great part of the higher orders are interested, are more likely to be well managed, than those which depend solely on the benevolent exertions of philanthropic individuals.

CHAPTER V

Working Conditions

Working conditions varied in different industries, in different parts of the country, and at different times. In the century from about 1780 onwards conditions of work in mines and factories provided the new type of environment of the industrial areas in which many were living for the first time.

A. MINES

The hard working conditions in the mines were intensified by Acts of 1606, 1641 and 1661 (q.v. W. C. Dickinson and G. Donaldson, *A Source Book of Scottish History* vol. iii (2nd edition, 1961) pp. 386-389) binding both underground and surface workers, and salters, to their place of work. They could not leave it without written permission from their employer or a magistrate, nor could another employer take them on, under pain of heavy fine. Colliers could be severely fined, and even beaten, for absenteeism and restricting output, and were denied the customary holidays.

Whatever the legal position, practice is by no means clear. Attempts to claim colliers who had fled were not always made and some were harboured even by other coalowners. There was a great variety of practice in spite of the law.

(1) Scottish Record Office. Carron Company Manuscripts. Letter to John Monro of Auchenbowie, Esq., Advocate at Auchenbowie, 11th October 1770 –

We give you this trouble to beg your opinion of the following case. We lately applied to the Lord Justic Clerk & obtained from him a Justiciary Warrant for apprehending upwards of twenty four Colliers who have deserted our works within these three months past. We sent Mr. Fish, Overseer of our Collieries with this Warrant in quest of these Colliers & he found one of them at Mr. Hope's Coalworks at Cowpitts near Inveresk. Mr. Fish took only with him one of the Town's Officers, but had no Messenger or Macer with him. When they were bringing him away the other Colliers belonging to the work set upon them, beat & bruised Mr. Fish most unmercifully, deforced the Constable & rescued the Prisoner who made his escape.

We do not think we ought to let such an Atrocious Insult pass unpunished & are resolved to prosecute the perpetrators of it, but we have a Doubt whether a Constable is the Proper Officer & has power to execute a Justiciary Warrant. If he has not we are afraid these people cannot be prosecuted for a Deforcement. The words of the Warrant are "These therefore grant warrant to & ordain Sheriffs of Shires, Stewards of Stewartries, Magistrates of Burghs, Macers of the Court of Justiciary, Messengers at arms & all other proper officers of the Law, To pass, search for seize & apprehend the Persons of the said David Dalrymple &c." We therefore beg to have your opinion whether the above was a Deforcement or not & if it would not be proper to apply to the Court of Justiciary for a warrant to apprehend & commit the guilty persons to stand trial & the sooner you can furnish us with this the better. There is one David Gardiner Overseer of the Coal works of Bonharr belonging to Capt. Robertson of Earnock who has harboured six of our colliers for some months & not only refuses to deliver them up but threatens vengence against any person coming to take them away. They were required from him under form of Instrument on 6th Augt. last. By the Act of Parliament we are informed he is liable in a Penalty of £100 Scots for each collier he detains & we intend to pursue him for it. Would you advise us to bring the Process before the Sheriff of the County or before the Court of Session?

Relatively high wages did not offset the disadvantages of a collier's life. When the demand for coal rose in the later eighteenth century, the coal-owners had occasion to complain of a shortage of labour. They then began to accept the need for a change in the legal status of the colliers.

(2) Scottish Record Office. Clerk of Penicuik Manuscripts. Copy of letter from Sir James Clerk to a committee of coalmasters on the servitude of colliers, 20th February 1772 –

I have always considered the present state of the laws regarding Coalieries in Scotland as highly subversive of the general interest of the Coall trade and particularly so to the Interest of the Coall maisters.

The servitude the Coaliers have now for more than one century been subjected to has not only been the real cause of the present great scarcity of hands We all justly complain of, but which is infinitely of worse consequence, has rais'd such a spirit of national prejudice and total aversion amongst the Inhabitants of this country to that particular business that I am much afraid that even the best regulated schemes we can possibly devise, will prove inefectual, at least for a great number of years, totaly to root out these national prejudices. Every Gentleman must be sensible how difficult a point it is to conquer the most trifling prejudices—far more so when they are so well founded as they are in the present case and we must naturally expect that tho the cause should be removed the prejudices themselves will still remain with us for many years, but that they should remain for ever would be highly culpable on our part, which however must be the case unless some remedy can be devised to prevent that evil, it becomes therefore our duty as well as our Interest to promote such schemes as may gradually advance the liberty of the Coalier, and likeways gradually recover the inhabitants of this Country for the prejudices they now ly under, which in the end may procure as many hands to be employed in this valuable trade as in any other.

Shortage of labour was the reason for the Colliers' and Salters' Emancipation Act of 1775. Freedom, however, was subject to important restrictions, which seriously limited the application of the Act.

(3) 15 George III, c. 28 (1775). An act for altering, explaining, and amending several Acts of Parliament of *Scotland*, respecting Colliers, Coal-bearers, and Salters –

'Whereas by the Statute Law of *Scotland*, as explained by the Judges of the Courts of Law there, many Colliers and Coal-bearers and Salters are in a State of Slavery or Bondage, bound to the Collieries and Salt-works where they work for Life, transferable with the Collieries and Salt-works, when their original Masters have no further Use for them: And whereas Persons are discouraged and prevented from learning the Art or Business of Colliers or Coal-bearers, and Salters, by their becoming bound to the Collieries and Salt-works for Life, where they shall work for the Space of one Year, by means whereof there are not a sufficient Number of Colliers, Coal-bearers, and Salters, in *Scotland*, for working the Quantities of Coal and Salt necessarily wanted; and many new-discovered Coals remain unwrought, and many are not sufficiently wrought, nor are there a sufficient Number of Salters for the Salt-works, to the great Loss of the Owners and Disadvantage to the Publick: And whereas the emancipating or setting free the Colliers, Coal-bearers, and Salters in *Scotland*, who are now in a State of Servitude, gradually and upon reasonable Conditions, and the preventing others from coming into such a State of Servitude, would be the Means of increasing the Number of Colliers, Coal-bearers, and Salters, to the great Benefit of the Publick, without doing any Injury to the present Masters, and would remove the Reproach of allowing such a State of Servitude to exist in a free Country; may it therefore please your Majesty that it may be enacted; ...

... That from and after the first Day of *July*, in this present Year one thousand seven hundred and seventy-five, no Person who shall begin to work as a Collier, Coal-bearer, or Salter, or in any other Way in a Colliery or Salt-work, in *Scotland*, shall be bound to such Colliery or Salt-work, or to the Owner thereof, in any other Way or Manner different from what is permitted by the Law of *Scotland* with regard to Servants and Labourers; and that they shall be deemed free, and shall enjoy the same Privileges, Rights, and Immunities with the rest of his Majesty's Subjects, any Law or Usage in *Scotland* to the contrary notwithstanding ...

III. And be it further enacted by the Authority aforesaid, That all Persons under the Age of Twenty-one Years, upon the said first Day of *July*, employed as Colliers, Coal-bearers, or Salters, in *Scotland*, and bound to any Colliery or Salt-work, shall, after seven Years Service from the said first Day of *July*, be free from their Service and Servitude, and at Liberty to engage themselves as Servants or Labourers in any other Colliery or Salt-work, or in any other Kind of Labour whatever.

IV. And be it further enacted by the Authority aforesaid, That all bound Colliers and Salters in *Scotland*, above the Age of twenty-one Years, and under the Age of thirty-five Years, upon the said first Day of *July*, after a Service of ten Years; and all Colliers and Salters above the Age of thirty-five Years, but under the Age of forty-five Years, at the said first Day of *July*, after a Service of seven Years; and after their having respectively found and sufficiently instructed a Person as an Apprentice, if required so to do by the Master or Lessee of the Colliery or Salt-work, within one Year after the said first Day of *July* next, in the Art or Mystery of Coal-hewing or making of Salt, of the Age of eighteen Years at least; when such

Instruction shall be perfected, shall be free from any other Servitude or Bondage to the Colliery or Salt-work to which they were bound.

V. And be it also enacted, That all Colliers and Salters, bound to any Colliery or Salt-work in *Scotland*, above the Age of forty-five Years upon the said first Day of July next, shall, after three Years, be free and discharged from any further Servitude or Bondage to the Colliery or Salt-work to which they are bound.

VI. Provided always, and be it enacted by the Authority aforesaid, That if any bound Collier or Salter shall not sufficiently instruct an Apprentice in the Art or Mystery of Coal-hewing or making of Salt, if required by the Master or Lessee of the Colliery or Salt-work to which he is bound, as directed by this Act, such Collier or Salter shall nevertheless be free, after the Performance of an additional Service of three Years at the Colliery or Salt-work to which he is bound.

VII. Provided always, That every Collier or Salter, claiming Liberty under the Authority of this Act, shall, prior to his being freed from his Servitude or Bondage, obtain a Decree of the Sheriff Court of the County in which he resides, finding and declaring that he is intitled unto his Freedom, under the Authority of this Act.

Because of the continuing restrictions difficulty was still experienced in recruiting an adequate supply of colliers to meet the rising demand for coal. Some coalmasters made a big effort to attract more labour under the new conditions, but with only moderate success.

(4) Scottish Record Office. Carron Company Manuscripts. Advertisement anent Colliers sent Mr. Balfour, 30th November 1775 –

Publish in the Newspapers

Whereas by the late Act of Parliament, no person entering as a Collier to any Colliery within Scotland can become bound to that Colliery, Carron Company to encourage labouring people to become Colliers do hereby give notice that they are ready to enter into agreement with able bodied labouring men and to employ them as Colliers for any space that shall be agreed on, not less than one year, and to pay them one shilling p. day of wages certain, and whenever they shall have attained such knowledge in their business as that they can work more Coal in a day than would cost the Company more than one shilling at the common rate of the field, the Company shall from thenceforth pay to such men in place of the certain wages of one shilling p. day, the same rates and prices for each Ton of Coals they shall work that are paid to the other Colliers in the field, employed in the same kind of work, and a diligent industrious Collier can easily earn from eighteen pence to half a crown each day.

The Company also propose to indent young lads from thirteen to eighteen years of age to serve as apprentices to the business of Coal hewing, lads of thirteen and fourteen years of age to bind for seven years and to receive ninepence p. day for the first three years and one shilling p. day for the remainder of their apprenticeship. Lads of fifteen and sixteen years of age to bind five years and lads of seventeen and eighteen years of age to bind three years, and both receive one shilling p. day until any of them can work more Coal in a day than to the amount of one shilling. The Company will from thenceforth pay them by the Ton of what they work at the same rates that are paid to the other Colliers in the field.

The shortcoming of the first Act necessitated another in 1799, making emancipation unconditional, though colliers still remained subject to normal restraints and conditions of employment.

(5) 39 George III, c. 56 (1799). An Act to explain and amend the Laws relative to Colliers in that Part of *Great Britain* called *Scotland*.—(13th *June* 1799) –

Notwithstanding which, many Colliers and Coal Bearers still continue in a State of Bondage, from not having complied with the Provisions, or from having become subject to the Penalties, in the said Act: [15 Geo. III, c. 28] May it therefore please your Majesty that it may be enacted; . . . 'That, from and after the passing of this Act, all the Colliers in that Part of *Great Britain* called *Scotland*, who were bound Colliers at the Time of passing the said Act, shall be and they are here hereby declared to be free from their Servitude, and in the same Situation in every Respect as if they had regularly obtained a Decree in the Manner directed by the said Act.'

After the Emancipation Acts, the legislators confined their attention to the employment of women and children underground. The general harshness of life and work in the mines was demonstrated convincingly by a remarkable Report of 1842. But the Report's chief concern was with the conditions of employment of women and children. In general, women were employed in the east but not in the west except in the ironstone mines. Children were found everywhere. One of the most striking features of the Report was a series of interviews aimed at bringing out forcefully the conditions under which people worked.

(6) Children's Employment Commission, 1842, vol. ii, pp. 436 and 458. Report on the Collieries and Iron-works in the East of Scotland, by R. H. Franks –

p. 436

No. 1 Janet Cumming, 11 years old, bears coals:–

Works with father; has done so for two years. Father gangs at two in the morning; I gang with the women at five, and come up at five at night; work all night on Fridays, and come away at twelve in the day.

I carry the large bits of coal from the wall-face to the pit bottom, and the small pieces called chows, in a creel; the weight is usually a hundred weight; does not know how many pounds there are in the hundred weight, but it is some work to carry; it takes three journies to fill a tub of 4 cwt. The distance varies, as the work is not always on the same wall; sometimes 150 fathom, whiles 250. The roof is very low; I have to bend my back and legs, and the water comes frequently up to the calves of my legs; has no likening for the work; father makes me like it; mother did carry coal, she is not needed now, as sisters and brothers work on father and uncle's account. Never got hurt, but often obliged to scramble out when bad air was in the pit.

Father lately got crushed by a big coal falling, and was by for seven weeks; was supported by William Bennet's and John Craig's societies, to which he subscribed; believes he got 8s. weekly from the two.

I am learning to read at the night school; am in the twopenny book; sometimes to Sabbath-school. Jesus was God; David wrote the Bible; has a slight knowledge of the first six questions in the shorter catechism.

No. 3. George Reid, 16 years old, coal-hewer:-

I pick the coal at the wall-face, and seldom do other work; have done so for six years; the seam is 26 inches high, and when I pick I am obliged to twist myself up; the men who work in this seam lie on their broadsides.

Father took me down early to prevent me from going o'erwild about the town; it is horrible sore work; none ever come up to meals. Pieces of bread are taken down; boys and girls sometimes drink the water below, when there is no metal in it; men take a bottle of small-beer. We get meat on Saturday nights and Sunday; the men say we could not work well if we had meat on other days.

I should not care about the work if we had not so much of it; have often been hurt; was off idle a short bit ago, the pick having torn my flesh while ascending the shaft. There is a good deal of quarrelling below, especially among the women people. Six of the family work with father below; he seldom does any on Monday, sometimes Tuesday; when work is good he takes away 2 *l.* to 50s. for the fortnight. A fortnight is two weeks.

There is 4 weeks in a month, 12 months in the year; 7 times 9 makes 63; and 12 times 11, 132. Reads, writes indifferently, cannot spell well; knows the question in the Catechism; was never in the maps but acquainted fairly with Scripture; goes to night-school for one hour, when open; the hard work prevents me from doing muckle.

p. 458.

No. 117. Jane Peacock Watson, age 40, coal-bearer:—

I have wrought in the bowels of the earth 33 years. Have been married 23 years, and had nine children; six are alive, three died of typhus a few years since; have had two dead born; thinks they were so from the oppressive work: a vast [number] of women have dead children and false births, which are worse, as they are not able to work after the latter.

I have always been obliged to work below till forced to go home to bear the bairn, and so have all the other women. We return as soon as able, never longer than 10 or 12 days; many less, if they are much needed.

It is only horse-work, and ruins the women; it crushes their haunches, bends their ankles, and makes them old women at 40.

Women so soon get weak that they are forced to take the little ones down to relieve them; even children of six years of age do much to relieve the burthen.

Knows it is bad to keep bairns from school, but every little helps; and even if inclined there is no school nearer than two miles, and it is a fearfu' road across the moor in summer, much more winter.

Coal-hewers are paid 4½d. for each load of 2 cwt., out of which they have to pay the bearers whom they hire.

Each collier has his place on the coal-hill, and gets his money just as the sale comes in which makes the pay uncertain.

The Commissioners' Report led to an Act of 1842 prohibiting the employment in mines and collieries of all women and of boys less than ten years old. Government Inspectors visited the coalfields to ensure that the Act was enforced. Some women excluded from the pits suffered hardship through lack of other work, but the Inspectors vigorously initiated prosecution against workmen or employers who flouted the Act.

(7) Report of the Commissioner on the state of the population of the Mining Districts, 1845, pp. 3-4 –

Sir,

I have to acquaint you with the progress made, since last year, in excluding females from the collieries, and in causing the other provisions of the Act of Parliament, with the execution of which I am charged, to be observed; . . .

Of the 2400 females employed in the collieries of Scotland at the passing of the Act (August, 1842), I had reason to believe that not many more than 200 were so employed at the date of my last Report (July, 1844).

That number has been still further reduced within the last year, though not without difficulty, and the necessity of resorting to legal proceeding in several cases. An attempt has also been made to introduce females into new works in a part of the coal-field of Stirlingshire, recently opened. This has, however, been checked by the measures promptly taken by the procurator fiscal of that district.

Early in September, three workmen of the Redding colliery, near Falkirk, were convicted in the penalty of 5 *l.* each, with 2 *l.* costs. I am informed by the procurator fiscal that this had the effect of preventing a repetition of the offence for about three months, when he discovered that 12 women had resumed work. Convictions have been since obtained against some of the men who employed them. An attempt was made, when the former case was pending, to obtain evidence sufficient to lead to the conviction of the manager, for connivance. He stated to me that he had received express directions from his superior (the agent of the Duke of Hamilton) to prevent the violations of the law; and he undertook to discharge any workman discovered employing a female, and also to appoint a trustworthy person to prevent their going down by the stair-pits.

These precautions not having been effectual, he has been desired by the Duke of Hamilton's agent to secure the entrance by a locked hatchway; a measure which for the present has, I believe, been found sufficient. 126 females were employed in these works when the Act passed. . . .

In all the localities where occasional violations of the Act occur, it is represented to me that the number of females persisting in their endeavours to return to their former work is few, and chiefly confined to those who, being widows or orphans, or the daughters of aged or infirm colliers, and having been long habituated to that kind of employment, find it more difficult to obtain any other. However much the sympathies may be excited in favour of this class of female, and however hard the Act depriving them of their accustomed means of earning a comfortable subsistence, may, and does sometimes unquestionably, bear upon them, it is necessary to discourage any tendency to relax the law in their favour, wherever it may appear. Numerous complaints have been addressed to me by the proprietors of works bordering upon those where the Act is not strictly observed, stating the increased difficulty they have in restraining their colliers from taking their wives and daughters again into the pits which they think it hard not to be allowed to do, while it is done by others. They point out, also, the unfair advantages that may be obtained by competing coal-owners, by using what is in some cases the cheaper labour of women. Instead, therefore, of allowing any hope to be indulged that the Act would not be put strictly in force, the course at once most humane and most consistent with duty has been to forward as much as possible the transference of the most suffering class of females to other occupations; or, failing that, the alleviation of their distress by benevolent assistance.

B. FACTORIES

Many of the new concerns which appeared in Scotland in the late eighteenth and early nineteenth centuries experienced difficulties in recruiting an adequate labour force. The supply of skilled labour was particularly scarce. As one of the pioneers of new methods in Scotland, Carron Company encountered these problems and had to try to attract labour to its works.

(1) Scottish Record Office. Carron Company Manuscripts. Letter to Benjamin Roebuck, Sheffield, 16th December 1760 –

We have been expecting to hear from you about one or two good founders which we imagined you would be able to get from Rotherham, & we cant help thinking from the information about them that if you would exert yourself one or two of Walker's hands might be procured. What we principally want is a man for Bushes & if he has been used to Potts & Sad Irons or loam work would be the more valuable. We would either have them work by the day or piece. If the former 10 week [10s. a week] or 12 for a very good man with any other moderate encouragement as you see proper. Travelling charge you know must be granted with a House & firing free. We shall be obliged to you to inform us distinctly how Walkers go on their Blast Furnace, as to what quantity of goods they make weekly & the prices, what sort of Mine & Coal they make use of & upon what terms they have them. We are afraid you wont succeed in getting a Finery man for the forge but if you could hear of a good hand that is not under Article we think he might be bribed to come to as good a Forge perhaps as any in Britain where he would have consumed good work & civil usage. You might venture to give him £10 in hand £20 more when he arrived in Scotland & if he should not like his situation when he arrived here we will pay his charges back again & risque the £10. We are in good hopes to Blow in about 10 days & shall then acquaint you with the success. In the meantime we beg to hear from you.

One method of alleviating the general shortage, followed by Carron Company as well as by other concerns, was to employ pauper children as apprentices. Sometimes they were ill-treated, and the device was only a means of obtaining cheap labour, but not always. Carron Company accepted some responsibility for their welfare and found them so troublesome that they stopped taking them.

(2) Scottish Record Office. Carron Company Manuscripts. Letter to Thomas Fairholme, Edinburgh. 29th November 1761 –

We do not think the Poorhouse boys can ever enter into a more certain business than the Nail Trade. A diligent person with a pair of tolerable hands can always make ten shillings a week and there is no danger of it ever turning out of fashion. The usual time of binding lads near Birmingham in this way is from the age of ten, eleven or twelve years until the age of twenty-one. But as this may not be agreeable to the Managers of the Poorhouse we agree to take lads at above twelve years old to bind for seven years. (E.R. thinks they might be bound to the age of 21. Its enough to be their masters.) The Carron Coy. agree to find them in meat drink & cloaths for that time. To learn them the art of making nails by good workmen & sober, decent characters. If the boys behave well the Company will probably give them some Gratuity beside meat & cloath, but this article must be left entirely to the Coy's generosity. Four or six lads may be sufficient for a beginning & we will want as many more within two months.

(3) Scottish Record Office. Carron Company Manuscripts. Letter to Mr. Archibald Mercer, Edinburgh, 20th January 1766 –

We deferred replying to your favour of 15th curt until we had an opportunity of enquiring abt. the boys & we are sorry to say that we have reason to believe the harbouring of them at Edinr. has had the effect to make them neglect their business & complain without sufficient cause. We refer you to the enclosed letter from R. Harrold by which it appears he is fully as much dissatisfied with the boys as they can be with him for which reason we determine to take them out of his hands within 3 or 4 weeks. The expenses of teaching the fourteen boys from the Poor House . . . has not been less than £15 each—after they have learnt their trade at so great an expense to us it is extremely hard that we should not have the benefit of their work. As the Guardians of the boys we hope you will either put us in possession of the whole of them or reimburse us for the money we are out—in the first case we will put them under the care of discreet men to maintain and oversee their work—in the last case which would be fully as agreeable we will deliver up the Indentures. We expect your reply by return of post. The trouble we have had with these boys prevents our taking any more of them.

The cotton mills built in the late eighteenth century to exploit the new methods of spinning intensified the labour shortage. The difficulties of recruitment lay in part in the reluctance of many to enter them. The condition of labour elsewhere, as in handloom weaving, was not easy, especially for children, but the new cotton mills were associated with regimentation and discipline, though conditions varied. Adam Bogle, manager of the cotton mill at Blantyre, was more typical than Robert Owen, the owner of New Lanark. Owen believed in paternal discipline, but his child labour was well cared for, particularly in respect of education.

(4) *Evidence to the Select Committee on the State of Children Employed in Manufactories, 1816*, pp. 167–171. Evidence of Adam Bogle –

... Do many persons apply to you for work from the Lanark works?—A good many do.

What are the reasons which have been stated to you by the workers which induce them to leave the works at Lanark?—I never inquired of any but one, though a great many have come lately; that one stated, that it was with a view of bettering her situation. I asked her what made her leave Lanark, because I understood they were to be better there than they could be any where else; she said, she did not think they were, because she had been better before, and she thought she might be better still; that there had been a number of new regulations introduced. That they had got a number of dancing-masters, a fidler, a band of music that there were drills and exercises, and that they were dancing together till they were more fatigued than if they were working.

Did the woman complain that she got no wages for the dancing?—No, she did not ...

At what age are children generally bred to hand-weaving in Scotland?—Of late years at a younger period than any other business I know.

At what age?—We have had a number of hand-weavers, with their families, that have come to our work within the last six months, and they have applied to me, many of them, to take their children into factories; and I have told them that they were too young, and too small, and they have told me they were surprised at that, for that some of them had been at it two years, and some of them one year.

Is it the general practice in Scotland to put children under ten years of age to hand-weaving?—It is universally the practice.

And to bind them apprentices?—Yes.

For how long?—Various periods; three, four, and five years, according to the age and circumstances of the parties.

Is that work hard labour?—For children of that age it is much harder labour than any employment that children under fourteen can have in cotton factories . . .

Have you known, or ever heard, of complaints of oppression in cotton factories?—No; I never heard of any complaints of over-working in our own or any other works.

Whether do you consider persons under sixteen years of age employed in factories, or persons under sixteen years of age, employed in the cotton manufactures out of factories, to be better off as to wages?—In the average of two or three years the factory children are very superior; but for one year now and then in hand-weaving, when it is brisk, they may be as well off, and perhaps a little better.

The wages for hand-weaving are very fluctuating?—Very fluctuating.

In regard to living, which do you think are best?—The persons in factories live much more comfortably than the hand-weavers.

With regard to the moral habits and general conduct of one class of persons as compared with the other, what is your opinion?—My opinion is, that taking our population at Blantyre, which is entirely a cotton one, being all employed at our works, it is equal to the same population in any of the surrounding parishes where there are no works, in point of regularity and moral conduct.

The Committee wish to know whether from your knowledge and long experience in all the branches of the manufacture, you conceive the children employed in the cotton manufactures out of factories, or the children employed within factories, may be considered best in respect to moral habits and general conduct?—I should consider that the children in cotton manufactories are not inferior in this respect to any mixed population of children in a town employed in other trades and occupations; there is nothing in the cotton trade that I know, that should endanger their moral habits more than in any other; but on the other hand, the regularity that is necessary to be kept in cotton works would be a guard to their morals.

(5) *Evidence to the Select Committee on the State of Children Employed in Manufactories, 1816*, pp. 20f. Evidence of Robert Owen – *see over*

What is your situation in life?—I am principal proprietor and sole acting partner of the establishment at New Lanark, in Scotland.

How many persons, young and old, are immediately supported by the New Lanark manufactory and establishment?—About 2,300: Upon the first of January last the numbers were 2,297, I believe.

To how many out of that number do you give employment?—This number varies occasionally, but upon the average about sixteen or seventeen hundred.

The remainder of the 2,300 are the wives and children?—Children too young, and persons too old, of the same families; some of the wives are employed.

Do you mean that the 2,300 are the number composing the whole of the families, some parts of which are employed in the works?—Yes; the difference between those immediately employed in the works and the number first stated, are those who are too young for work, or too old, or wives who are obliged to attend families too young for work.

What is the population of the village?—About 2,300.

At what age do you take children into your mills?—At ten and upwards.

What are your regular hours of labour per day, exclusive of meal times?—Ten hours and three quarters.

What time do you allow for meals?—Three quarters of an hour for dinner, and half an hour for breakfast.

Then your full time of work per day is twelve hours, out of which time you allow the mills to cease work for an hour and a quarter?—Yes.

Why do you not employ children at an earlier age?—Because I consider it would be injurious to the children, and not beneficial to the proprietors.

What reason have you to suppose it is injurious to the children to be employed in regular manufactories at an earlier age?—The evidence of very strong facts.

What are those facts?—Seventeen years ago, a number of individuals, with myself, purchased the New Lanark establishment from the late Mr. Dale of Glasgow; At that period I found there were 500 children, who had been taken from poor-houses, chiefly in Edinburgh, and those children were generally from the age of five and six, to seven and eight; they were so taken because Mr. Dale could not, I learned afterwards, obtain them at a more advanced period of life; if he did not take them at those ages, he could not obtain them at all. The hours of work at that time were thirteen inclusive of meal times, and an hour and a half was allowed for meals. I very soon discovered that, although those children were extremely well fed, well clothed, well lodged, and very great care taken of them when out of the mills, their growth and their minds were materially injured by being employed at those ages within the cotton mills for eleven hours and a half per day. It is true that those children, in consequence of being so well fed and clothed and lodged, looked fresh, and, to a superficial observer, healthy in their countenances; yet their limbs were very generally deformed, their growth was stunted, and, although one of the best schoolmasters upon the old plan was engaged to instruct those children regularly every night, in general they made but a very slow progress, even in learning the common alphabet. Those appearances strongly impressed themselves upon my mind to proceed solely from the number of hours they were employed in those mills during the day, because in every other respect they were as well taken care of, and as well looked after, as any children could be. Those were some, and perhaps they may be considered by the Committee sufficient, facts to induce me to suppose that the children were injured by being taken into the mills at this early age, and employed for so many hours; therefore, as soon as I had it in my power, I adopted regulations to put an end to a system which appeared to me to be so injurious.

In consequence then of your conviction that children are injured by being employed the usual daily hours in manufacturies, when under ten years of age, you have for some time refused to receive children into your works till they are ten years of age?—Yes.

Do you think the age of ten to be the best period for the admission of children into full and constant employment for ten or eleven hours per day, within woollen, cotton, or other mills or manufactories?—I do not.

What other period would you recommend for the admission to full work?—Twelve years.

How then would you employ them from ten to the age of twelve?—For the two years preceding, to be partially instructed; to be instructed one half the day, and the other half to be initiated into the manufactories by parties employing two sets of children in the day, on the same principle that two sets of children were employed when proprietors thought it their interest to work day and night.

If such be your opinion, how happen you not to have acted upon it?—Had the works been entirely my own, I should have acted upon that principle some time ago, but being connected with other gentlemen, I deem it necessary in practice not to deviate so much from the common regulations of the country as I otherwise would have done; and, besides, it required some time to prepare the population for so material a change from that to which they had been previously accustomed . . .

Do you give instruction to any part of your population?—Yes.

What part?—To the children from three years old, upwards; and to every other part of the population that chuse to receive it.

Will you state the particulars?—There is a preparatory school, into which all the children, from the age of three to six, are admitted at the option of the parents; there is a second school, in which all the children of the population, from six to ten, are admitted; and if any of the parents, from being more easy in their circumstances, and setting a higher value upon instruction, which to continue their children at school for one, two, three, or four years longer, they are at liberty to do so; they are never asked to take the children from the school to the works.

Will you state who supports the schools?—The schools are supported immediately at the expense of the establishment; they are indeed literally and truly supported by the people themselves.

Will you explain how that is?—New Lanark was a new settlement formed by Mr. Dale; the part of the country in which these works were erected was very thinly inhabited, and the Scotch peasantry generally were disinclined to work in cotton mills; it was necessary that great efforts should therefore be made to collect a new population in such a situation, and such population was collected before the usual and customary means for conveniently supplying a population with food were formed, the work people therefore were obliged to buy their food and other articles at a very high price, and under many great disadvantages; to counterbalance this inconvenience, a store was opened at the establishment, into which provisions of the best quality, and clothes of the most useful kind, were introduced, to be sold at the option of the people, at a price sufficient to cover prime-cost and charges, and to cover the accidents of such a business, it being understood at the time that whatever profits arose from this establishment, those profits should be employed for the general benefit of the work people themselves; and these school establishments have been supported, as well as other things, by the surplus profits, because in consequence of the pretty general moral habits of the people, there have been very few losses by bad debts, and although they have been supplied considerably under the price of provisions in the neighbourhood, yet the surplus profits have in all cases been sufficient to bear the expense of these school establishments; therefore, they have literally been supported by the people themselves.

What effects have you experienced from these plans of instruction?—The best possible. It perhaps may be useful, as there are many gentlemen present who are interested in these questions, and who may not have had the experience I have had, to state, that when these schools were opened, it was not considered sufficient that attention should be paid merely to instructing the children in what are called the common rudiments of learning, that is, in reading, writing, arithmetic, and the girls also in sewing, but was deemed of much greater importance, that attention should be given by the masters to form the moral habits of the children, and their dispositions; and in consequence, the moral habits of the children have been improved in such a manner as that from the 1st of January last to the time I left the establishment, about a week ago, out of two hundred and about twenty children, who are in school in the day, and three hundred and eighty or ninety, who are in school at night, there has not been occasion to punish one single individual; and as the school is arranged upon such principles as are calculated to give the children a good deal of exercise and some amusement, the children are more willing and more desirous of attending the school and the occupations which they are engaged in there, than of going to their ordinary play; the most unpleasant time they have in the week is the Saturday afternoon, which is necessarily a holiday, in consequence of the schools, in which they are taught, being washed and cleaned on that day. I have found other and very important advantages, in a pecuniary view, from this arrangement and these plans. In consequence of the individuals observing that real attention is given to their comforts and to their improvements, they are willing to work at much lower wages at that establishment, than at others at no great distance, which are esteemed to be upon the best plans in the country, with all the newest improvements . . .

What length of time per day, at school, do you conceive would be necessary to give boys common instruction in reading and writing?

—That depends very much upon the capacity of the children, and more materially upon the plans adopted by the teachers: Under the best system I have ever witnessed, at which indeed I was present this morning at the National School, the children are taught to read not only well, but better than any other children I have heard, not only in a small number but in the gross, in twelve months: There can be no doubt, children may be taught to read and write, and understand accounts, and the girls also to sew, by attending to those rudiments one hour a day for a given number of years; but if they attend two hours a day, it will be done in less than one half of that time.

The town of Lanark is entirely dependent upon your manufactory?—Entirely so.

Do you think that the regulations which are in force at New Lanark, would apply to a large populous manufacturing town, where the inhabitants are not entirely dependent upon a manufactory?—The same principles, I conceive, may be applied, under different modifications, to any situation, either where there are few or many.

What employment could be found for the children of the poor, in those situations, till ten years of age?—It does not appear to me that it is necessary for children to be employed, under ten years of age, in any regular work.

If you did not employ them in any regular work, what would you do with them?—Instruct them, and give them exercise.

Would not there be a danger of their acquiring, by that time, vicious habits, for want of regular occupation?—My own experience leads me to say that I have found quite the reverse, that their habits have been good in proportion to the extent of their instruction.

That proceeds upon the supposition that they are to be instructed? —Most assuredly: if the children are not to be instructed, they had better be employed in any occupation that should keep them out of mischief.

The result of the Report of 1816 was the Factory Act of 1819, which was only of limited scope. A satisfactory attack on the problem required the acceptance of the principle of inspection, which came only with the Factory Act of 1833. Parliamentary investigations and subsequently the reports of the inspectors showed that there were substantial differences between the practices of the large and of the small mills.

(6) *Factories Inquiry Commission, 1833*. Report of the District Commissioner for the Northern District, pp. 50-51 –

Yesterday we saw the magnificent cotton-mill establishment of Stanley Mills on the river Tay, about seven miles from Perth, belonging to Messrs. Dennistoun, Buchanan, and Company of Glasgow . . . We afterwards proceeded to Blairgowrie, fifteen miles from hence, where we saw four flax-mills . . .

The situation of Stanley Mills is peculiarly beautiful and picturesque, and entitles them to a visit from a stranger, not less on account of the romantic scenery and fine river to be seen from almost every window of this great factory, than on account of the extent and arrangement of their buildings, all their own property, comprehending every description of building necessary for a population of about two thousand persons, and including a peculiarly handsome church, erected at an expense of about 3,000 *l.*, and endowed by the company, a school, school-house, and very neat range of dwelling-houses for the workpeople.

The cotton yarn spun at Stanley Mills is not fine, so that the general temperature is only from fifty-five to sixty-five degrees, excepting in that apartment where webs are dressed for the loom, and a temperature from seventy-five to eighty degrees is required. The sallow complexion of the workers here, who are not numerous, but some of them youthful, proves the confinement in this room to be unfavourable to health. The general appearance of the workers, who were on our account dismissed for dinner at an earlier hour than usual, that we might have a good opportunity of seeing them in passing us in small numbers at the gate, was very gratifying in point of good looks, health, apparel, etc. The porter at the gate, who was a worker at the mills from the period when they were set a-going, is eighty-four years of age, and in the enjoyment of good health. So is his wife, though now eighty-eight. One of the female workers, who has been at this work for many years, emphatically replied to my question, how she liked it? "real weel." . . .

I have few remarks to make respecting the small flax-mills on the road from Aberdeen to Perth, and near Blairgowrie, . . . The small mills are uniformly ill cleaned and ventilated, and there is more dust in the preparing-rooms, and less attention to the boxing in of the machinery, than in large establishments. If any thing like abuse in respect to punishment now takes place, it is in the smaller mills, where a strap, as it appears from the evidence, is not unfrequently in the possession of the overseer; but I doubt very much whether any such abuse exists, or has of late years existed in this country, in any degree worthy of notice. My impression, founded on previous knowledge, and on what has transpired in this investigation, being decidedly, that country schoolmasters in Scotland are far more apt than mill-owners or overseers to exert their authority by applying the taws with undue severity. The accusation of cruelty or severity, which was in the course of the parliamentary investigation of last year brought against the owners and overseers of flax spinning-mills in this country, whatever may have happened formerly, seems to me to be utterly and entirely unfounded at the present day.

C. TRUCK AND ARRESTMENT: TRUCK

The practice of truck (obliging employees to spend their wages in shops run by the employers) was prohibited by an Act of 1831, but remained common in certain parts of Scotland and in certain industries. The Report of 1854, compiled by the historian J. Hill Burton, explained how the law could be evaded.

(1) *Report on . . . the Arrestment of Wages in Scotland, 1854*, pp. 81-84 –

I was prepared beforehand to find the system in operation in the coal and iron districts, but the vast extent to which it developed its presence, on local investigation, certainly surprised me. It is to be found in Lanarkshire, in Ayrshire, in some parts of Stirlingshire, in Linlithgowshire, in the western district of Fife, and to a small extent in Mid-Lothian. Though it be found in some works which are mere collieries, it is the prevailing feature of iron-works, and accompanies, as I shall have to show, the rapid local increase of the industrial population which attends the establishment of blast furnaces. Its great centre is the Airdrie iron district. There it is skilfully carried to perfection, with a powerful simplicity of action, creditable to the ingenuity of its inventors, and to their knowledge of human nature. It is pursued in various forms, but they are all worked as it were with one engine—the reckless improvidence and consequent pecuniary helplessness of the people employed. The first step for taking advantage of these defects is long payments. From a traditional difference in practice, the underground workers—colliers and ironstone miners—are sometimes paid fortnightly, and the furnace men and other surface workers monthly; but the prevailing practice is monthly payment. This applies to a class so thoroughly and organically improvident, that they not only cannot wait a month for their wages, but often will not wait two days. The arrangement adopted is to permit them systematically to draw advances between pay terms, to be spent at the store. I shall briefly describe, after an examination of several methods of accomplishing this object, what appeared to me to be the most neat and efficacious arrangement.

A special office is kept called "the cash advance office", distinct from the monthly pay-office, and in large concerns managed by a separate set of officers. In this office the amount of work or output by each man in the establishment is daily given in, and the corresponding remuneration is made up . . .

When a man wants to draw money—whether all that he is entitled to draw, or a portion—he goes to the cash advance office and obtains it. It is his duty then to pass over to a ticket office, which may be at the store or separate from it, put down his money on the counter, and obtain a ticket for the amount. This ticket is a note good for its amount at the store. The ticket-keeper preserves printed tickets of all grades in even money, from 1s. up to 20s., just as a banker keeps his several kinds of notes. The sum is printed on the ticket, which is otherwise in the shape of an invoice, with two columns for figures, so that the goods obtained may be entered from time to time and balances struck. As a check, the tickets are stamped with the day of issue as they are given out, as railway tickets are . . .

There is no excuse for delaying to take the ticket, and the offices are conveniently situated for the completion of the transaction. There is something, too, in its neatness and regularity that makes a failure to conform with it seem like a fraud. The money is obtained for the purpose of getting the ticket, and the workman learns the routine of the operation as a matter of course. It appeared to me that the whole was founded on very sagacious calculations.

By another method the ticket may be handed to the worker along with his money, and he may go to the store and lay down the money, purchasing with the ticket. By this arrangement, the storekeeper who receives back the money gets it with an advice of its amount, in the shape of the ticket shown to him, and the man cannot surreptitiously carry a portion of it away . . .

By another method, very extensively practised, the worker selects his goods before he draws his money, and brings a note of them from the store to the cash-advance office . . .

In smaller works the proceedings are not so systematic. There may be no establishment like the cash-advance office, but the workman goes from time to time to the employer, or the pay-clerk, for an advance. He gets a ticket or slip of paper along with it, in which the amount is entered and initialed, and he takes this to the store, where the goods are entered on it. In other establishments the worker puts down the money at the store, and having got so much goods, if he do not want to take the whole amount, receives a back-line for the balance. In some instances the master draws on a store, not kept by himself, but in which he has some specified interest. The drafts are for a certain sum in cash, and the arrangement for spending it at the store lies with the worker and the shopkeeper. In these cases there is no cash paid, but the arrangement for giving goods is not ostensibly made by the employer.

In the smaller establishments, indeed, the arrangements vary greatly, and matters are not so rigidly managed as at the great works; for the motions of each man are better known, and perhaps there is more reliance on what he will do. The great object is not so much to evade the penalties of the Truck Act as to avoid the danger of the Compensation section, which, on a prosecution by the workman for wages earned, renders it incompetent for the employer to plead set-off or claim reduction . . .

Some people spoke about the local position of the store, and the place of payment, as if it were thence to be inferred that the motions of each worker were watched, and he was seen to pass from the one to the other . . . I was told, too, of arrangements by which the money laid down at the ticket-office, or the store, finds its way by a movable till back to the cash-office, so as to economise the amount of money required to make a large number of payments, and shew that the workman professedly paid in cash was merely entrusted with the money, as the evidence of the draft he was entitled to make on the store; but the mechanical arrangement did not appear necessary to prove what was very obvious in the nature of the transactions. People offered also to mention instances where violence had been used to prevent men from receiving their earnings, but I declined hearing any statements involving charges of such illegal conduct, nor did they appear to me to bear on the real question, since, if there were not a stronger hold over colliers and iron-workers, the personal prowess of a pay-clerk or overseer would do little to carry out the system.

It was sometimes stated on the part of the men, that they knew they were liable to dismissal if they carried money past the store, or even if they waited for their money until the pay-day, declining to draw advances to be spent at the store; but naturally enough, the testimony I received on this head was of a vague character, since such dismissals, if they took place, would not in general be avowedly attributed to such a cause. On the other, and I believe far more potent means of influence over them—the refusal of the advances on which they make themselves so dependent—the workers naturally enough did not enlarge, as everything they would say of the power of the coercive force was so far an admission of their own extreme weakness and improvidence.

The Burton Report did not lead to the abolition of truck or the associated practice of poundage (deduction by the employer of one or two shillings per £ in return for an advance of wages). According to the miners' leader, Alexander McDonald, in 1871 truck was prevalent in almost exactly the same areas as in 1853. It was particularly rigorous in small or branch works, various forms of compulsion or inducement were used to enforce it on the men, and it was a contributory factor in all industrial disputes.

Workers and their wives objected to truck chiefly because the goods were dearer and inferior to those which could be obtained elsewhere. Some managers agreed with them and found the existence of a store made the recruitment of labour more difficult.

(2) *Report of the Royal Commission on the Truck System, 1871*, pp. 38-39. Evidence of James Gray, manager of the Drumpellier colliery –

Do you find any difficulty in getting men to come to you?—Yes.

More difficulty than your neighbours?—I don't know for my neighbours, but I find a difficulty myself.

Do you find more difficulty than you did in your former place?—Yes.

Can you account for that?—I may give my opinion.

There is a store at the work, is there not?—Yes.

Do you suppose that that has anything to do with it?—The workmen say so.

Was there a store at the place where you were formerly?—Yes.

And there was no difficulty there?—None.

Do you consider that there is a difference between this store and the other?—Yes.

Is it that this store is more severely worked than the store at the work where you formerly were?—Exactly.

Do you mean that there is more compulsion put upon the men to go to the store?—There is no compulsion, but the next money is stopped if they don't leave it there.

Was it not stopped at the former store?—Not so rigidly.

Have you ever heard of any complaints about the quality of the article at the store?—Yes.

Recently?—It is everyday in fact; but there were at one time more complaints than at others, and I investigated the case then.

How long ago is that?—About 15 months ago, I think.

Did a deputation of the men come to you on that occasion?—No; but I had a general complaint in the whole work from the men, and I stated to Mr. Henderson that such was the complaint amongst the whole workmen.

Did you yourself investigate the truth of the complaints?—I did.

What were the complaints chiefly?—High prices and inferior articles.

Did you consider that the complaints were well founded?—I proved it.

That the prices were high?—Yes.

And that the articles were inferior?—Yes.

Throughout the whole store?—No, not the whole articles.

Do the men complain still?—There are always complaints.

Your men don't like the store much, do they?—They don't like the store.

And the better men don't go to it if they can help it?—They never go to it.

Do you think it is rather a drawback having a store for your purpose of getting good men?—Yes.

Do they often talk to you about the store?—Almost every day.

Is it any part of your duty to pass on the complaints to Mr. Henderson?—Yes.

Or is it only when they get very bad that you do so?—It is part of my duty, because my interest is hurt by the store.

How?—If you cannot get men to give a supply of coal it is considered that the manager is not doing his duty.

Are you interested in the store in any way?—Not the slightest.

Do the men give as a reason why they don't take their advances to the store that they cannot get what they want at the store?—That they cannot get it at the price they want it. The reason they give is that the articles are dearer, and that they are inferior.

Do you think that is the true reason?—I proved it at once.

Do you think that possibly there is something in it?—It may be.

It is the rule of the works that you should persuade the men to spend their advances at the store?—Not at all. I would not do it. I think a man should get his money and go where he likes with it.

Then I may take it that you don't approve of the store system?—I don't approve of it on the system that is carried on.

You think there is no check on the store to make sure that the articles are good enough and cheap enough. Do you think the store system is defective in that respect?—It is defective in so far that there might be reason for the complaint, and no one takes it up and looks after it . . .

Do you find men complaining that when the price of bread goes down in the shops the store keeps on the old price longer?—I have heard that said.

Do you think it is true?—I believe there is some truth in it.

Public opinion, co-operation, and trade union action gradually eliminated the truck system; but an Act of 1887 finally closed all loopholes in existing legislation.

TRUCK AND ARRESTMENT: ARRESTMENT

Associated with the practice of truck was that of arrestment, by which a retailer or other creditor could obtain payment from the debtor's employers, the amount then being "arrested" from the debtor's wages. Some traders depended upon arrestment for much or all of their business.

(1) *Report on . . . the Arrestment of Wages in Scotland, 1854*, pp. 16-17 –

As there is no official record of arrestments, there are scarcely more available means of knowing the number issued in such a town as Glasgow in any given time, than of ascertaining the number of applications for payment of tradesmen's accounts. Nor have employers generally the means of showing the precise number which may at any given period have been served at their works, since, unless they be so numerous as to require a separate system of book-keeping by themselves, the whole wages are entered as paid, and the proportion kept for the arrester is set aside along with the arrestment, which, when he is paid, is destroyed . . . It is only in a few instances that a permanent record of arrestments appears to be preserved. In general, therefore, employers can only speak by guess to the numbers received by them.

Among the instances of such estimates, it was stated that at the power-loom weaving-factory of Bishop's Garden, in Anderston, where, of 400 workers, 350 were female, the arrestments served were, on an average, 7 in the month, or 84 in the year. In the West Street factory, Tradeston, of the same kind, where, of 190 workers, 170 were female, the number was estimated at five in the month. At the Barrowfield Print-works, where there are 800 people, it was said that there had been between the beginning of the year and the end of July, about 60. Though a print-work, half of the workers here are female, having been brought in during a strike. In the spinning work of Messrs. William Hussey & Son, Dale Street, where also about half the workers, amounting in all to between three and four hundred, are female, the number was estimated at sixteen per month, but it was said that this number was frequently doubled, and on one fortnight's pay-day during a strike—so long ago, however, as 1835—there had been 40 on the table. The Thornlie Bank works, where about 1000 people are employed, two-thirds of them males, in bleaching, printing, and machine-making, is one of the establishments in which a war has been kept up against arresters, and it was the opinion of the cashier, that while there would sometimes be 15 arrestments on one fortnightly pay-day, they did not now average above 4 in each month . . .

One of the notable peculiarities of the arrestment system in Glasgow is its operation on the humble earnings of factory girls, and other female workers, who in other parts of the country are . . . almost exempt from its operation . . .

The testimony to this preponderance of female liability has been chiefly afforded from weaving manufactories; and while it may be in some measure owing to the considerable respectability of the few male workers employed in power-loom weaving, perhaps there has been a tendency, from the great preponderance of female hands employed in this department, to exaggerate their comparative liability. But of this there can be no doubt, that arrestment of the humble wages made by factory girls is a systematic practice in Glasgow.

CHAPTER VI

Poor Law

The need for aid to the poor was always evident in Scotland, especially during periods of extreme hardship and famine such as occurred in the late seventeenth century.

(1) Sir Robert Sibbald, *Provision for the Poor in time of Dearth and Scarcity* (1699), pp. 2-3 –

God Almighty . . . requireth of us, a due Care for the Relief of the Poor; This is one of the Tributes we owe to Him, and he hath Dispersed the Poor amongst us, as his Substitutes and Receivers, to whom it is to be payed . . . This Charity to the Poor . . . is an Act of the greatest Policy and civil Prudence: For Poverty and Want Emasculate the Mindes of many, and make those who are of dull Natures, Stupid and Indisciplinable, and unfit for the Service of their Countrey; these that are of a firy and active Temperament, it maketh them unquiet, Rapacious, Frantick or Desperate. Thus, where there are many Poor, the Rich cannot be secure in the Possession of what they have . . . And such Considerations ought now to be lai'd to Heart, when the Bad Seasons these several Years past, hath made so much Scarcity and so great a Dearth, that for Want, some Die by the Way-side, some drop down in the Streets, the poor sucking Babs are starving for want of Milk, which the empty Breasts of their Mothers cannot furnish them: Every one may see Death in the Face of the Poor, that abound everywhere; the Thinness of their Visage, their Ghostly Looks, their Feebleness, their Agues and their Fluxes threaten them with sudden Death, if Care be not taken of them. And it is not only common wandering Beggars, that are in this Case; But many House-keepers, who lived well by their Labour and their Industrie, are now by Want, forced to abandon their Dwellings, and they and their little Ones must Beg; and in this their Necessity they take what they can get: Spoiled Victual; yea some eat these Beasts which have died of some Disease, which may occasion Plague amongst them.

Legislation on the poor was common for centuries, partly because of Christian charity, partly because of self-interest. (For information on early practice see W. C. Dickinson and G. Donaldson, *A Source Book of Scottish History*, vol. iii (second edition, 1961), pp. 374f.)

As a result the Scottish poor law acquired several distinct characteristics. Administration lay in the hands of heritors and kirk session; finance came from collections at the church door, from various fines for breaches of ecclesiastical discipline and from other minor sources; the able-bodied were refused help in normal circumstances, though exceptionally they could receive occasional help. In short the administration was conceived as a personal matter where an individual would be given such help as was necessary, normally as a supplement to his own resources or to the assistance of friends, and only after his entire needs had been investigated. The details were described by a Committee of the General Assembly in 1839.

(2) *Report by a Committee of the General Assembly on the Management of the Poor in Scotland, 1839*, pp. 4-8 –

I. The characteristic distinction of that part of the system, the object of which is to provide the necessary supplies for the poor, is, that it places its main reliance on the voluntary contributions of the public, and never imposes a compulsory assessment so long as hopes can be reasonably entertained of procuring without it the needful assistance . . .

It is true, that a compulsory assessment for the support of the impotent poor was, at a very early period, permitted in Scotland. It was introduced by the Act 1579, c. 74, and was thus nearly contemporaneous with the measure of somewhat similar import in England, which originated in the reign of Queen Elizabeth . . . This radical distinction between the two systems has from the outset prevailed, that while in England, the scheme of assessment soon became general over the whole country, in Scotland, no assessment was imposed for upwards of a century after the date of the statutes above referred to; and when at length this measure became necessary in certain parishes the use of it was confined to these parishes; the rule in practice, which was acted upon in this end of the island, having been that an assessment is not to be laid on in any parish, while a sufficiency of funds for the maintenance of the poor therein is voluntarily contributed.

The power to assess, although apparently in the original intention of the framers of the Act 1579, introduced mainly for securing the suppression of common begging, has been in practice, construed as a security to prevent the risk of the poor in any parish suffering from the want of funds to support them, and therefore to be resorted to in supplement of, or rather as a substitute, when such has become necessary for the church collections and other voluntary contributions. No attempt was ever made to apply the measure at once and simultaneously in all the parishes throughout the land, in whatever circumstances their poor, and the funds for their maintenance, might stand . . .

Hence it is that recourse has been had to the measure of assessment, at very different dates, in different parishes. The returns exhibit instances of certain parishes which, after having struggled long with scanty funds, have at length yielded to the pressure, and have levied an assessment—of others, chiefly in towns, or on the English border, which have succumbed more readily, and without so long or so strenuous resistance—of a third class, more numerous than either of the former, which has with greater energy and activity persevered in the ancient practice; and even of some which, having tried an assessment, have abandoned it, and returned to the old usage. Throughout all this variety there may be traced a decided preference of the system of church collections and voluntary alms over that of assessment.

Until nearly the middle of the last century the funds derived from church collections, and other voluntary contributions, were found to be sufficient for the maintenance of the poor in the whole of Scotland.

The first occasion of the church collections proving permanently inadequate in any parish for the maintenance of the ordinary poor, was the rise and progress of Presbyterian secession from the Established Church. This commenced in 1733, but some years elapsed before the effect of the measure on the funds appropriated to the poor was sensibly felt . . .

Since the date of the former Report, made by the General Assembly to the House of Commons in 1820, the difficulty in many parishes of maintaining the poor, by means of the collections made at the churches, has been greatly augmented by the rapid increase of population in the country, without a corresponding increase of the Ecclesiastical Establishment. In this way, and particularly in the manufacturing districts, the number of paupers has been greatly multiplied, while the ordinary funds for their maintenance have continued unimproved . . .

The deficiency of adequate means of religious instruction has also greatly tended to increase pauperism, by allowing the population to grow up free from those religious and moral restraints which operate so powerfully to induce habits of industry, prudence, and temperance, and so to check the progress towards want and pauperism.

These occurrences have rendered assessment unavoidable in some of the suburban parishes of commercial and manufacturing towns, in which the ordinary poor were previously maintained from the church collections and other funds voluntarily contributed . . .

But the old system still prevails over the greater part of Scotland. The people in general are persuaded of its expediency, and, with very few exceptions, are anxious to preserve it . . . The offerings of the greater number of them may be of the smallest denomination of coin in circulation, but when the contributors are numerous, and their contributions frequently and regularly repeated, a sufficient fund is raised by them. The moral consequences also of the institution on the country are of a highly beneficial nature. It has been remarked as one of the peculiar beauties of the Scottish system, that the prevalence of the custom among the least wealthy of the people, of putting, every Sunday, their mite into the poor's box, increases their repugnance in later life, till absolutely compelled by want to become pensioners on this fund.

II . . . In England provision was made by statute, not only in favour of the impotent poor, but also of those who are able to work and are destitute of employment . . . In Scotland, on the contrary, a legal right in the able-bodied poor was never acknowledged. The claims of this class of persons, as shall immediately be seen, was put on a totally different footing. The Act 1579 did not admit of such claims, and hence those evils, so oppressive to the rich, and so destructive to the poorer orders themselves, which prevailed in England, have, in this part of the island, been avoided. The system also of poor-houses and correction-houses never took place as a general measure in Scotland. Such establishments have been formed in one or two of the principal cities; but, with these exceptions, the relief given to paupers is entirely what is termed "out-door" relief . . .

If the poor were to be provided for by the spontaneous contributions of individuals, and chiefly by the collections made at the churches, it was impossible that this fund could supply work for the industrious poor and defray the expense of workhouses, and of other necessary arrangements for the purpose. It seems not improbable, then, that such considerations as these aided the other arguments for limiting the right of relief to the impotent poor, and that thus political and moral reasons concurred together in establishing the distinction between these two classes of persons . . .

At the same time it was obvious that the situation of such people, destitute of employment, was not to be overlooked, and that many cases might occur in which men of this class ought to obtain temporary relief, in times of occasional sickness or unusual calamity, although not as a matter of right . . .

Such are the rules of the law of Scotland on this subject—such the origin and foundation of the distinction between these who are called the "*ordinary*", and those who are denominated "*occasional*" poor . . .

III. The amount of the allowances to the parochial poor in Scotland exhibits another and striking peculiarity in the system. In all cases remarkably moderate, it varies according to the circumstances and situation of the parties who are to be assisted. The principle on which the amount of allowances to paupers is fixed, is, that, except in very rare instances of total and absolute destitution, the aliment to be provided by the parish is not to be such as would render the pauper independent of all other resources—that in the general cases poor persons are not so entirely destitute as not to be capable of procuring a part of their sustenance by their own labour, or by the assistance of relatives, or the benevolence of neighbours and others; and that it is only what may be necessary for their support, in addition to these separate means, that the parish ought to supply.

From such an arrangement as this many and great benefits result. The poor are led to be industrious and provident; their relatives and neighbours are encouraged to assist them; a spirit of independence is cherished; an unwillingness arises to come on the parish for the pittance which it yields; the burden to the industrious part of the community of the ordinary poor is lessened; a compulsory assessment is avoided; and the church collections prove in general sufficient to provide the necessary fund . . .

IV. The system which has now been generally described is, in each of the country parishes, placed under the superintendence and administration of the Kirk Session and landholders or heritors of the parish. In the towns the jurisdiction in these matters belongs to the magistrates, but generally, if not uniformly, they devolve the management on the Kirk Sessions within their bounds.

A great social reformer, the originator of savings banks, gave a more intimate picture of how the system operated in his own parish.

(3) *Evidence to the Committee on the Poor Laws, 1819*, pp. 11f. Evidence of Rev. Henry Duncan –

In what part of Scotland do you reside?—In the parish of Ruthwell and presbytery of Annan, in Dumfries-shire.

In what manner are the indigent poor of your parish supported?—By collections in the church, by private charities, but chiefly by their own relations.

What is the amount annually of the funds under the management of your session, and in what manner are these funds raised?—The annual amount is about £.24; these funds are raised by collections in the church, and by fines, which the session has in its power to impose on irregular marriages, on the parents of illegitimate children, and on proclamations for marriage.

Are there any other funds out of which the poor of your parish are supported?—No; there are no other funds.

What is the population of your parish?—About 1,160.

Have the goodness to detail to the Committee the mode of management by which the sessions of Scotland become acquainted with the wants of the poor, and afford them supply?—I believe the Committee is aware, that the session of a parish consists of the minister and elders, and that the minister is the moderator or president; the elders are chosen from the respectable householders, and the selection is made from particular districts of the parish, as far apart as circumstances will admit; they supply vacancies by election of their own body. The parish is by a mutual understanding divided into districts, over which each elder exercises a kind of superintendence, and he is perfectly acquainted with the situation of all the inhabitants of his own particular district; he gains this acquaintance not only by his residence among them, but also from the exercise of the duties of his office, which consist in visiting the sick and in praying with them, on which occasion he takes an opportunity of inquiring into their circumstances, and of ascertaining whether they are in pecuniary distress, or otherwise. Every Sunday, if necessary, there is a meeting of the session, which generally takes place immediately after divine service. The affairs of the poor are then talked over, and if there are any who require immediate relief, it is ordered to be given.

Relief, however, is only ordered at these meetings, in cases of remarkable distress, the usual time of making distributions being at a quarterly meeting of the session; at that quarterly meeting, the minister and elders look over the poor list, and appoint the different allowances to the indigent. I should mention also, that the heritors (that is to say, the landed proprietors) have it in their power to attend these meetings of session. In point of fact, however, they never do attend excepting when specially summoned on ten days notice; they are never called upon but in cases where it may be necessary to levy some particular contribution for the exigencies of the poor.

Is it customary to suffer indigent persons connected with the parish to ask alms and what method is adopted to restrain or modify the practice?—It is sometimes but not very frequently the custom, to grant certificates to poor persons to beg in the parish. Occasionally, in cases of particular distress, the certificate is given to extend to the whole presbytery. By a resolution of the Synod of Dumfries, passed some years ago, it was recommended to the different ministers within their bounds, to grant no certificates, the operation of which should extend beyond their own presbytery; and to take care that no person should be permitted to beg in any parish till the minister of that parish had signed the certificate. Where this recommendation has been enforced, it has been productive of useful consequences.

What is the amount of the poor on the poor roll of your parish, and what are the average allowances made to each person?—The amount of the poor on our roll is from 16 to 18, and the average allowances are from half a crown to seven shillings a quarter.

What other means of support do these poor persons possess?—The poor are principally supported by their own relations. There is that feeling in Scotland of independence, that laudable desire among the poor to provide for themselves, and that dislike of any thing approaching to reliance upon charity, that the labouring classes in those quarters, where poor rates have not been introduced, universally consider it to be their duty to make every sacrifice in support of their poor relations. There is another mode pretty frequently adopted for the support of the poor. In the particular district to which I belong, it has been customary for persons in indigent circumstances to have what is called a *drinking*. This is a kind of rustic *charity-ball*. The person for whose benefit it is intended, employs some friends or some persons for hire, to go through the parish, and invite the parishioners to this drinking. Those who do not wish any of their family to attend, generally give a contribution, either in meal or money. Ale and spirits are distributed at the ball, as well as other refreshments; and a contribution is made by the individuals present, which, after clearing all expenses, generally leaves to the entertainer about £.1 or £.2 of clear gain. This was the usual mode of relief in the parish of Ruthwell, for persons under particular circumstances of distress, when I came to it. I found, however, that there were irregularities (as might be supposed) consequent upon this mode of giving relief, and I discouraged it; but it was necessary to find some substitute. I therefore proposed, that instead of having this ball, the poor persons, who would have resorted to it, should confine themselves to the raising of a contribution. This has generally been adopted in the parish of Ruthwell and, I believe, in some other parishes. And now a common mode of obtaining relief for such persons, is to hire two individuals, who go through the parish with a certificate from the minister, stating the circumstances of the case, and who obtain for them a supply in meal or money. This is a substitute for begging; and though it may be attended with disadvantages, is probably better than permitting the individual himself to ask alms, because it has not so great a tendency to bring down the spirit of the lower classes, by degrading them in their own eyes, or in public opinion, and possesses other recommendations which will readily occur.

Ruthwell showed the favourable side of a poor law designed for rura parishes without any considerable degree of dissent. Such parishes were decreasingly common in the nineteenth century.

In most parishes the traditional methods of financing the old poor law proved inadequate. Voluntary assessments were sometimes levied by the heritors on themselves, but increasingly the reluctance of heritors to meet such demands forced legal assessments to be made. Even an appeal such as was issued at Cupar proved fruitless.

(4) Scottish Record Office. Records of the Heritors of Cupar. Minute of meeting of committee of heritors, 21st July 1841 –

There was laid before the meeting a state of the money paid by Mr. Dryburgh to the Kirk Session for the relief of the poor of the parish from which it appears that the funds raised by voluntary subscription for that purpose were exhausted.

The Clerk stated that a few of the Heritors had refused to pay their share of the subscription and that under these circumstances it would be necessary to raise a greater sum than they did last year to make up the deficiency and also to meet the increasing demands made upon them by the Kirk Session.

The Committee view with deep regret this state of matters and are extremely sorry that any of their brethren should be so unjust, callous and cold hearted as to throw a burden upon others, and not to join them in an Act of Charity, which by the laws of God and of the land is binding upon all and they would recommend to the Heritors that if those Gentlemen who are in arrears refuse to pay or to contribute in future along with the other Heritors for the support of the indigent that a legal assessment should be resorted to. They however would only make this a last resource as they have always considered that the mode of providing for and managing the poor in Scotland by Kirk Sessions when faithfully exercised is the best and cheapest which has ever been devised. Were a legal assessment once introduced the machinery for managing the whole would fall into the hands of people appointed by the rate payers and the expense of raising & distributing the funds, and of disputed Settlements etc. would soon amount to a great deal more than the sum at present contributed. It would also have this effect that the poor belonging to the different denominations of Christians in the parish and who are just now supported in part, and in some cases wholly by the congregations to which they belong would be thrown upon the general fund, and from the numerous applications which would then be made a fearful amount of destitution would soon be brought to bear upon the legal amount of assessment. They would therefore address themselves to the humanity & the common sense as well as the selfish principles of their brother Heritors, and implore them to contribute their share of the means for supplying the wants of their indigent fellow creatures.

In cities plagued by the unemployment of industrial depressions the old poor law met its greatest challenge. Even in such conditions it was defended by its greatest supporter, Thomas Chalmers.

(5) *Report for the Directors of the Town's Hospital of Glasgow on the Management of the City Poor* (1818), pp. 45-47. Remarks by Thomas Chalmers –

What in fact is the best defence of a people against the evils of a state of fluctuation? Their own providential habits, and these are what a compulsory provision goes directly to extinguish. What is it that most increases the difficulty of providing for *occasional* poor? The being previously burdened with a number of regular and ordinary poor, and this number it is the lesson of all experience is sure to be augmented by a compulsory provision. What is it that most discourages the wealthy from putting forth their liberalities to meet any incidental visitation of distress?—The apprehension that by so doing they will familiarize all the temporary sufferers to the habit of receiving, and so lay a permanent augmentation on the regular and established pauperism of the place: and therefore if there was no such system, the extra cases which occur in a season of difficulties would be far more cheerfully and amply provided for. But if instead of arguments we are required to produce facts upon this subject—we ask, what were the towns which felt most helpless and embarrassed in the last great fluctuation that came over the trading world?—Just those towns where the method of compulsory provision had been longest in operation. After all, these were the towns where an effort of gratuitous and extraordinary benevolence was most called for. And as if to prove, not the peculiar suitableness, but the peculiar inaptitude of any compulsory or legal establishment to the needs of a manufacturing population, these were the towns where benevolence was most heavily discouraged by the burden and the exhaustion of the already existing pauperism. We have therefore to implore the Committee that they will bethink themselves of these facts and these considerations, ere they give way to the delusion that a compulsory provision is indispensible to Glasgow, because it is just that peculiar expedient which meets the peculiar necessities of a great and manufacturing community. We affirm the entire and diametrical reverse of this. If there be one thing for which such a provision is more peculiarly fitted than another, it is to bring a sorer aggravation on all the distresses to which an operative population are liable. The way of meeting their distresses is not by setting up and extending a system of relief that shall be regular and constant in its operation, for this just brings a constant pressure upon the town, that weakens and incapacitates it for all such extraordinary efforts of benevolence as are called for by extraordinary visitations. The distress arising from fluctuations of trade ought in fact to be committed to those impulses of public benevolence, which the occurrence of such fluctuations is ever sure to awaken. And the Committee may rest assured, that when benevolence is not weighed down by a load of previous assessments, and where it is not discouraged by the apprehension, that with all its efforts it is just nursing the disease of ordinary pauperism—it will come forth in every season of incidental suffering with an alacrity and a power altogether commensurate to the urgency of the occasion.

The problem of relieving the large numbers of able-bodied poor thrown up by depression in the industrial areas forced a revision of the system. Following the depression of 1843 a Royal Commission was appointed to investigate the problem. The Commission's Report was inconclusive, but an Act was passed providing for a new form of central control, with power no longer chiefly in the heritors' hands, and with the right to authorise assessment to provide more adequate finance.

(6) 8 and 9 Vict., c. 83 (1845). – An Act for the Amendment and better Administration of the Laws relating to the Relief of the Poor in Scotland –

II. Be it enacted, That a Board of Supervision shall be and is hereby established . . . and . . . shall consist of the following Persons; . . . the Lord Provost of *Edinburgh*, the Lord Provost of *Glasgow*, the Solicitor General of *Scotland*, the Sheriff Depute of the County of *Perth*, the Sheriff Depute of the County of *Renfrew*, the Sheriff Depute of the County of *Ross* and *Cromarty*, all for the Time being together with three other Persons whom it shall be lawful for Her Majesty . . . to appoint.

XVII. And be it enacted, that in every Burghal Parish or Combination of Parishes there shall be a Parochial Board of Managers of the Poor; and the whole Administration of the Laws for the Relief of the Poor shall be under the Direction and Control of Such Parochial Board . . .; and until it shall have been resolved . . . to raise the Funds requisite for the Relief of the Poor . . . by Assessment, the Board shall . . . consist of the Persons who, if this Act had not been passed, would have been entitled to administer the Laws for the Relief of the Poor . . .; and when in any Burghal Parish or Combination in which it shall have been resolved . . . to raise the Funds requisite for the Relief of the Poor by Assessment the Parochial Board . . . shall be . . . chosen as follows; . . . the Persons assessed for the Support of the Poor . . . shall elect . . . such Number of Managers, not being more than Thirty, as the . . . Board of Supervision . . . may from time to time fix, such Qualification being in no Case fixed at a higher annual Value than Fifty Pounds . . . ; and the Magistrates of the Burgh shall nominate Four Persons . . . and the Kirk Session of each Parish shall nominate not exceeding Four Members of such Kirk Session: Provided always, that those Parishes only shall be held to be separate Parishes which at the Date of this Act are separate Parishes for the Purposes of Settlement and Relief of the Poor; and that where there shall be in any such Parish Two or more Kirk Sessions the Members of such several Kirk Sessions shall meet together and nominate not exceeding Four of their Number to be Members of the Parochial Board.

XXXII. And be it enacted, That each Parochial Board shall . . . meet for the Purpose of making up or causing to be made up a Roll of the poor Persons claiming and by Law entitled to Relief from the Parish or Combination, and of the Amount of Relief given or to be given to each of such Persons, and for the Purpose of appointing an Inspector or Inspectors of the Poor in such Parish.

XXXIII. And be it enacted, That it shall be lawful for the Parochial Board . . . to resolve that the Funds requisite for the Relief of the poor Persons . . ., including the Expenses connected with the Management and Administration thereof, shall be raised by Assessment . . .

XXXIV. And be it enacted, That when the Parochial Board . . . shall have resolved to raise by Assessment the Funds requisite . . .; . . . it shall be lawful for any such Board to resolve that one Half of such Assessment shall be imposed upon the Owners, and the other Half upon the Tenants . . . of all Lands and Heritages within the Parish or Combination rateably according to the annual Value of such Lands and Heritages, or to resolve that one Half shall be imposed upon the Owners . . . and the other Half upon the whole Inhabitants, according to their Means and Substance, other than Lands and Heritages situated in *Great Britain* or *Ireland*, or to resolve that such Assessment shall be imposed as an equal Percentage upon the annual Value of all Lands and Heritages within the Parish or Combination, and upon the estimated annual Income of the whole Inhabitants from Means and Substance, other than Lands and Heritages situated in *Great Britain* or *Ireland*; and when the Parochial Board shall have resolved on the Manner in which the Assessment is to be imposed, such Resolution shall be forthwith reported to the Board of Supervision for Approval . . .

LV. And be it enacted, That . . . it shall be the Duty of the . . . Inspector of the Poor . . . to visit and inspect personally, at least Twice in the Year, or oftener if required by the Parochial Board or Board of Supervision, at their Places of Residence, all the Poor Persons belonging to the Parish . . . in Receipt of Parochial Relief . . .

LX. And whereas for more effectually administering to the wants of the aged and other friendless impotent Poor, and also for providing for those poor persons who from Weakness or Facility of Mind, or by reason of dissipated and improvident Habits, are unable or unfit to take charge of their own Affairs, it is expedient that Poorhouses should be erected in populous Parishes; be it enacted, That in every Case in which a Parish . . . contains more than Five thousand Inhabitants . . . it shall be lawful for the Parochial Board . . . to take into consideration the propriety of erecting a Poorhouse . . .; and if . . . the said Parochial Board . . . shall come to a Resolution to that effect, such Resolution shall be forthwith reported to the Board of Supervision, and if approved of by the Board of Supervision the same shall be carried into execution by the said Parochial Board.

LXXIV. And be it enacted, That in every Case in which any Poor Person shall consider the Relief granted him to be inadequate, such poor Person shall lodge . . . a Complaint with the Board of Supervision . . .; and if upon Inquiry, it shall appear that the Grounds of such Complaint are well founded . . . the said Board shall by a Minute declare that . . . such poor Person has a just Cause of Action against the Parish . . . from which he claims Relief . . . and upon the Production . . . of such Minute or certified Copy thereof such poor Person shall forthwith . . . be entitled to the Benefit of the Poor's Roll in the Court of Session; and it shall be lawful for the Board of Supervision, after any Action has actually been commenced by or on behalf of such poor Person, to award to him such interim Aliment as to the said Board shall seem just during the Dependency of such Action, which Award the Parochial Board of every such Parish or Combination shall be bound to obey.

LXXV. Provided always, and be it enacted, That it shall not be competent for any Court of Law to entertain or decide any Action relative to the Amount of Relief granted by the Parochial Boards, unless the Board of Supervision shall previously have declared that there is a just Cause of Action as herein before provided.

After 1845 the administration of the Scottish poor law was brought closer to that of England. Previously, following the idea that assistance from the parish was supplementary to other aid, outdoor relief was common. After 1845 admission to a poorhouse was often offered as a test of whether an applicant was genuine. The Fifth Report of the Board of Supervision made this change clear.

(7) Fifth Annual Report of the Board of Supervision for the Relief of the Poor in Scotland. In Parliamentary Papers, 1851, XXVI. Circular as to Poorhouses (from Board of Supervision to local Inspectors of Poor), 2nd February 1850 –

So long as relief to the poor was looked upon, both by the givers and recipients, as the fulfilment of a charitable, rather than a legal, obligation, poorhouses were naturally regarded merely in the light of almshouses for the reception of the more deserving amongst the aged, infirm or friendless poor. The inmates were therefore, generally speaking, of but one class, consisting wholly of persons whose destitution and disability were beyond a doubt, and by whom admission to the poorhouse was held to be a favour or indulgence of which they might at any time be deprived by their own misconduct. The whole establishment was managed in a corresponding spirit. The inmates had regular liberty—days once a-week, when they went to visit their friends, or to amuse themselves; and it was not uncommon to find some of them begging on the streets or highways. In like manner, once a-week their friends were freely admitted to visit their inmates in the poorhouse, which, on such occasions, exhibited a promiscuous throng of paupers and their visitors mingled together. The friends of the paupers were permitted to bring to them, in the house, tobacco and such other articles of luxury (excepting ardent spirits) as they were able to procure. The inmates were induced to engage in some kind of industrious occupation, by a weekly payment of part of the proceeds of their work, to be expended as they might think proper on their liberty-days; and one of the first petitions presented to the Board of Supervision was from the male inmates of a poorhouse, complaining that the weekly sum allowed them as pocket-money was unreasonably small. It was deemed unnecessary to enforce strictly any system of rules or discipline where flagrant breaches of order or decorum were punished by expulsion from the house. But, while poorhouses ought always to afford a fit and safe asylum for helpless and friendless paupers, they must now be prepared to receive a new and wholly different class of inmates.

The altered feelings of the poor in regard to parochial relief, their more perfect knowledge of their rights, and the facilities which the law now affords for enforcing these rights have caused a strong pressure on parochial boards from a class, whose claims it would be unsafe to admit without testing the truth of allegations on which these claims are founded. For this purpose a well regulated poorhouse is the best of all tests. While it furnishes sufficient, and even ample, relief to the really necessitous, it affords the only available security that the funds raised for the relief of the poor are not perverted to the maintenance of idleness and vice. But a poorhouse will be wholly useless as a test, or rather it will not be a test at all, unless it is conducted under rules and regulations, as to discipline and restraint, so strict as to render the more irksome than labour, without such discipline and restraint, those who are not truly fit objects of parochial relief. Hence the necessity which has arisen for placing the management of poorhouses upon a footing essentially different from that on which it formerly stood. It is with the view of meeting this necessity that these rules have been issued.

RULES and Regulations for the Management of Poorhouses

XIV. The Poorhouse shall be visited once at least in every week, by a committee of two or more members of the Parochial Board. The Visiting-Committee shall carefully examine the Poorhouse—shall satisfy themselves as to the quantity and quality of the provisions issued to the inmates—shall ascertain whether the house is kept clean, well ventilated, and sufficiently warm, and whether the inmates are properly attended to and accommodated . . .

LV. Any inmate who shall neglect to observe such of the Rules and Regulations of the Poorhouse as are applicable to, and binding upon him;

Or who shall make any noise when silence is ordered to be kept;

Or who shall use obscene or profane language;

Or shall, by word or deed, revile or insult any person;

Or shall threaten to strike or assault any person;

Or shall not duly cleanse his person;

Or shall refuse or neglect to work, having been required to do so;

Or shall pretend sickness;

Or shall play at cards, or other game of chance;

Or shall enter, or attempt to enter, without permission, the ward or

part of the premises appropriated to any class of inmates other than that to which he belongs;
Or shall behave improperly at public worship, or at prayers;
Or shall not return till after the appointed time, when allowed to quit the Poorhouse on temporary leave of absence;
Or shall wilfully disobey any lawful order of any officer of the Poorhouse; shall be deemed DISORDERLY, and the House-Governor may punish any such inmate by requiring him, for a time not exceeding two days, to perform one or two hours of extra work each day, and by withholding, for the like time, all milk or butter and milk which such inmate would otherwise receive with his meals . . .
LXVII. (Diet of adult inmates of either sex who are working)

Breakfast . . .	Meal, four ounces, and milk, three-fourths pint imperial.
Dinner . . .	Bread, eight ounces; broth, one-and-half pint imperial; and boiled meat, four ounces.
Supper . . .	Meal, four ounces; and milk, three-fourths pint imperial.

CHAPTER VII

Labour Movements

A. EARLY COMBINATIONS AND THE LAW

From at least the eighteenth century, and probably earlier, organisations of workmen were found in many industries. Conditions in coalmining—with its physical danger, servile status and close, isolated communities—were particularly conducive to combinations, normally for welfare purposes, but capable also of industrial action. Frequently the guise of friendly societies had to be adopted because of opposition from employers, some of whom tried to enforce detailed codes of conduct. Among them was Sir John Clerk of Penicuik.

(1) Scottish Record Office. Clerk of Penicuik Manuscripts. Memorandum by Sir John Clerk –

I loosed the whole Coaliers and bearers of Lonhead from their work upon Wednesday the 20 of January 1703 till they should condescend to the whole following articles.

1. To guard agst. all profanness and immorality particularly agst. excessive drinking and tipling, fighting and flyting, cursing and swearing or taking the lords name in vain, and in case of failzie to make their publick acknoulegement and Confession before the Congregation of Lasswade and to Submitt themselves to the censure of the Kirk Session as they shall be appointed by the minister and Elders. And to be liable in payment of their fines imposed or to be imposed by the Master conform to the acts made by him against all such profanness and gross abominations.
2. The hail Coaliers shall work whole days to witt twelve hours Space each day of the week at least so many hours dayly as may furnish to their bearers twelve hours work dayly to bear out yr masters wrought coals.
3. That every Coalier keep and employ as many Coal bearers as will be Suitable to the Coal-wall and to the Coaliers strength.

4. That every Coalier pay dayly 5/- Scots to each bearer who are not hired for meat and fee within there houses.
5. That every Coalier pay to the master (for each day he lies idle) ... as much money as by his work he hath gained to him upon any other work day of that or the preceeding week Except the Said Coalier get liberty to ly idle of yt. day either from the master or in his absence from the Oursman and Grieve both together or that he be really Sick as an Sure evidence yr of either keep his house or if he go to walk abroad to take the air for his health that he make it appear he hath abstained from drinking and tipling: Because for the most part it hath been found yt. Such as lay idle did nothing but go up and down Seeking people to drink and tipple wt. them, to make them yt., which they pretended to be, to wit, Seek indeed, not with too much work, but with too much drink.
10. ... the Coaliers do oblige themselves ... to lay quite aside the unprecedented and unusual way of working quarter and half days which hath creeped in amongst ym to the loss of all parties and which is inconsistent with the old Custom of yr. place.
17. That if any of the Coaliers or bearers be injured by any of the neighbours Coalkaers or others yt. they presume not by flyting cursing and beating ym, to take satisfaction at yr own hand but complain to the Oursman and Grieve who is presently to determine the quarrell and to give Satisfaction to the partie injured according to justice.

(Signed by Sir John Clerk, 17 Colliers and 2 witnesses)

In the eighteenth century the employers invoked the aid of the law and of the military to ensure adherence to the terms of contract. In most cases they succeeded, but not always. In particular, then and later, the landowners, who exercised much of the judicial power, were not always sympathetic to the views of the industrialists. Bruce and Dundas were two landowners who frequently quarrelled with Carron Company when it started mining operations on their lands.

(2) Scottish Record Office. Carron Company Manuscripts. Letter to John McGowan, Edinburgh, 23rd June 1778 –

We are favd. with Mr. Campbell's letter of yesterday covering copy of the Bill of Suspension offered for Abraham Laird, which we wish had been sent us before now, as you found it necessary to give in answer to it, which we did not know was the case. With respect to the question you ask whether the sum in the Bill was for fore wages or not, you may with great truth affirm that it was not for fore wages, but was extorted by force from Mr. Gascoigne by Laird & about 100 Colliers at his back, for whom he was spokesman & of whom he was the ring leader in all the combination and disturbances that happened at that time. This will appear from a copy of a letter, sent you enclosed, which Mr. Gascoigne wrote to Mr Bruce of Kinnaird, on that subject, and in consequence of his Factor's having applied to Mr. Gascoigne to stop the prosecution then going on against Laird.

When Laird was brought to trial he signed a Declaration in presence of the Jury, that he was concerned in & had signed the Combination with the other Colliers to desist from working, until they had obliged the Company to increase their wages. Notwithstanding of which the Jury brought him in *not guilty*. This we could not help, but his signed confession is certainly legal evidence against him in this case. Not only that, he was engaged in an unlawful combination, but the Bill charged on is legal evidence that the value of it was paid to him and the other accepters. How he or they might distribute it afterwards we have no opportunity of knowing, nor did we enquire. So far from being the active, industrious servant and careful of the Works with which he was entrusted that he pretends to be, he has been the very reverse, for he has been fomentar & ringleader of all the disturbances & combinations that have happened among the Colliers for these several years past, in which he has been but too much countenanced & encouraged by Mr. Bruce & Mr. Dundas, whose servant he has been, more than the Company's. We therefore beg you'l give in answer to the Bill and endeavour to get it refused or at least passed upon caution. Indeed we never doubted but that it had been passed upon caution with your consent long ere now, and are surprised you did not sooner write us anything about it . . .

Towards the end of the eighteenth century the old agitations began to assume a new edge. Under the influence of the French Revolution and of Thomas Paine's *Rights of Man* (published in 1791-92), economic grievances were expressed strongly in ideological and political terms. Repressive measures followed the British Convention of the Friends of the People at Edinburgh in 1793. The popular political movement was crushed; but industrial organisation continued.

The illegality of combinations as *contra utilitatem publicam* was well established under the common law of Scotland. In the mid-eighteenth century the Court of Session declared illegal two associations, one of weavers in Paisley the other of woolcombers in Aberdeen, though both were at least superficially only friendly societies. Consequently, though the Combination Acts of 1799 and 1800 (39 Geo. III, c. 81 and 39 and 40 Geo. III, c. 106) were drawn up in English terms, were not invoked in Scotland, and according to the best legal opinion did not apply there, the legal standing of combinations was weak.

(3) *Evidence to the Committee on Artizans and Machinery, 1824*, pp. 484-486. Evidence of John Archibald Murray, Advocate –

Is the combination of workmen a crime under the statute law of Scotland?—It is not.

Is the combination of workmen, without violence or intimidation, a crime under the common law of Scotland?—It has been held to be so by the decisions of the supreme court, for some years.

Can you state what was the practice in Scotland, in cases of combination of workmen, prior to the year 1808?—I beg leave to refer, on that point, to the opinions that appear to have been delivered by the judges of the court of justiciary, upon a trial that took place in 1808 . . .

What trial was that?—The trial of James Taylor, and other journeymen paper makers at Edinburgh, the 21st of March and 10th May 1808 . . .

What instances of prosecution have taken place since that time?—I beg leave to refer upon that point to the statement of Baron Hume, in his work on Criminal Law . . . , where he refers to the cases of Mackininnie and others, on the 12th and 13th of March 1813; then to the case of Alexander Richmond and Arthur Ferrier and others on the 16th March 1813; to the case of John Wilson and David Ross, on the 18th of March 1813; and to the case of John Folhaus Wilson and Charles Banks in January, February and May 1818; . . . and he observes, after these cases, the law was considered as fully established to make combination a crime . . .

Were all those individuals punished under the common law, for combination?—All the sentences against those individuals proceeded upon the common law.

Were any of those parties guilty of any acts of violence?—I think in some of the cases violence is stated as an exaggeration of the crime; but the essence of the crime was, I conceive, held to be the act of combination; and in some cases it is stated that acts of violence were not proved . . .

Are the Committee to understand, that these decisions have settled the law in Scotland, and rendered combination of workmen to raise wages, although unattended with any acts of violence, liable to be punishable by the Common Law?—I conceive they have, as long as the judges of the Court of Justiciary shall remain of that opinion.

The position of the individual worker was also weak under the common law. A workman leaving his employment without notice could be imprisoned by summary warrant.

In 1823 the common law was reinforced by the Act of Master and Servant. A defaulting workman could be treated criminally; but masters in breach of contract were liable only to civil proceedings.

(4) 4 Geo. IV, c. 34 (1823). An Act to enlarge the Powers of Justices in determining Complaints between Masters and Servants –

And be it further enacted, That if any Servant in Husbandry, or any Artificer, Calico Printer, Handicraftsman, Miner, Collier, Keelman, Pitman, Glassman, Potter, Labourer or other Person, shall contract with any Person or Persons whomsoever, to serve him, her or them for any Time or Times whatsoever, or in any other Manner, and shall not enter into or commence his or her Service according to his or her Contract, or shall absent himself or herself from his or her Service before the term of his or her Contract, whether such Contract shall be in Writing or not in Writing, shall be completed, or neglect to fulfil the same, or be guilty of any other Misconduct or Misdemeanour in the Execution thereof, or otherwise respecting the same, then and in every such case it shall and may be lawful for any Justice of the Peace of the County or Place where such Servant in Husbandry (etc.) . . . shall have so contracted, or be employed, or be found, and such Justice is hereby authorised and empowered, upon Complaint thereof made upon Oath to him, by the Person or Persons, of any of them, with whom such Servant in Husbandry (etc.) . . . shall have so contracted, or by his, her, or their Steward, Manager or Agent, which Oath such Justice is hereby empowered to administer, to issue his Warrant for the apprehending of every such Servant in Husbandry (etc.) . . . and to examine into the Nature of the Complaint; and if it shall appear to such Justice that any such Servant in Husbandry (etc.) . . . shall not have fulfilled such Contract, or hath been guilty of any other Misconduct or Misdemeanor as aforesaid, it shall and may be lawful for such Justice to commit every such Person to the House of Correction, there to remain and be held to Hard Labour for a reasonable Time, not exceeding Three Months, and to abate a proportionable Part of his or her Wages . . . or in lieu thereof, to punish the Offender by abating the Whole or any Part of his or her Wages, or to discharge such Servant in Husbandry (etc.) . . . from his or her Contract, Service or Employment . . .

The law was particularly resented in Scotland, where magistrates generally issued summary warrants rather than summonses. Accordingly Glasgow Trades Council, supported by the Miners' Unions, began the agitation which led to reform. A conference was called in London in 1864. In evidence to a Select Committee which investigated the problem in 1866 the chairman of the Glasgow Trades Council pointed out the nature of the problem.

(5) *Evidence to the Select Committee on Master and Servant, 1866*, pp. 29–34. Evidence of Alexander Campbell (formerly a joiner and builder, editor of the *Glasgow Sentinel*, a working-man's newspaper, and Chairman of Glasgow Trades Council).

. . . The Conference held in London two years ago, which was constituted of delegates from the principal branches of industry in the country, and representing the large masses of the organised societies, unanimously agreed that the Glasgow committee, who had originated the meeting, should be constituted the executive committee to carry out the movement, and that all other committees, wherever they might exist, should be subordinate to their direction . . .

. . . We meet regularly every two weeks, and specially when any business comes before us. We have correspondence from all parts of the kingdom, and we reply to that correspondence, and we have the power of calling a conference in London or any other place, if we deem proper, to carry on the movement. We alone possess those powers, as vested in us by that conference . . .

Will you mention the trades in which those cases of proceedings, being taken for breach of contract, most frequently occur ?—A great many cases used to arise amongst the iron ship builders, and, in fact, I might say, with some exceptions, in almost all the trades. Amongst the factory workers they used repeatedly to occur . . .

The following trades have been given to me as among those in which those cases occur:-brickmakers, glass workers, moulders in iron, iron workers, carpenters, and miners?—There are not so many cases arising among the carpenters; there are cases constantly occurring among the miners, and there used to be a great many cases among the iron moulders, and brickmakers, and factory workers . . .

You have heard Mr. Newton's evidence; do you generally agree with the tenor of his evidence?—Generally.

Do you agree as to the objections which he takes as to the inequality between master and servant?—Decidedly.

The apprehension by warrant instead of summons, and the treatment of those cases by criminal instead of civil procedure; upon those points you agree with him?—Yes, the primary object of all who have moved in this matter is to put the employer and employed before the law exactly in the same condition, as far as that is possible.

So far you agree with Mr. Newton; do you agree with him as to the persons by whom those cases should be tried?—Yes; there are objections to those cases being tried by justices, and I would prefer their being brought before some constituted legal authority, such as the sheriff or substitute in Scotland, or the county judge in England.

Why do you wish for that change; is it a theoretical objection that you have to the existing state of things, or have you seen any practical evil result from the present administration of the law by the justices? —In the first place, many justices, although they are gentlemen who, no doubt, desire to do all the justice they can, are not sufficiently acquainted with the law to be enabled to come to a decision in a critical case which might occur; they are not posted up in law.

Is your objection merely the want of legal knowledge as to the different bearings of law upon these questions, or do you also object to partiality in the administration of the law?—I object on the two grounds, the want of knowledge of the law, and the tendency towards partiality in the administration of it on the part of the justices sitting in such cases . . .

You object because you believe that they will be influenced by class interests and feeling?—I will tell you how I come to that conclusion; for instance, when a factory worker, male or female, is taken before the justices, it is no uncommon thing to find a justice presiding who is actually in the same branch of business as the worker belongs to; that is quite a common occurrence, and the same with regard to other branches of trade.

The law of master and servant was modified in 1867 following the report of the Select Committee. In 1875 the Employers and Workmen Act made contract of employment a purely civil engagement.

Whatever the legal position, the masters had always other powerful sanctions to ensure their way. Workmen's leaders could be blacklisted (6); the social prestige of the masters and their personal acquaintance with the magistrate secured improper convictions of workmen in inferior courts (7) and in some places, especially mining communities, men could be evicted from their homes (8). It was especially easy to break strikes if any dissension among the strikers could be exploited.

(6) *Evidence to the Committee on Combinations of Workmen, 1838*, pp. 71–72; 74–75. Evidence of James McNish –

Have you yourself been the subject of any severe treatment by masters, in consequence of belonging to the Cotton Spinners' Association?—Yes.

Describe it?—At the period of our strike, in 1824, I happened to be secretary to the association for about eight days. I had to sign some public document; and for that I was kept three years out of employment. My father had 49 men under his employment, and he was not allowed to employ me.

By whom was he prevented?—By the proprietors of works.

Do you know whether masters are in the habit of sending the names of proscribed men to masters at distant places?—Yes; I am aware that they are.

And if a man is prevented obtaining employment in Glasgow, it is possible that he would be prevented from obtaining employment in Dublin or in Belfast, or in any other place in this country?—I am aware that my name was in Belfast, for I sought for employment there.

How was it that your father was at the head of 49 men?—He was the manager of a cotton factory.

Were you totally idle during the three years?—Totally idle, with the exception of a month or two in works that were not connected with the combination; but such works that a man could not make wages to support his family . . .

Have you any reason to believe that there is an understanding in the association of masters, that an operative dismissed from any one of their mills shall not be employed in another?—I have every reason to believe that such an understanding does exist. A number of our late committee are still kept out of employment; some of them have had to leave the country, and go to Belgium; they have been informed by their employers that dismissed them, that they would not be employed.

Was this because they were bad workmen?—No; we understand it was because they were connected with the committee for conducting the last strike . . .

Have they been dismissed, and consequently refused employment, for other causes than that they were unionists, and therefore obnoxious?—The causes are not given them; they pretty well understand when a man is dismissed for being a unionist. The master does not state what he is dismissed for.

To your knowledge, have men been dismissed for having rendered themselves obnoxious in any other way?—Yes; there are a good many who have rendered themselves obnoxious by their own bad character, but they generally obtain employment in other factories.

(7) *Evidence to the Committee on Combinations of Workmen, 1838*, pp. 198-199. Evidence of Andrew Gemmill –

. . . Do you recollect the committal of five persons in the village of Catrine, in Ayrshire, to Ayr gaol, also upon illegal warrants?—I do; those were upon the statute of 6 Geo. 4, c. 129. A strike had taken place at Catrine works, of which Mr. Buchanan, one of the justices of the peace for the county of Ayr, is a partner; Mr. Buchanan sent for two of his brother justices to his counting-house, got hold of the five individuals, carried them in before the justices, and a sort of trial was gone through before the relations of the parties were aware, and the justices sentenced them to imprisonment without the benefit of consulting with their relations, or having a legal adviser; they were escorted to Ayr gaol by a party of cavalry, and there imprisoned. I made inquiries into the circumstances of the case, and I found that after the conviction had taken place, and before the removal of the persons, the relations had got some notice of it, and had gone to Mr. Buchanan and the justices, and had tendered bail for their appearance upon any day, and claimed for them a fair trial, and requested that they might be set at liberty in the meantime till they obtained legal advice; that was refused; the parties were sent to gaol. Upon examining more particularly into the nature of the proceedings, I found that the justices had not proceeded according to the statute; in fact, they had overlooked some of the most important provisions; I therefore presented bills of suspension and liberation to the Court of Justiciary; in this I was also successful, the Court of Justiciary holding that the proceedings were altogether illegal; actions of damages were subsequently brought, and the question revived anew in the Court of Session, and the Court of new held unanimously that the proceedings were illegal, and that the prisoners were entitled to damages at the hands of the masters.

Is not Mr. Buchanan partner of Mr. Kirkman Finley?—I believe he is. In connexion with this I may state another circumstance; as charges are brought here against the men, it is right that the committee should also know something of what is going on with the masters: Mr. Buchanan went to a person of the name of Reed, a public-house keeper, in which the united body were in the habit of meeting, and told him that he should not have his licence renewed, because he permitted unionists to meet in his house; he objected to his licence being renewed in consequence, and it was only upon Reed apologising to Mr. Buchanan, the master, and promising never afterwards to offend in that particular, that the justices granted a renewal of the licence.

(8) Manuscripts belonging to the Duke of Hamilton. Factor's Letters –

Letters of Wm. Leighton to R. Brown. 5th Dec. 1833.

Mr. Bauchop would tell you that I explained to the colliers on Saturday, that their wages were now as good as when the prices of provisions were fully a third dearer, that although the price of coal had been restricted 1/6 per ton, yet *their* rates had only been lowered about 4d per ton and as they might earn from 2/6 to 3/ per day (if they choosed to work) they could not expect any advance, but on the contrary their wages would be taken down, that as they had improperly struck work without giving any warning, and forefeited all right to their Homes, they were dismissed from the Duke's service, and I concluded by telling them that they would not be again allowed to work at the Redding unless at 1d per ton of reduction from their former rates, and if they did not think proper to comply with this, or remove, their homes would be unroofed.

Since Saturday, a number of men agreed to begin work, but these have been intimidated by the others, and the whole are still idle. I saw Staffa today along with Mr. Rutherford. He is very much against the unroofing of the houses, and says it would look as if the law was not strong enough. He *promises* to grant warrants or ejection in course of three days after application, by allowing the colliers 24 hours to give in answers, and failing of their doing so, to hold them as confessed, or if answers should be lodged, to consider the replies immediately, and decide. I am to try him with several of the colliers in this way, and if he does not succeed and go through with it, we will have recourse to the more summary method of unroofing the others. The applications are to be made tonight.

In regard to the colliers who have been using intimidating language, one or two of them will be apprehended in the course of this evening or tomorrow morning, and transmitted to Stirling, along with the witnesses, and Staffa *says* that he will immediately call them before him, and if the case is proved, sentence them to three months confinement.

I hope therefore we will get through this business and crush it in the Bud, for it does not yet seem to be a serious strike, and the colliers are not receiving any support from their other Brethren in the East or West. I have said to Staffa that it would not do to be simple with them, the same as last time, and that whatsoever was to be done, must be done immediately. Staffa has gone off to Stirling this evening, and will be there holding Criminal Courts for 4 or 5 days. I am going to the Redding and Falkirk tomorrow.

11th Dec. 1833.

I am now glad to inform you that the combination at the Redding appears to be fairly broke up. I refused to treat with the Colliers as a body, and when at the Redding yesterday made every man appear and answer for himself holding the whole as dismissed. They then individually came forward, and made application to be again allowed to work, when several of the Ringleaders were refused, and the others told that they could only begin if they choosed to take a penny per ton less than they got before the Strike to which they agreed. Today the same process has been gone through with a number of others, and by tomorrow night I expect to be able to inform you that they are all at work—with the exception of from 25 to 30 who are to be put away from the Redding altogether, as an example to those that are to be kept. There have as yet been no ejections, but the process is before the Sheriff and no answers lodged, so that the warrants will be got this week, if necessary and these Ringleaders put out. There is one of the men in Stirling Jail for using intimidating language.

13th Dec. 1833.

The colliers have all individually applied to be again employed and today and yesterday have been at work, so that the Combination is completely suppressed and I hope there will be no further trouble with them. They now work at a penny per ton less than they were doing before they struck work. I am sorry that so many of them will be turned out of their Homes but am afraid that resolution cannot be relaxed. I am going out to the Redding tomorrow and if there is any counter movement I shall write you.

Letter of Robert Bauchop to R. Brown 16th Dec. 1833.

When at Redding on Saturday we found that all the colliers that were permitted had commenced working at the reduced price. Those that had got warnings to remove from their homes were petitioning very hard to be employed also, but Mr. Leighton resisted all their solicitations. I suppose he will dismiss at least 20 of the ring leaders and may probably employ some of the rest after punishing them by a week or two idleness. There is a complete quarrel among the colliers themselves and some of the dismissed ones were offering to work in some of the pits at a farther reduction of 1d per ton. This Mr. Leighton will make his own use of.

B. LABOUR ASSOCIATIONS

In the nineteenth century associations of workmen became organised in forms which increasingly approximated to modern unions. As early as 1837 the widespread nature of the organisations was evident. In the sharp trade depression which began in that year, all associations had similar difficulties in maintaining their wages. Archibald Alison, Sheriff of Lanarkshire, described the ensuing strikes and his attempts to maintain order.

(1) Sir Archibald Alison, *Some Account of My Life and Writings* (1842), pp. 369 ff. –

With the steady contraction of the currency by the Bank of England, which began in July 1836, prices fell during the whole of the ensuing winter, and in the spring of 1837 the panic was universal. Many bankruptcies took place, though fewer in Glasgow than might have been expected from the severity of the pressure, owing to the amount of solid wealth which had been made in the preceding five years. But as prices of all sorts of manufactured produce had sunk nearly a half, the manufacturers were under the necessity of lowering wages; and this soon induced strikes in nearly all the branches of skilled industry. The cotton-spinners, the sawyers, the carpenters, the masons, the iron-moulders, the dyers, were soon out on strike; and as the whole of these trades possessed thoroughly organised trades-unions, under the direction of small committees, which communicated with each other, they were enabled to act simultaneously, and in the way most calculated to embarrass their employers and prove most distressing to society. The avowed object of these strikes was to retain wages forcibly, during adversity and low prices, at the elevated level which they had attained during the previous prosperity and high prices. Extravagant, and apparently hopeless, as such an attempt must appear to be, and as it really is in the long-run, it was universally embraced by the united trades over the whole island; and in a great many instances, and for a considerable period, was attended with success. The reasons were, that during the previous period of prosperity, when prices were rising, the workmen had found that, in almost every instance, a strike had been attended by concession on the masters' part; and that, even when the tide had turned, and prices were stationary or declining, they had frequently, by similar means, succeeded in keeping up their wages, from the reluctance of the masters to lose a body of skilled workmen. They trusted, too, in the good fortune which led the master to go on manufacturing for months, or even years, at a loss, in the hope of being indemnified by a rise of prices in more prosperous times.

All these strikes began with the profession of pacific intentions on the part of the workmen, and of a desire to avoid any breach of the law. But before many weeks had elapsed these professions were forgotten, and the usual system of intimidating and assaulting the new hands commenced. I was beseiged with applications for protection by the masters and new workmen who were suffering under this system, which were the more distressing as their complaints were evidently well-founded . . .

During the whole of May and June the strikes continued, threatening meetings and processions were frequent, and assaults on the new hands were of almost daily occurrence ... Convictions were almost impossible, in consequence of the extreme difficulty of getting witnesses to come forward, from the dread of experiencing similar treatment at the hands of the trades-unions; the convicted persons were not unfrequently rewarded for their imprisonment of three months by a box of sovereigns from the members of the strike.

The strike of cotton spinners in 1837 was especially serious and led to a government investigation. From it much valuable information is available on the strike itself, which, like many others, was to resist a reduction in wages, and, of greater importance, on the general organisation and development of the unions.

(2) *Evidence to the Committee on Combinations of Workmen, 1838*, pp. 30-37. Evidence of Angus Campbell –

Are you a member of the Cotton Spinners' Association in Glasgow?—Yes ...

What induced you to become a member of the Cotton Spinners' Association?—I found from my own experience, and the opinion of the rest of my brother cotton-spinners, that, if an association of that kind did not exist, our wages would be gradually reduced to the lowest possible pittance, and that we would be unable to live ...

Can you state the cause of the cotton-spinners forming themselves into an association?—The cause of the cotton-spinners forming themselves into an association was to resist, as far as their moral power and united efforts would allow them, a gradual reduction of wages made upon them by the masters.

Did any change take place in the state of your trade between the years 1825 and 1827?—Yes.

State in what it consisted.—During the existence of the combination laws the society did exist, but under the combination laws it was illegal, and consequently it was necessary to keep it private. After the repeal of the combination laws, it was a short time, perhaps a few months, before the spinners could bring themselves regularly to open up all their private affairs to the public; but immediately afterwards, finding themselves connected with a legal association, they did open their affairs to the public, and the masters then joined in an association to resist the cotton-spinners. In the latter end of the year 1824 a general strike took place, and after that the masters insisted upon an equalization of the wages, which forced on one strike after another, until the association of cotton-spinners became almost dissolved. A change then took place in the constitution of the association, to the effect that all our public affairs should be laid open, and the masters recognised an equality in the wages, and the spinners recognised the same in the year 1827

In 1826 was any reduction of wages proposed by the masters?—Yes.

What was the amount of that proposed reduction?—First, there was a reduction of 15½ per cent.; secondly, there was a reduction of seven and about one-third per cent., which together amounted to between 22 and 23 per cent. of reduction.

Did the master succeed in establishing a reduction for any length of time?—Yes.

Was there any rise in your wages between 1827 and 1836?—No.

Did any strikes take place between the years 1825 and 1827? Yes . . .

What measures did the spinners adopt in order to avoid the evils which were threatened towards them by the majority of the master spinners at that time?—The practice adopted by the spinners to avoid those evils was, that when any intimation was given by any of the masters to any portion of the men, that any given master was paying at a lower rate of wages, and if the spinners did not cause him to pay a higher rate of wages, they would strike; the measure taken to provide against that was, that the spinners immediately convened a public meeting for the purpose of discussing the question, and appointing a deputation, composed of members of the trade, the most judicious and talented that could be found, and sent them to the various masters who were paying the lower rate of wages, and investigated into the matter, whether the report was correct or not; and, after finding that the report was correct, they exercised their talents to the best purpose they could to induce the master to pay a higher rate of wages. If he did not comply with their views, they came back to the members of the association again, and reported at a public meeting the result. If they were not satisfied with the master's answer, they sometimes, though not generally, sent another deputation, perhaps of the same men, perhaps of other men, to the master again, for the purpose of knowing whether the arrangements that the first deputation had entered into were proper or correct; and that was done with another intention to induce the employer to come to a higher rate of wages, in order to prevent any dissensions between the masters and the men; and the result was, that, if he did not agree on the second or third application by the men, a strike was the consequence . . .

Did the majority of the mill-owners recommend the spinners to combine and agitate the question?—They did . . .

Did the operative spinners succeed upon that occasion in establishing equality of wages?—Yes . . .

That is, the majority of the mill-owners, who had recommended the spinners to agitate, did not raise the amount of wages that they were giving; but the result of the agitation was to bring up the low amount of wages to their level?—Just so . . .

Between the repeal of the combination laws and the year 1827, was it necessary for the names of the spinners' finance committee to be kept secret?—Yes.

On what account?—If any of the members of the association were known to have taken an active part in the affairs of the association, the effect was, that they were thrown out of employment, and afterwards prevented from getting work in any of the rest of the mills; at least, generally.

Then, although the masters had themselves induced the men to combine, and to agitate for an equality of wages, yet it was not unusual for them afterwards to persecute the men who they knew took an active part in conducting the affairs of the association?—Just so . . .

Have the spinners a public hall for conducting their business?—Yes.

How were those public meetings constituted?—They have regular weekly meetings composed of delegates. Those delegates were appointed one or two from every factory or mill, according to the number of men in the factory. They met once a week, overlooked the affairs of the association, and decided thereupon.

Did the delegates overlook the affairs of the finance committee?—Yes . . .

How were the weekly subscriptions of the members of the association collected?—By the delegates, and they were carried on the Saturday evening to the finance committee . . .

Did you hear any complaints as to the mode in which the money was expended?—I have heard many individuals say 'That is too much; you must account for why you have spent so much,' and so on. If the expenditure was any way extravagant, they were necessitated to account for every farthing of it . . .

Were the admissions into the room in which the business of the association was conducted confined to the members of the association?—Yes, except when any other association or any other party found it convenient to solicit admission; if they had any business with the members of the association, they sent in a card, and it was always granted that they should be heard, and take precedence of any other business . . .

You considered that they had as much right to conduct their own business in private as the mill-owners had, or as the members of any joint-stock company would have had?—Certainly . . .

The standard rate of wages is fixed by the masters themselves?—Yes, it has been acknowledged by both parties these many years . . .

Do you know of any strikes having taken place from the spinners asking an advance beyond the standard price?—No.

Do you know of any strikes having taken place in consequence of the masters having attempted to reduce the wages below the standard price?—Yes.

In the early nineteenth century the most important unions were among the cotton operatives, but the growth of the heavy industries encouraged combinations among the miners. They assumed increasing importance in the labour movement generally. Like the cotton operatives, the miners frequently struck to maintain, not to raise, wages. At such times stagnant demand and the availability of Irish labour strengthened the employers' resistance. But any dispute in coalmining usually had two distinctive features. First, a main function of colliers' combinations was to restrict output (the 'darg') in order to keep stocks of coal low; they also aimed, by this means, to limit working hours, and to equalise the earnings of younger and older men. The masters, conversely, complained of increased costs and consequent danger to masters. The second problem was that the interests of employers who worked coal for sale and those who needed it for use in their own iron-works were not identical, and the unions had to negotiate differently in each case. Both points of view are illustrated in a report of the Inspector of Mines in 1845.

(3) *Report of the Commissioner on the state of the population in the Mining Districts, 1845*, pp. 7-9 –

The combination of the colliers which, though directed against their masters' and the public interests, must be ultimately far more disastrous to their own, still continues. Nearly all the colliers of the central parts of the district, from which the supply of Glasgow and the iron works is chiefly derived, are in the Union.

... The temporary success they have had in obtaining a higher rate of wages for a less amount of work, has given them increased confidence, and blinds all but the more intelligent among them to the severity of the reaction which they are preparing for themselves.

The successive reductions of day's work and increase of rate paid for it, are shown by the following examples:-

Whiflat Colliery

				s.	d.
September, 1843, to May, 1844—Day's work,		3	carts, at	1	2½
May, 1844, to August.	"	2½	"	1	5½
August to December.	"	2	"	1	6

Thus one-third had been taken from the day's work, and above one-fifth added to the wages; making the enormous difference of 53¼ per cent. against the master in the price he pays for working the coal.

Monkland Iron and Steel-works

Before reduction of 'Darg', in April, 1844		*Since reduction*	
Day's work—average of 11 coal pits	*Average wages per day*	*Day's work—average of 11 coal pits*	*Average wages per day*
	s. d.		s. d.
8 hutches per day	3 0	5½ hutches	3 4

In this case the addition is 36 per cent. upon the price of coals against the master.

While this great additional burden of one-third to one-half on the cost of coal is thrown upon the master, the additional rate paid to the collier is not more than from one-ninth to one-fifth.

His actual earnings in the case first quoted, and in numerous other collieries, are even less than they were before.

Wherever, as in the second case quoted, they are more, he might or might not be entitled to public sympathy, according to the previous rate of his wages in proportion to the work required of him. At all events, at the present rate he does not do much more than half a day's work, as he might get through it easily in the short space of six or seven hours, for which he receives from 3s. to 3s. 4d., and has nothing to do for the rest of the four-and twenty.

The two parties first affected by this forced rise in the rate of wages, are the sale-master (who supplies the domestic consumption and the manufactories of the district) and the iron-master.

The first, finding his stocks reduced, (the amount of the reduction was, according to an accurate estimate, from 171,680 tons on 11th June, to 68,100 tons on 21st December, 1844, or five-eighths in six months) and that the commodity has therefore become more valuable, raises the price to the consumer, and thereby compensates himself for the higher wages paid to the collier. The rise of price between those two periods was 1s. to 2s. per ton. In the mean time the price enables supplies to come in from a greater distance. If they arrive, new competitors are brought into the market; while the high price has limited the sales of those who before occupied it, and has either caused a falling off in the general demand, or prevented the growth and extension of their dealings. The latter effect has been very marked upon the export trade in coal from the Clyde, as the following returns plainly show:-

Coals exported from the Harbour of Glasgow

1838-9	199,476 tons
1839-40	192,593 "
1840-1	193,619 "
1841-2	163,777 "
1842-3	142,563 "
1843-4	119,150 "

The combinations and strikes of the last three years may not have been the sole, but they have in all probability been a very active cause of the decline.

As soon as a falling off in demand, from whatever cause, showed itself, the sale-masters would naturally have been impelled to seek for fresh openings in new and distant markets. This they could only hope to effect by lowness of price. But the combination of their colliers to raise the price would restrict, if not effectually prevent, any such enterprise. Hence less immediate employment, and the more inevitable certainty of wages being the more depressed, and for a longer period, from the moment that the decline of demand occurs in the comparatively limited market. From this decline the colliers will find it all the more difficult to recover, because . . . their combination has been the means of bringing one-third more men into their trade than are required to raise the quantity of coal in ordinary demand.

When the sale-masters are thus compelled to raise the wages of their colliers, the iron-masters, in order to retain their men, are obliged to raise theirs. If at that time the price of iron is low, the injury to the iron-master is great, because, having to compete with Welsh and Staffordshire iron, he is not able to raise the price of his own commodity at pleasure. Therefore when the amount he has to pay in wages is unduly raised, his profits are restricted, and his trade restricted, and he can find less employment for his men at the very time when, in consequence of the depression in their trade, they most require it. According to the opinions of those most competent to form sound ones, the clear policy of master and men, at these frequently recurring periods of slackness of demand, is to produce the article cheap, in order to revive demand, by enabling the master to seek for and open new markets. If the workmen of any locality, by forcing up their wages at such a time, create an artificial dearness of their commodity, the only effect is that they tie the hands of their master and their own, and allow others to enter the field of enterprise without them.

If iron is high, the collier is entitled to increased wages, which are cheerfully paid, provided the master obtains an equivalent in the amount of work done. But this is prevented in the present case by the combination; the men working only about six hours a-day, and "putting out" at least one-third less coal; demanding for this, at the same time, a higher rate. The effects are manifold, and are injurious to both parties. The iron-master, if restricted in the quantity of coal at his command, is deprived of the opportunity of taking full advantage of the revival of trade. He is obliged to refuse contracts, which are carried elsewhere, and his men lose the employment they would have afforded. If, in order to maintain his full supply of coal, he is obliged to purchase, instead of raising it from his own pits, he does so at a great disadvantage. A certain portion of the cost of raising it from his own pits consists of interest on fixed capital; in the cost and maintenance of the shafts, road-ways, steam-engine and other machinery, waggons, etc, etc., together with salaries of clerks and overlookers. It is obvious that these fixed charges are lightened in proportion as they are distributed over a larger quantity of coal raised. The colliers by limiting their labour increase this burden. It was shown to me that at some works the increase was considerable; and that taking the total amount of coal required for the iron-furnaces of the district, when in full operation as at present, . . . the total burden thrown on the fixed capital by this restriction upon the "output", rose to a formidable sum. Upon the sale-masters the restriction operates in the same manner, in proportion to the amount of capital employed. It must be admitted that the loss occasioned to both is one among the many results naturally arising from the low state of intelligence in which the colliers, as a class, have been allowed to grow up, and of the absence of that general good understanding and confidence between the men and their employers, which, in the few fortunate cases where it exists in this district, is a great element of comfort and prosperity to both parties . . .

The present effect of this voluntary limitation of their labour by the men of the Union, is that they are earning from 3d. to 1s. a-day less then they might do. They are unfortunately under the delusion that by still further limiting their labour they will compel further advances in the rate of wages, and will be able to keep wages at that higher rate for this limited amount of work. No clearer index could be given of the degree of intelligence among this collier population than the bare statement of such a proposition, while there is a field of coal unworked, capital seeking employment, and Irish labourers ready at hand.

Many of the industrial movements were ephemeral. Geographical diversity, especially in the mining industry, alone made a national union difficult to organise. Political movements were a means of promoting greater national unity.

Chartism made an early appeal. The six demands of the People's Charter of 1838—manhood suffrage, vote by ballot, equal electoral districts, no property qualification for Members of Parliament, payment of Members and annual Parliaments—were the basis of Chartism in Scotland as elsewhere. The first number of the Glasgow *Chartist Circular* made explicit the movement's theoretical, religious, political, economic and patriotic ideals—and its belief in enfranchisement as a complete implement of reform.

(4) *The Chartist Circular*, no. 1, 28th September 1839. Appeal to the People of Scotland –

Fellow-Countrymen,

The great question of our national liberty, as embraced in the people's charter is of all others connected with our individual and social well-being, the most important . . . It must decide whether a proud and useless oligarchy, whose ambition and avarice are unbounded, are to crush beneath their power a great, an industrious, a generous and brave people, and to fill the land with poverty, crime, and turbulence; or whether that people will throw aside the unnatural pressure, be free, and establish the reign of honour, happiness, and tranquillity . . . Whether we look into the annals of antiquity or of modern times, it is the efforts of the patriot who braved the frowns of tyranny, and dared to seek his country's liberty, that call forth our admiration and love; . . . the vivid imagination beholds a Wallace, a Tell, a Hampden, and a Washington, leading on their heroes to the rescue of their country . . .

But it is not merely to our moral sensibilities that we are to look for evidence of the divine origin of liberty; NATURE DECLARES IT OUR INHERITANT RIGHT . . . In vain do we search in her institutions for the badges of exclusive rank, or the charter of wealth and power; superior virtue and wisdom constitute her only nobility; and these qualities have not been made hereditary; it is the assumption of artificial rights that makes one man a lord, and the presumption of supposed obligations that makes another man a slave. The God of nature never instituted such invidious distinctions . . . He consigned not the execution of his laws to an aristocracy, knowing that men inflated with absolute irresponsible power, would themselves become the greatest transgressors; a simple democracy was the only order of government he instituted; . . . Thus the liberty for which we contend is an emanation from the Deity . . .

Here then is the origin of our cause—here is the omnipotent authority on which we rest the glorious charter of the people's liberties; nay more, here is our charter itself, let the aristocracy show theirs—let them present the public with their old blood-crusted weapons, and moth-eaten parchments, and we will bow to the decision of that public, on the validity of our respective rights; theirs rest on the munificence of kings who gave what was not theirs to give; ours on the beneficence of heaven, to whom the universe belongs; . . .

Unfortunately, however, for the country, . . . there are other arguments than these embraced in the philosophy of political justice that tend to show the necessity of an organic change in the principles of legislation, . . . it is in the wretched state of the country that these arguments are to be found—it is the excessive toil—the gaunt poverty, and the haggard looks of a vast proportion of the working classes—in their utter hopelessness and despair . . . in the desperate motives that have impelled the legislature to make poverty a crime, and to sink the industrious poor below the level of felons . . .

Where is the source, and what are the operating causes of this dreadful state of things? . . . It is not because the productive power of this country is inadequate to support the working population, and keep the necessary machinery of society in proper motion. There is an abundance of wealth created by our industry for all the moderate wants of the nation—enough to give riches to the master, competence to the workman, and sufficient finances to any well regulated state . . . It is not, indeed, because we have not produced enough of wealth that disaffection is raging over the land . . . No, it is because the abundance which is created is most unjustly distributed—it is because the lords of the middle classes turn the power of their capital against the producers, and unite with the aristocracy in the wholesale plunder of the people—it is because this heterogeneous confederacy of wealth and title constitute the government . . . and direct its operations exclusively to their own benefit. Hence the huge commercial monopolies that exist, some of which crush beneath their power more than a hundred millions of human beings—hence the iniquitous corn laws . . . —hence the unnatural laws of primogeniture, which confer the right of succession on the first-born in the *higher orders*, and leave the rest to eat the taxes which must be wrung from the people . . . and hence the barbarous penal laws . . . poor laws, and hundreds of other laws too numerous to detail, . . . hence the enormous salaries, pensions, sinecures, and emoluments of statesmen, . . . —and hence the exorbitant livings of the reverend fathers . . . —and hence the unparalleled expenditure of the court . . . —and hence the magnificent establishment of our land, and cotton, and coal, and iron lords, who are, as they say themselves the very *first gentlemen* in the world . . . The exclusive exercise, then, of political power is the source, and its effects are the operating causes of all our misery—it is these, and these alone that have brought our great and enlightened, our enterprising and generous country to its present distracted and abject condition . . .

Have we not for eight years past experienced the workings of an elective franchise stretched far beyond its preceding boundaries? but what has it done for us? . . . it was the work of a fraction who were evidently impelled by no other motive, and had no other object in view than that of exalting themselves to power, dignity, and wealth, and of leaguing together all the wealthier classes against the poor, for the protection of the privileges of the aristocracy . . . But no sooner did they acquire the ascendancy than they threw off the mask of patriotism and grasping the iron rod of the tyrant, placed Ireland under military law for resisting the heinous oppression of its overgrown church—banished the Dorchester labourers for uniting to protect their industry . . . —tantalized half a million of hand-loom weavers with mock enquiries into their distress, without ever attempting to relieve it—treated even the middle classes themselves with superlative contempt when they asked a repeal of the corn laws, and latterly spurned indignantly from them the petition of the people who demanded their just—their heaven-born rights . . . It is these astounding facts that depict with overwhelming power the state of our affairs. In language nerved with the irresistible force of truth they declare to the middle and working classes that an entire change in the constitution of the House of Commons is indispensable to the political salvation of the country . . . The honour, prosperity, and exigencies of the country, therefore, demand a House of Commons in whom the voice of the whole people will be concentrated, and who will be under the proper control of those whom it represents. Then, and not till then will we have a sternly virtuous parliament, . . . harmonizing the interests of the nation—and in legislating for the protection, instruction, independence, and happiness of all.

Fellow-Countrymen, It must be obvious, however, to you, that the attainment of such a legislature is altogether dependent on our acquisition of Universal Suffrage, and the other principles of the People's Charter. To you, the working men of Scotland, we therefore, appeal by all your hopes of happiness and your love of liberty, to use every means which God and the laws of your country allow, to obtain your inheritant—your necessary but long withheld rights. If you have ever regarded the noble deeds of your ancestors with feelings of manly pride—if ever you have estimated your own natural dignity and acquired truth—if ever you have felt your breast heave with indignity at the great and manifold injuries which you have sustained—if ever you have seen, with parental solicitude, your children the victims of necessities, which you ought, but had not the power to relieve— . . . then divest yourselves of every prejudice, . . . and unite, with heart and soul, in the present great and momentous movement, determined never more to abandon the cause of liberty, till it finally triumphs over all the machinations of its enemies. Agitate and organise in every direction; let not a town, nor a hamlet, nor a rural district in the kingdom be without its patriotic unions; but be legal, and peaceful, and constitutional in your every action . . . Onward, then, Brother Chartists,—onward in the glorious cause of freedom. Let peace, order, and union be your watchword, and the day of our emancipation will soon be proclaimed amongst men, and registered in heaven.

Signed in name of the Universal Suffrage Central Committee for Scotland,

William Thomson, Secretary.

Though five of Chartism's demands have been achieved the movement failed at the time. For a generation thereafter Scottish working-class organisation was entirely industrial. When the Scottish miners' leader, Alexander Macdonald, was returned to Parliament as a Liberal member in 1874, it was for an English constituency. But impatience with the Liberals, and universal male suffrage after 1885, revived the demand for a separate Labour Party. In April 1888 James Keir Hardie stood as Independent Labour candidate in the Mid-Lanarkshire by-election, and in August the Scottish Labour Party was formed (5). The new party adopted a more distinctly socialist programme than any previous labour organisation (6).

(5) *The Democrat*, 1st September, 1888 –

Scottish Parliamentary Labour Party

The result of the Mid-Lanark election showed the pressing need there was for an organisation in Scotland which would enable the workers to exercise their voting power to their own advantage. Hitherto a number of isolated bodies have been at work in this direction, but the hold they have obtained on the working classes has been but slight, probably owing to the fact that they were content to sink their identity when the supposed interests of the Liberal party were concerned. Since April last Mr. Keir-Hardie has been devoting most of his spare time to the work of organising a distinct labour party, and on Saturday, 25th August, a conference was held in Glasgow to formally give birth to the new movement. In all, thirty-one representatives were present, representing the whole country from Dumfries in the south to Caithness in the north. Mr. Cunninghame Graham, M.P., presided . . . The programme adopted included nationalization of the land, minerals, railways and banking systems, an eight hour bill, second ballot, payment of members, home rule, abolition of the House of Lords, disestablishment, free education (boards to have power to provide food for children), adult suffrage, etc. etc. The office bearers elected were —hon. president, R. B. C. Graham, M.P. . . . secretary, J. Keir-Hardie . . .

A monster demonstration was held on the Green after the conference, when the proceedings of the conference were unanimously ratified. Speeches were delivered by Mr. Graham (who again presided), J. Robertson (Dundee), Rev. W. L. Walker, Keir-Hardie, A. le Morton (London), Donald Stewart, and Wm. Small. A spirit of hopefulness prevailed throughout, and the enthusiasm at the demonstration was unbounded. Being now fully equipped for service, the Scottish Parliamentary Labour Party should be a power in the land.

(Signed) J. Keir-Hardie.

(6) *Scottish Parliamentary Labour Party* –

Constitution

I. That the association be called the Scottish Parliamentary Labour Party.

II. That its object be to educate the people politically, and to secure the return to Parliament and all local bodies of members pledged to its programme.

Programme

1st. Adult suffrage, with abolition of plural voting.

2nd. Triennial Parliaments, elections to be all on one day.

3rd. Simplification of Registration Laws, so as to prevent removal from one constituency to another disfranchising a voter.

4th. Payment of Members by the State, and of official election expenses from the rates.

5th. Home Rule for each separate nationality or country in the British Empire, with an Imperial Parliament for Imperial affairs.
6th. Abolition of the House of Lords and all hereditary offices.
7th. A Second Ballot.
8th. Nationalisation of Land and Minerals.
9th. Labour Legislation—(a) An Eight Hours' Bill; (b) Abolition of present Poor Law System and substitution of State Insurance to provide for Sickness, Accident, Death, or Old Age; (c) Arbitration Courts with power to settle disputes and fix a minimum wage; (d) Weekly Pays; (e) Homestead Law to protect furniture and tools to the value of £20 from seizure for debt; (f) Application of the Factories and Workshops Acts to all premises, whether public or private, in which work is performed.
10th. Prohibition of the Liquor Traffic.
11th. No War to be entered upon without the consent of the House of Commons.
12th. Free Education, Boards to have power to provide food for children.
13th. Disestablishment.
14th. Reform in the system of civil government and abolition of sinecure offices and pensions.
15th. Simplification and codification of the civil and criminal law.
16th. State acquisition of railways, waterways, and tramways.
17th. National Banking System and the issue of State money only.
18th. Cumulative Income Tax beginning at £300 per annum.

Following the formation of the Scottish Labour Party similar organisations were founded in the north of England. Those, together with representatives of the Fabian Society and the Social Democratic Federation, formed the basis of the Independent Labour Party, founded in 1893. The following year the Scottish Labour Party was wound up.

Scottish labour, though no longer an independent organisation, still showed an independent spirit, especially during the First World War. When the Munitions Act and the Defence of the Realm Acts restricted the activities of trade unions, the legislation was accepted officially by the unions but was strongly opposed by some radical opinion, especially on the Clyde. This led to the formation of the Clyde Workers' Committee, based on the shop stewards' movements, which was stronger on the Clyde than elsewhere. The C.W.C. also led Clydeside opposition to conscription.

(7) Department of Economic History, University of Glasgow. Highton Manuscripts.

Clyde Workers' Committee—To all Clyde Workers
Fellow-workers,

Since the outbreak of the European War, many changes have been brought about of vital interest to the workers. Foremost amongst these has been the *scrapping* of Trade Union Rules, and the consequent undermining of the whole Trade Union Movement. To the intelligent workers it has been increasingly clear that the officials have failed to grasp the significance of these changes, and as a result have been unable to formulate a policy that would adequately protect the interests of those workers whom they are supposed to represent.

The support given to the Munitions Act by the Officials was an act of Treachery to the Working Class. Those of us who refused to be *Sold* have organised the above Committee, representative of *All Trades* in the Clyde area, determined to retain what liberties we have, and to take the first opportunity of forcing the repeal of all the pernicious legislation that has recently been imposed upon us . . .

What the Committee is and Its Purpose.

It is composed of Delegates or Shop Stewards from all Trades in the Glasgow area, and is open to all such *bona fide* workers. The progressives in all Trades are invited to attend. Its origin goes back to the last big strike of February, 1915, when action was taken to force the demand put forward for an increase of 2d. per hour in the Engineering industry. At that time a Committee known as the *Labour With-holding Committee* was set up, representative of the different Trades in the industry, to organise the strike, and notwithstanding the fierce opposition from public opinion, employers, Government, and *our own officials* alike, that Committee managed and carried through probably the best organised strike in the annals of Clyde history, and brought about closer working unity amongst the rank and file of the different Trades than years of official effort. It becomes obvious then that such a Committee permanently established would be valuable to workers, and with that purpose in view the Committee was kept in being after the termination of the strike.

Recently, when the three Govan shipwrights were locked up under the Munitions Act, many appeals were sent to the Committee to again take action. In answer to those appeals the Committee called its forces together and discussed certain lines of action, and, despite all reports to the contrary, it was through 'the powers that be' getting to know that the Committee was again at work, that ultimately forced the release of the three shipwrights.

At this juncture it was considered advisable to change the name of this body, and from now on it will be known as the *Clyde Workers' Committee* (*C.W.C.*)

Our purpose must not be misconstrued, we are out for unity and closer organisation of all trades in the industry, one Union being the ultimate aim. We will support the officials just so long as they rightly represent the workers, but we will act independently immediately they misrepresent them. Being composed of Delegates from every shop, and untrammelled by obsolete rule or law, we claim to represent the true feeling of the workers. We can act immediately according to the merits of the case and the desire of the rank and file.

The following Trades are at present represented on the Committee. All other Trades are kindly invited to become attached. All Shop Stewards welcome:- A.S.E., Toolmakers, Boilermakers, Blacksmiths, Shipwrights, Coppersmiths, Brassfinishers, Patternmakers, Miners, Tinsmiths, Sheet-iron Workers, Electrical Trades, Joiners, Gas and General Workers, School Teachers, Coopers.

For further information see your Shop Steward, Speakers will be sent on request to Work Gates, Districts, and generally be at the convenience of the workers.

Signed on behalf of the Committee,
Wm. Gallacher, President. J. M. Messer, Secretary.

Clyde Workers' Committee
Objects.

1. To obtain an ever increasing control over workshop conditions.
2. To regulate the terms upon which the workers shall be employed.
3. To organise the workers upon a Class basis and to maintain the Class Struggle, until the overthrow of the Wages System, the freedom of the workers, and the establishment of Industrial Democracy have been obtained.

Structure.

The unit of organisation shall be the Workshop Committee, composed of Shop Stewards or Delegates elected by the Workers in the Shop.

From every Shop Committee shall be elected two Conveners, one of whom shall be a woman, where women are employed, who are to be the delegates forming the Clyde Workers' Committee.

No Committee shall have executive power, all questions of policy being referred back to the Rank & File.

The early demand of the Scottish Labour party for home rule was not dropped when the Scottish Labour Party lost its separate identity. It seemed a means whereby a socialist government could be introduced to Scotland earlier than through a British parliament.

In spite of revolutionary ideas and suggestions for home rule the Scottish labour movement approximated more and more closely to that of the rest of the United Kingdom.

CHAPTER VIII

Living Conditions

A. HOUSING

Scottish housing conditions were notorious long before the Industrial Revolution. The need for reform was not a problem created by the new industrial concentrations. In the Highlands and Islands the accommodation described by Dr. Johnson had been normal for centuries.

(1) S. Johnson, *Journey to the Western Islands of Scotland in 1773*. (Oxford Standard Authors edn., pp. 91–93) –

The habitations of men in the *Hebrides* may be distinguished into huts and houses. By a *house*, I mean a building with one story over another; by a *hut*, a dwelling with only one floor. The Laird, who formerly lived in a castle, now lives in a house; sometimes sufficiently neat, but seldom very spacious or splendid . . .

Of the houses little can be said. They are small, and by the necessity of accumulating stores, where there are so few opportunities of purchase, the rooms are very heterogeneously filled. With want of cleanliness it were ingratitude to reproach them. The servants having been bred upon the naked earth, think every floor clean, and the quick succession of guests, perhaps not always overelegant, does not allow much time for adjusting their apartments.

Huts are of many gradations; from murky dens, to commodious dwellings.

The wall of a common hut is always built without mortar, by a skilful adaptation of loose stones. Sometimes perhaps a double wall of stones is raised, and the intermediate space filled with earth. The air is thus completely excluded. Some walls are, I think, formed of turfs, held together by a wattle, or texture of twigs. Of the meanest huts, the first room is lighted by the entrance, and the second by the smoke-hole. The fire is usually made in the middle. But there are huts, or dwellings of only one story, inhabited by gentlemen, which have walls cemented with mortar, glass windows, and boarded floors. Of these all have chimneys, and some chimneys have grates.

The house and the furniture are not always nicely suited. We were driven once, by missing a passage, to the hut of a gentleman, where, after a very liberal supper, when I was conducted to my chamber, I found an elegant bed of Indian cotton, spread with fine sheets. The accommodation was flattering; I undressed myself, and felt my feet in the mire. The bed stood upon the bare earth, which a long course of rain had softened to a puddle. . . .

The petty tenants, and labouring peasants, live in miserable cabins, which afford them little more than shelter from the storms. The Boor of *Norway* is said to make all his own utensils. In the *Hebrides*, whatever might be their ingenuity, the want of wood leaves them no materials. They are probably content with such accommodations as stones of different forms and sizes can afford them.

Their food is not better than their lodging. They seldom taste the flesh of land animals; for here are no markets. What each man eats is from his own stock. The great effect of money is to break property into small parts. In towns, he that has a shilling may have a piece of meat; but where there is no commerce, no man can eat mutton but by killing a sheep.

Fish in fair weather they need not want; but, I believe, man never lives long on fish, but by constraint; he will rather feed upon roots and berries.

Later, even in more prosperous agricultural districts, many workers lived in bothies, a system which roused Cobbett's indignation when he saw one near Dunfermline.

(2) William Cobbett, *Tour in Scotland*, 1832 (1833), pp. 130–133 –

I went to the '*boothie*' between twelve and one o'clock, in order that I might find the men at home, and see what they had for their dinner. I found the 'boothie' to be a shed, with a fire-place in it to burn coals in, with one doorway, and one little window. The floor was the ground. There were three wooden bedsteads, nailed together like the berths in a barrack-room, with boards for the bottom of them. The bedding seemed to be very coarse sheeting with coarse woollen things at the top; and all seemed to be such as similar things must be where there is nobody but men to look after them. There were six men, all at home; one sitting upon a stool, four upon the sides of the berths, and one standing talking to me. Though it was Monday, their beards, especially of two of them, appeared to be some days old. There were ten or twelve bushels of coals lying in a heap in one corner of the place, which was, as nearly as I could guess, about sixteen or eighteen feet square. There was no back-door to the place, and no privy. There were some loose potatoes lying under one of the berths.

Now, for the wages of these men. In the first place the average wages of these single farming men are about ten pounds a year, or not quite four shillings a week. Then, they are found provisions in the following manner: each has allowed him two pecks of coarse oatmeal a week, and three '*choppins*' of milk a day, and a '*choppin*' is, I believe, equal to an English quart. They have to use this meal, which weighs about seventeen pounds, either by mixing it with cold water or with hot; they put some of it into a bowl, pour some boiling water upon it, then stir it about and eat it; and they call this BROSE; and you will be sure to remember that name. When they use milk with the meal, they use it in the same way that they do the water. I saw some of the brose mixed up ready to eat; and this is by no means bad stuff, only there ought to be half-a-pound of good meat to eat along with it. The Americans make 'brose' of the corn-meal; but, then, they make their brose with milk instead of water, and they send it down their throats in company with buttered beef-steaks. And if here was some bacon along with the brose, I should think the brose very proper; because, in this country, oats are more easily grown in some parts than the wheat is. These men were not troubled with cooking utensils. They had a large iron saucepan and five or six brose-bowls; and are never troubled with those clattering things, knives, forks, plates, vinegar-cruets, salt-cellars, pepper-boxes, mustard-pots, tablecloths, or tables.

Now, I shall not attempt any general description of this treatment of those who make all the crops to come; but I advise you to *look well at it*; and I recommend to you to do everything within your power that it is lawful for you to do, in order to show your hatred of, and to *cause to suffer*, any one that shall attempt to reduce you to this state. The meal and the milk are not worth more than eighteen-pence a week; the shed is worth nothing; and here are these men, who work for so many hours in a day, who are so laborious, so obedient, so civil, so honest, and amongst the best people in the world, receiving for a whole week less than an American labourer receives for one day's work not half so hard as the work of these men. This shed is stuck up generally away from the farm-yard, which is surrounded with good buildings, in which the cattle are lodged quite as well as these men, and in which young pigs are fed a great deal better. There were three sacks of meal standing in this shed, just as you see them standing in our farmhouses filled with barley-meal for the feeding of pigs. The *farm-house*, standing on one side of the yard, is always a sort of gentleman's house, in which there are several maids to wait upon the gentleman and lady, and a boy to wait upon them too. There is, generally, a BAILIFF upon these farms, who is very often a relation of the farmer; and, if he be a single man, he has either a small '*boothie*' to himself, or a place boarded off in a larger 'boothie'; and he is a sort of sergeant or corporal over the common men, who are continually under his eye day and night; and who being firmly bound for the year, cannot quit their service till the year be out.

In districts where the bothy system did not prevail, agricultural labourers might be better housed; but standards varied, and many dwellings were defective both in design and construction.

(3) *Reports on the Sanitary Condition of the Labouring Population of Scotland*, 1842, pp. 84–85 –

Dr. S. Scott Alison. Report on Tranent and District. Condition of houses.

The cottages inhabited by hinds in the county of Haddington are divisible into two classes, a superior and an inferior. The former are constantly increasing, while the latter are as constantly diminishing in number. The old cottages are almost all very inferior, while those which have been recently built are much better finished and more comfortable. The habitations of the hinds are almost invariably the property of the landlords, and are situated on the farms near the offices. A few hinds live in villages adjoining the farms on which they work. A cottage of the inferior class consists of one apartment about 14 feet long and 12 broad. The habitation is formed of the front and back walls, about 8 feet high, two side walls or gables rising pyramidically to the height of about 20 feet. The roof is composed of thatch or straw, resting upon rafters or beams of wood. There is one fire-place, which is provided with a capacious chimney. The walls are in general substantial, there being plenty of stone on the spot, and lime being abundant in the county. The roof is, in many cases, very inferior. The thatch is often quite rotten, and pervious to rain and wind; and the rafters in many cottages are much decayed. These cottages are not supplied with any ceiling or partition to hide the thatch and rafters, or to protect against the wind and rain that may penetrate the thatch covering when they are given up to the hinds. This great defect is remedied in part in the cottages of some of the more respectable and comfortable hinds, by their putting up a wooden ceiling which they purchase and carry about with them from cottage to cottage, as a piece of house furniture. In other cottages another and cheaper contrivance is adopted: this is the placing of canvas in the place of wood; and when, as is often the case, this canvas covering is whitewashed, it gives the apartment the appearance, if not the reality, of comfort. In some cottages no ceiling of any kind is used. The appearance of the cottage is then very bad: there appears an immense dark and dingy space, bounded above by ugly thatch, and rafters generally covered with much dust and multitudes of spiders' webs. The floor of these cottages is generally beneath the level of the soil outside. For what purpose this arrangement is adopted I cannot understand, unless it be to counteract the inability to keep the cold out, through insufficiency of the door and roof, by its rendering the apartment as much like a hole as possible, and thereby to keep the heat in. The walls in the inside are bare, or only whitewashed. There is one window which is generally about two feet square, and unprovided with hinges, or other appliances, to admit of being opened. The expense, I suppose, is the only reason for this defect. The door is seldom well fitted, is frequently decayed, and admits strong currents of air. The superior cottages are, with very few exceptions, about the same size as those just described, have only one apartment, and the floors are below the level of the ground outside; but the walls are plastered, and comfortable ceilings are supplied, the doors are well fitted, the windows are constructed so as to open, and the roofs are covered with slates or tiles.

In spite of publicity, the bothy system persisted, especially in the Mearns and the north-east. The findings of the Commission on the Employment of Children in Agriculture in 1867 (4) were confirmed by the

Royal Commission on Scottish Housing of 1917-18, which could report only limited improvements (5).

(4) Commission on the Employment of Children in Agriculture, 1867. Report of Commissioner for Forfar, Kincardine, Aberdeen, Banff, Moray and Nairn, pp. 40–41 –

I had frequent opportunities of examining bothies, and availed myself of every opportunity which presented itself of doing so. A bothy is to be found on almost every farm in the lowland district of Forfarshire and Kincardineshire; they are also numerous in Moray and Nairn, but there are very few in Banffshire and Aberdeenshire. They vary very much in character, the best consist of a large sitting room with a separate sleeping closet for each servant, and a supply of fresh water for washing purposes. These bothies where they are kept clean by a woman employed for that purpose appear to me to be as good a mode of lodging unmarried men as any that can be adopted. Bothies of this character are unfortunately very rare; I have only met with five or six, and these on the farms of landowners and large farmers. As a general rule the bothy consists of a portion of the farm buildings or steading formed into a single room of moderate size. It is supplied with no separate sleeping apartments, and nobody is employed to clean it or to make the beds (and the bothy men if left to themselves never attempt to keep it clean and tidy); a heap of coals will be seen in one corner and of firewood in another; it is furnished with no tables and no seats, so that on returning from work the only place which the servants have to sit down upon is their chests; and the flags with which it is paved are generally broken into small pieces by having the firewood chopped upon them. The bothies are but rarely well ventilated. In a few cases I have met with bothies attached to the stables where the ventilation (if indeed it can be so called) was of the worst description. I recollect two which consisted of portions of the stables in which cart horses were kept and were only separated from the stables themselves by thin wooden partitions, which were broken and defective in many places. These bothies had no means of obtaining air except what came through the stables; and the stables themselves were badly ventilated and contained several horses each. The air, therefore, which the men breathed must have been most impure. The bothy men are in general provided with separate beds, but they do not at all object to sleeping two in a bed. I recollect visiting one bothy which was occupied by four men and which contained four beds, bedding being provided by the proprietor for all the four, only two, however, were occupied, and this was owing to the men preferring to sleep two in a bed. There can be no question that a life in such bothies as I have last been describing must have the effect of making the men rude and boorish, and this appears to me to be the great objection to them. I did not understand that they led directly to vice or immorality, in fact the reverse appears to be rather the truth . . .

It is quite clear that when left to themselves the bothy men are likely to become careless and untidy, and to lose their self-pride and self-respect. The effect of the bothy upon the character of the men must depend greatly upon the amount of supervision exercised by the master. The men who live in these bothies are always provided with meal and milk which they cook for themselves, and the sameness of diet which is thus entailed is certainly an objection to the system . . .

In Aberdeenshire and Banffshire, and to a less extent in the other counties, what is called the "kitchen plan" is adopted: where this is done the men servants sleep either in a loft above the stable or in a small apartment in the steading, and take their meals either in the farmer's kitchen, or in the cases of large farms in a room expressly provided for them.

The difference between this and the bothy system is, that in the bothy the men receive their meal and milk and cook it for themselves, on the kitchen plan meals are regularly provided by the farmer and cooked by his wife or one of his servants for the men. Much discussion has arisen between the advocates of these two systems of providing for farm servants as to their comparative advantages and disadvantages. It may be said in general that those who live where bothies prevail condemn the kitchen plan, and vice versa. The advantages of the kitchen plan are that the men have more variety of food, that their food is better prepared and more wholesome, and that they pass their evening in the farmer's house and often under his eye, and that they are therefore under a better supervision than the bothy men who live out of the house in a place which their master rarely enters, and further it is said that the "kitchen" system gives better opportunities for study and self-improvement than the bothy, a clean, well-lighted, and warm kitchen being more comfortable than a cold, dim, untidy, and ill-lighted bothy; on the other hand the advocates of the "bothy" system say that it is impossible at the present day to adhere to the kitchen plan, because the men are far more independent than they used to be, they are far more particular about their food, and that it is difficult to provide for them without giving them dissatisfaction, and further that the kitchen plan gives the men opportunities of associating with the women servants in the house, which lead to immorality. For my own part it seems to me to be impossible to say that either one or the other system is absolutely the best; they are suited to entirely different conditions of things. The original plan was the kitchen plan, which is suited to a system of small farms, where the farmer is but little raised above his servants in the social scale. Where this state of things still exists the farmer is willing to associate and dine at the same table with his servants; but gradually, as the science of farming advances, the farmer becomes a far more important man than he previously was, and occupies a much higher social position than his servants. As soon as this condition of things is arrived at the farmer is no longer willing to sit at the same table with his servants or even to have them in his house; he becomes more refined and will not expose himself to the inconvenience caused by a troop of dirty field labourers invading his kitchen for three meals a day. This state of feeling gives rise to the bothy system, which is now to be found wherever large farms exist and which will, I should expect, be gradually introduced wherever small holdings are consolidated into large farms.

(5) *Report of Royal Commission on the Housing of the Industrial Population in Scotland, 1918*, para. 171 –

The Bothy System.—Probably no aspect of rural housing has received so much attention as the bothy, and no system has been so roundly condemned; yet it survives, little changed from the days when the first onslaught was made on it about seventy years ago. The worst of the old hovels have disappeared, but there still remain instances of bothies that are not fit to house animals. Generally speaking, however, the actual structures of the bothies will compare quite favourably with the cottages. Where the bothies fail is in the internal arrangements and the social conditions produced by herding young men together with no proper provision for food or comfort. It combines a maximum of discomfort with a minimum of civilized conditions.

The condition of urban housing was different but equally notorious. Visually its most characteristic feature was the tenement. In so building Scotland followed continental traditions and had thereby a method which enabled the urban population of the country to become heavily concentrated. Yet the tenement had many advantages. They were pointed out by a Glasgow builder to the Royal Commission on Housing of 1917-18.

(6) *Report of the Royal Commission on the Housing of the Industrial Population in Scotland, 1918*, para. 476 –

Perhaps the best summary of the arguments for the tenement was given by Mr. Mactaggart, who stated, however, that personally he felt the arguments against to be stronger. He gave the following summary of the advantages enjoyed by tenants living in flatted houses:—

(a) Tenants suffer less from cold, rain, and storms, owing to more substantial construction. In Glasgow 2-feet stone walls strapped, against London County Council 9-inch brick walls unstrapped.
(b) Being nearer their employment tenants save time in going to and from house, and have better-lit streets at night.
(c) In four-storey tenements three-fourths of the tenants are further from the damp ground, and also less liable to have their drains choked.
(d) Flats having no inside stairs are more easily worked, especially in illness.
(e) Tenants suffer less from burglars, and parties living alone are more secure.
(f) In flatted houses only good-sized apartments can be let.
(g) The statistics of the Glasgow Medical Officer with reference to Kelvinside and Pollokshields, where four-fifths of the people live in flatted houses, seem to suggest that the death-rate among fairly well-educated and well-fed tenants of flats is as low as among cottage residents.

Whatever the advantages of the tenement, they increased the density of the population. In Glasgow the peak was reached with 94 persons to the acre in 1871. The tenements had many small houses, or flats, so that in 1871 32.5 per cent of Scottish houses had only one room; 37.6 per cent had only two rooms. By 1911 the proportions were 12.8 per cent and 40.4 per cent. Moreover in 1911, 56 per cent of one-roomed houses had more than two persons in each room, so had 47 per cent of those with two rooms. The number of persons to the acre was, therefore, very high.

This is the background to important papers by Dr. James B. Russell, Glasgow's medical officer of health from 1872 to 1892. In Glasgow an attempt was made to control overcrowding by issuing 'tickets' stating the number of persons permitted to live in a house. Russell's paper on the subject was an objective analysis of conditions in these houses (7), but his eloquent address on life in a one-roomed house was much more effective in stirring the public conscience (8).

(7) J. B. Russell, 'On the "Ticketed Houses" of Glasgow' in the *Proceedings of the Philosophical Society of Glasgow*, vol. 20 (1888–89), pp. 13–15 –

Let us now go inside the ticketed house. We find that the average air-space of a one-room house is 1,058 cubic feet; the average number of inmates is 3.17, so that the average air-space per inmate is 334 cubic feet. I make no distinction between adults and children, because it is one which is not physiologically justifiable, and besides it would involve more complicated calculations. The average air-space of a one-room house in the Model Buildings is 2,213 cubic feet, the average number of inmates 2.92, and the average air-space per inmate 758 cubic feet. This is also a high standard. The ordinary non-ticketed one-room house ranges in capacity between 1,200 and 1,350 cubic feet, and is never crowded down to the legal minimum per inmate. Turning to the ticketed two-room house, we find that the average total air-space is 1,725 cubic feet, the average number of inmates 4.66, and the average air-space per inmate 370 cubic feet. In the Model Buildings the average air-space of a two-room house is 3,158 cubic feet, the average number of inmates 4.29, and the average air-space per inmate 736 cubic feet. The non-ticketed two-room house is simply a duplication, or a little more than a duplication, of a one-room house, and is always occupied so as to keep far above the legal minimum. The ticketed house, then, is small of its kind to begin with, and owes its ticket to the constant disposition to overcrowding of its inmates. In fact, 13 to 14 per cent. of the one-room houses are found overcrowded when inspected during the night, and 6 to 7 per cent. of the two-room houses. Of the inmates of the ticketed one-room houses, 5 per cent. are lodgers; of the inmates of the two-room houses, 6 per cent.

What do these people pay for this accommodation? These houses are taken by the month or by the week. I therefore give monthly rents. These vary slightly in different districts. A ticketed one-room house reaches the lowest average rent in the "Calton", namely, 6s. 1d.; and the highest average, in the small district of "Brownfield", is 9s. 9d. A ticketed two-room house reaches the lowest average in a bad part of the district we call "Monteith Row", namely, 7s. 9d.; and the highest, which is in "Anderston", is 12s. 6d. But if I were to go into the details of the districts I should weary and puzzle you. Let us discuss the average for the whole city. The rent of a one-room house is 7s. 11d. This is 29.96 pence per inmate, and at the rate of 90 pence per 1000 cubic feet of air-space. The rent of a two-room house is 10s. 3d. This is 26.39 per inmate, and at the rate of 71 pence per 1000 cubic feet of air-space. If, therefore, we look to the inmates accommodated, the inmate of a two-room house pays 3.57 pence less for 36 cubic feet more air-space than the inmate of a one-room house. If, again, we regard the rent as coming from one pocket, the tenant of a two-room house pays fully 29 per cent. more rent for 63 per cent. more air-space than the tenant of a one-room house. He pays 71 pence per 1000 cubic feet, while the one-room tenant pays 90 pence. We shall be better able to discern the full meaning of these points if we turn to the Model Buildings and consider the whole facts together. There the rent of a one-room house is 13s. 4d. This is 54.8 pence per inmate, and at the rate of 72 pence per 1000 cubic feet of air-space. The rent of a two-room house is 16s. 4d. This is 45.7 pence per inmate, and 62 pence per 1000 cubic feet of air-space. There the inmate of a two-room house pays 9.1 pence less for 22 cubic feet less air-space than the inmate of a one-room house; but the tenant of a two-room house pays 22½ per cent. more rent for 42 per cent. more air-space. He pays 62 pence per 1000 cubic feet, while the one-room tenant pays 72 pence.

(8) J. B. Russell, *Life in One Room* (A lecture delivered to the Park Parish Literary Institute, Glasgow, 27th February, 1888).

Reprinted in A. K. Chalmers (ed.), *Public Health Administration in Glasgow* (1905), pp. 195–198 –

I have told you that in 1881 the population of Glasgow was 511,520 persons, and that of those 25 per cent. lived in one-room, and 45 per cent. in two-roomed houses; but what does that mean? It means that 126,000 persons *live* in those one-roomed, and 228,000 in those two-roomed houses. But is that all I can say? I might throw down that statement before you, and ask you to imagine yourselves, with all your appetites and passions, your bodily necessities and functions, your feelings of modesty, your sense of propriety, your births, your sicknesses, your deaths, your children,— in short, your *lives* in the whole round of their relationship with the seen and the unseen, suddenly shrivelled and shrunk into such conditions of space. I *might* ask you, I *do* ask you, to consider and honestly confess what would be the result to you. But I would fain do more. Generalities are so feeble. Yet how can I speak to you decently of details? . . .

It is those small houses which produce the high death-rate of Glasgow. It is those small houses which give to that death-rate the striking characteristics of an enormous proportion of deaths in childhood, and of deaths from diseases of the lungs at all ages. Their exhausted air and poor and perverse feeding fill our streets with bandy-legged children. There you will find year after year a death-rate of 38 per 1000, while in the districts with larger houses it is only 16 or 17. Of all the children who die in Glasgow before they complete their fifth year, 32 per cent. die in houses of one apartment; and not 2 per cent. in houses of five apartments and upwards. There they die, and their little bodies are laid on a table or on the dresser, so as to be somewhat out of the way of their brothers and sisters, who play and sleep and eat in their ghastly company. From beginning to rapid-ending the lives of these children are short parts in a continuous tragedy. A large proportion enter life by the side-door of illegitimacy. One in every five of all who are born there never see the end of their first year. Of those who so prematurely die, a third have never been seen in their sickness by any doctor. "The tongue of the sucking child cleaveth to the roof of his mouth for thirst; the young children ask bread and no man breaketh it unto them." Every year in Glasgow the deaths of from 60 to 70 children under five years of age are classified by the Registrar-

General as due to accident or negligence; and it is wholly in these small houses that such deaths occur. Half of that number are overlain by drunken mothers, others fall over windows and down stairs, are drowned in tubs and pails of water, scalded, or burned, or poisoned with whisky. I can only venture to lift a corner of the curtain which veils the life which is lived in these houses. It is impossible to show you more.

B. ENVIRONMENT

The environment was as unwholesome as the houses. In the early nineteenth century Sir John Sinclair found little he could commend in the rural districts (1). The condition of the manufacturing districts, dependent chiefly on the cotton industry, varied (2). In the industrial areas which appeared with the development of the coal and iron industries the harshness and brutality of the surroundings were unsurpassed (3).

(1) Sir John Sinclair, *Analysis of the Statistical Account of Scotland* (1825), 1831 edn., vol. i, pp. 174–179 –

Nothing could be more detestable, than the method in which villages were originally constructed in Scotland. The houses were not built according to any regular plan, but scattered in every direction. The roads and alleys were inconceivably bad, especially in wet weather, as few of them were paved; and what added greatly to their miserable state, was the abominable practice of placing the dunghill, in which every species of filth was accumulated, before their doors; a practice highly injurious to the health of the inhabitants . . . though the politician is apt to consider the want of villages and manufactures as an evil, because it is unfriendly to the increase of wealth; yet the philosopher forbears to lament the loss, when he considers their pernicious influence on the morals, and health of mankind, compared to residing in distinct habitations. In villages, it is alleged by some, that numbers of the most worthless and wretched part of society are apt to resort; that thither the dregs of the community, from all quarters, pour in; that incentives to vice are presented, and that frequently no proper police is established to check the evil. Where villages are founded, manufactures ought invariably to be established, as the best means to give encouragement to industry. This operates as a more effectual check to the progress of vice, and contributes more to the felicity of the inhabitants, than the best code of municipal laws, or the most rigid exercise of any power with which magistrates are invested.

It may be admitted, that the inhabitants of villages are apparently more dissipated, than those persons who live in separate and sequestered hamlets, and who are employed in agriculture. But then it is to be observed, that this often arises, not from any superior purity of heart, but from the greater difficulty of indulging bad propensities; and that the inhabitants of sequestered spots, are generally more ignorant, duller, and more uncouth, than those who are assembled in villages . . .

The houses should be of a comfortable description. It is much to be regretted, that the lower class of villagers, who are often a numerous, useful, and virtuous body, are not in general better lodged. After toiling hard through the day, they return home to be involved in smoke, or suffer from other inconveniences.

This evil will remain, till the landed proprietors build, at their own expense, all the houses necessary for the good accommodation of the labourers upon their estates. And considering that, by doing so, they beautify the country, and augment the happiness of those, by whose industry and labour they enjoy ease, affluence, and splendour, and may receive an adequate interest for the money they expend, it is surprising, that the gentlemen have, in this respect, been so long inattentive to their own interests, and the comfort of their fellow-creatures.

(2) Parliamentary Papers, 1842, XXII, p. 24. Report of James Stuart, Inspector of Factories –

In the manufacturing towns of my district, viz. Glasgow, Belfast, Dundee, Aberdeen, Arbroath, Montrose etc. the connexion between the factory owners and the persons employed by them of course ceases for the day when the hours of work expire; the operatives procure their lodgings as they best can, frequently, in the large towns, in unhealthy, damp, and airless apartments most injurious to their constitutions. No one exercises any control over their mode of life, or sees that they employ their gains in obtaining the ordinary necessities for its preservation, wholesome provisions, sufficient clothing, education for their children, and medical attendance, when requisite for their families. In fact, the factory owner in a town knows little or nothing of the people he employs but during the hours of work. A very different state of things exists in the great factories situated in the country districts in Scotland . . . In country districts the owners of the factories pay scrupulous attention to the wants of the population which they have been the means of collecting, and of which they consider themselves the heads, retaining no one in their employment of notoriously dissipated or demoralized habits. With exceptions so trifling that they are unworthy of notice, they put it in the power of all whom they employ to be comfortably lodged, and to have their children educated at good schools, and provide medical attendance at their doors . . . The villages established by the factory owners of my district in situations where hardly a house was previously to be seen, at New Lanark, in Lanarkshire; Deanston and Stanley, in Perthshire; Catrine, in Ayrshire; Prinlaws, in Fifeshire . . . and in many other factories in my district in similar situations, afford far better and more comfortable accommodation than, so far as I have observed, is to be found for any other part of the working population in any other part of Scotland or Ireland. Although working for the same number of hours as in the towns, the persons employed in such factories enjoy as uninterruptedly good health, and are almost as ruddy and robust-looking as the agricultural labourers in their neighbourhood, and are certainly far better educated, and in their manners and appearance more civilized. That this representation strictly accords with the truth, will, I am confident, readily be admitted by every unprejudiced person who will take the trouble of minutely inspecting, as I necessarily have frequently had occasion to do, the population in the extensive cotton factories of New Lanark, and Deanston, and Stanley, as well as in the flax factories of Prinlaws, to which I particularly refer, as affording the best example in my district of perfect cleanliness and freedom from dust, which are with difficulty maintained in a flax factory, especially where wet spinning is carried on, and of most expensive, and, for the population, most advantageous outlays of money in the admirable accommodation in houses lately erected for the operatives, and in other comforts afforded to them.

(3) *Children's Employment Commission*, 1842. Report on the Collieries and Iron-works of the West of Scotland by Thomas Tancred, pp. 313–314 –

The Monklands district.

This vast and sudden accession of population, consisting for the most part of irregular and dissolute characters from all parts—from Wales, England, Scotland, and Ireland—has produced a state of society, upon the existence of which, in a civilized country, we cannot reflect without a deep feeling that it manifests something essentially defective in our religious and educational institutions . . .

Everything that meets the eye or ear tells of slavish labour united to brutal intemperance. At night, ascending to the hill on which the Established Church stands, the groups of blast-furnaces on all sides might be imagined to be blazing volcanoes, at most of which the smelting is continued Sundays and week-days, by day and night, without intermission. By day a perpetual steam arises from the whole length of the canal where it receives the waste water from the blast-engines on both sides of it; and railroads, traversed by long trains of waggons drawn by locomotive engines, intersect the country in all directions, and are the cause of frequent accidents, into which, by the law of Scotland, no inquiry is made.

The population consists almost exclusively of colliers and iron-workers, with no gentry or middle class beyond a few managers of works and their clerks. I visited many of the houses attached to some of the works, and usually found them in a most neglected state, bespeaking an absence of all domestic comfort or attention to social duties. The garden-ground usually lay a mere waste, unenclosed, and not a spade put into it; the children, in rags and filth, were allowed to corrupt each other, exempt from all the restraints of school or of domestic control. This domestic discomfort seemed attributable, amongst other causes, to the crowded state of the habitations, which, from the want of buildings to contain the rapidly increasing population, were filled with lodgers. I was assured that some houses, with a family and only two rooms, took in as many as 14 single men as lodgers. It is needless to observe how impossible it must be for a woman to preserve decency, cleanliness, or comfort, under such circumstances. An infatuated love of money, for no purpose but to minister to a degrading passion for ardent spirits, seems the all pervading motive of action in this quarter. I remember particularly the house of a workman, in which I found the wife in tears, and hardly an article of furniture; a board supported on lumps of coal being the only apology for a seat, the bed-places and walls completely denuded. The poor woman, on being questioned as to the cause of this appearance of wretchedness, bitterly complained of the drunken habits of her husband; and what was my surprise to learn from the manager of the works, that he was a very skilful workman, a furnace-keeper, and could earn when he chose from 7s. to 10s. per day! We afterwards met him in liquor at the store, where he was insisting upon getting more spirits, and so violent was his behaviour that at last the manager took him by the shoulders and turned him out, barring the door after him . . .

Another reason why they are generally careless of the state of their houses, I take to be that they have no feeling that they are their homes, or likely to be their permanent habitations. The houses being for the most part built by the several works, and quite inadequate to the demand, it is always understood that when a man leaves his work he and his family must remove from the house, or "flit", as it is termed. Thus the houses are held only from fortnight to fortnight, or from one pay-day to another. The greatest contrast is observable in other parts of the country where the workmen are engaged by the year, and where, consequently, they are secure of their houses for that time at least, as in the Duke of Portland's collieries, and others, in the valley of the Irvine, in Ayrshire, or where some houses have been built by workmen themselves, or can be hired by them independently of their employers, as at Chapel Hall iron and coal works, Lanarkshire.

C. SANITATION

Even before the industrial age Scottish cities were notoriously squalid. Many visitors were particularly struck by Edinburgh's combination of splendour and squalor.

(1) John Wesley, *Journal* –

Monday, May 11, 1761. I took my leave of Edinburgh for the present. The situation of the city, on a hill shelving down on both sides, as well as to the east, with the stately castle upon a craggy rock on the west, is inexpressibly fine; and the main street so broad and finely paved, with the lofty houses on either hand (many of them seven or eight stories high), is far beyond any in Great Britain. But how can it be suffered, that all manner of filth should still be thrown even into this street continually? Where are the magistracy, the gentry, the nobility of the land? Have they no concern for the honour of their nation? How long shall the capital city of Scotland, yea, and the chief street of it, stink worse than a common sewer? Will no lover of his country, or of decency and common sense, find a remedy for this?

Industrial development and the consequential rapid and uncontrolled growth of towns produced a serious sanitary problem. Its horrors were described in the classic Reports on the Sanitary Conditions of the Labouring Population of Scotland in 1842.

(2) *Report on the Sanitary Conditions of the Labouring Population of Scotland*, 1842, pp. 153–155. Wm. Stevenson, Surgeon. Report on Musselburgh and District. Sanitation –

The construction of the town, therefore, is radically unfavourable to health; but as this is now beyond a remedy, it is needless to insist upon it, and I proceed to mention those circumstances which come immediately within the means of improvement. Throughout the whole of the older portions of the town there cannot, generally speaking, be said to be any water-closets in the dwellings, and there are no kind of back courts (as in English towns) in which other conveniences are placed. In a word, the excrementitious matter of some forty or fifty thousand individuals is thrown daily into the gutters, at certain hours appointed by the police, or poured into carts which are sent about the principal streets. In all the narrow and worse ventilated closes, this practice of throwing out every kind of liquid refuse into the gutters is universally prevalent. Scavengers are appointed by the police to sweep the streets and lanes daily, and clear away all that appears offensive; but this may be pronounced an impossible task. The evil is too monstrous for cure by any such superficial means. In spite of vigorous regulations to the contrary, the closes which are inhabited by the poorer classes continue in a most filthy condition both night and day, and there is an incessant exhalation of foetid substances, which I should consider highly injurious to health. Independently, however, of the insalubrity from this cause, I feel convinced that there is as great a moral evil. The eyes of the people, old and young, become familiarized with the spectacle of filth, and thus habits of uncleanliness and debased ideas of propriety and decency are ingrafted.

Within these few years, the practice of introducing water-closets into houses has become pretty general, wherever it is practicable; but in the greater part of the Old Town nothing of the kind can be accomplished from the want of drains. There are drains in the leading thoroughfares, but few closes possess these conveniences, and water is also sparingly introduced into these confined situations. You will therefore understand that *a want of tributary drains and water* is a fundamental cause of the uncleanly condition of the town. Of water of the finest kind there is indeed a plenteous supply, but unfortunately this is a monopoly in the hands of a joint-stock company, and, excepting at two, or three wells, all the water introduced into the town has to be specially paid for, in the form of a tax upon the rental, by those who use it.

It is clear that the existing institutions and police regulations in Edinburgh are incompetent to cleanse the town of its impurities. The police bye-laws have done much, but they utterly fail to cure the evil at its root. If I were permitted to suggest a means of remedy, I should mention the following:—

1. A common covered sewer or drain to be made in every close, court, and street, in connexion with a main drain. Each of these drains to have one or more openings with swing-doors to admit the inpourings of all liquid refuse, but to prevent the escape of effluvia.
2. A much more plenteous distribution of common wells.
3. The erection of several public necessaries.
4. All overhanging parts of old buildings to be removed, so as to admit the action of the sun on the ground, and assist ventilation. Any old buildings, valued at a limited price, likewise to be removed, where they evidently intercept a current of fresh air.
5. Powers to be given to the Commissioners of Police to carry these arrangements into effect at the public expense, providing that the outlay was not above say 3000 *l.* or 4000 *l.* annually.

These arrangements fall short of what would be desirable, but I fear that anything more would not be practicable in the present posture of affairs. I am not disposed to undervalue the advantages of a prevention of the odious foul water irrigation in the neighbourhood of Edinburgh, but I think that much more mischief is done by the foul irrigation *within* than *without* the town, and is more within the power of the inhabitants to remove. With respect to measures of medical police, in the strict sense of the term, I do not require to say anything. All who know the private condition of the town are well acquainted with the fact of there being an immense amount of destitution and misery. Society, in the densely peopled closes which I have alluded to, has sunk to something indescribably vile and abject. Human beings are living in a state worse than brutes. They have gravitated to a point of wretchedness from which no effort of the pulpit, the press, or the schoolmaster, can raise them. Were we to plant a clergyman in every alley, and scatter the most elevating products of literature gratuitously into every dwelling, the benefits would, I verily believe, be imperceptible. The class of whom I speak are too deeply sunk in physical distress, and far too obtuse in their moral perceptions, to derive advantage from any such means of melioration.

During the first half of the nineteenth century medical opinion had no doubt of the connection between bad housing and disease (3). At the same time some of the more perceptive among them realised the connection between trade depression and unemployment on the one hand and disease and death on the other (4).

(3) 'Report of Medical Inspector for the relief of epidemic cholera in Glasgow' in *The Glasgow Herald*, 3rd August 1848 –

Those frightful abodes of human wretchedness which lie along the High Street, Saltmarket, and Bridgegate, and constitute the bulk of that district known as the 'Wynds and Closes of Glasgow'—it is in these localities that all sanitary evils exist in perfection. These places consist of ranges of narrow closes, only some four or five feet in width, and of great length. The houses are so lofty that the direct light of the sky never reaches a large proportion of the dwellings. The ordinary atmospheric ventilation is impossible. The cleansing until lately was most inefficient, and from structural causes will always, under existing arrangements, be difficult and expensive. There are large square middensteads, some of them actually under the houses, and all of them in the immediate vicinity of the windows and doors of human dwellings. These receptacles hold the entire filth and offal of large masses of people and households, until country farmers can be bargained with for their removal. There is no drainage in these neighbourhoods, except in a few cases; and from the want of any means of flushing, the sewers, where they do exist, are extended cesspools polluting the air. So little is the use of sewers known, that on one occasion I saw the entire surface of a back-yard covered for several inches with green putrid water, although there was a sewer in the close within a few feet, into which it might have been drained away. The water supply is also very defective; such a thing as a household supply is unknown, and I have been informed that from the state of the law, the Water Companies find it impossible to recover rates, and that, had the cholera not appeared, it was in contemplation to have cut off the entire supply from this class of property.

The interior of the houses is in perfect keeping with their exterior. The approaches are generally kept in a state of filthiness beyond belief. The common stairs and passages are often the receptacles of the most disgusting nuisances. The houses themselves are dark, and without the means of ventilation, the walls dilapidated and filthy, and in many cases ruinous. There are no domestic conveniences even in the loftiest tenements, where they are most needed, except a kind of wooden sink placed outside some stair window, and communicating by a square wooden pipe with the surface of the close or court beneath. Down this contrivance, where it does exist, is poured the entire filth of the household or flat to which it belongs, and the solid refuse not unfrequently takes the same direction till the tube becomes obstructed. In Edinburgh it is no unusual thing for the whole refuse, solid and fluid, to be tossed out of the windows, into the closes below, and this in spite of Acts of Parliament and police regulations centuries old. The necessities of nature are stronger than any police laws, and will always set them successfully at defiance.

(4) R. Cowan, *Vital Statistics of Glasgow* (1838), pp. 38–39 –

From the mortality bills of 1836 and 1837, the following table of the deaths from fever monthly has been compiled. It is to be regretted that the bill for 1835 was deficient in this respect, otherwise a more accurate account of the rise and progress of the present epidemic might have been obtained.

TABLE of the Deaths from Fever each month, in the years 1836 and 1837, distinguishing the Males and Females, and giving the monthly proportion which the deaths from Fever bear to the whole number of ascertained deaths.

	1836			1837			1836	1837
Months	*Males*	*Females*	*Total*	*Males*	*Females*	*Total*	*Proportion to whole deaths*	
							1 in	1 in
January,	31	14	45	108	93	201	17.55	9.81
February,	16	11	27	77	61	138	24.74	7.13
March,	33	24	57	124	100	224	11.82	4.20
April,	27	37	64	114	88	202	10.00	4.08
May,	39	28	67	120	113	233	10.29	3.22
June,	38	33	71	109	90	199	8.91	3.34
July,	31	30	61	106	88	194	11.14	3.67
August,	51	31	82	101	71	172	8.89	4.93
September,	32	24	56	73	53	126	11.46	5.11
October,	52	37	89	74	75	149	7.71	3.79
November,	42	47	89	83	64	147	8.86	4.28
December,	73	60	133	98	97	195	6.15	3.73
	465	376	841	1187	993	2180		
1st Quarter	80	49	129	309	254	561		
2nd Quarter	104	98	202	343	291	634		
3rd Quarter	114	85	199	280	212	492		
4th Quarter	167	144	311	255	236	491		
	465	376	841	1187	993	2180		

Many interesting observations may be drawn from this Table. It shows the slow progress of an epidemic disease when trade is prosperous, compared with what occurs in seasons of distress. Up to November 1836, the period at which the commercial embarrassments were felt, the mortality from fever had not been rapidly increasing. In November it was just about double what it had been in January preceding, the number of deaths being 45 in January, and 89 in November.

The moment, however, the effects of the stagnation in trade extended to the working classes, the mortality increased with fearful rapidity, aided no doubt by the season of the year, the high price of grain, and the scarcity or high price of fuel. The deaths from fever in the four months preceding 1st December, 1836, were 316; for the four months following, 696.

The Table also marks the period at which the epidemic reached its maximum amount of mortality, viz., in the second quarter of 1837, and in the month of May in that quarter, being the month succeeding that in which the strike of the cotton spinners took place, by which 8000 individuals were thrown out of employment.

The establishment of soup kitchens, and the provision of work for the unemployed operatives in the months of May, June, and July, must have materially aided in arresting the progress of the epidemic.

Many expect that fever is to subside suddenly, but an examination of the above table and of the mortality bill for 1838, will prove the fallacy of such opinions by exhibiting a gradual diminution in the numbers attacked.

In spite of improvements inadequate sanitary arrangements persisted especially in the mining districts of the West of Scotland. The Royal Commission on Housing during the First World War brought the continuing horrors to the attention of the public.

(5) *Report of the Royal Commission on the Housing of the Industrial Population in Scotland, 1918*, paras. 919–920 –

It is in the West of Scotland, where the "conservancy system" of sanitation has persisted longer than in the East, that the worst conditions are most commonly found in mining villages. Here the privy-midden, or common dry-closet combined with the ashpit for a group of houses, till recently formed the rule, and is still found in full offensiveness in not a few places. It seems necessary to quote [a description] of these erections, . . . by Dr. Dittmar of the Local Government Board . . .

"For 20 inhabited houses (with about 100 people) there are two sets of public privy ashpits, one with two privies and the other with a single privy. These erections are of brick, with brick floors and wooden roofs, and wooden unlocked doors; a low brick wall with wooden cope provides a seat for the users of the privy; a large ashpit behind receives the droppings and the refuse of the houses. It might be added that not only are there no locks on the doors, there are not even catches or hooks or any means provided to close them from the inside. The ashpits behind the privies are large, and enclosed by brick walls about 2 feet high, with earth floors and without any roof. The floors of the privies were littered with faeces on the day of my visit. They constituted a nuisance of a recurring type." This last opinion is confirmed by the fact that, although reported on by representatives of the Local Government Board in April 1903 and March 1905, yet, when another of their inspectors saw these privies in October 1912 they were still in the same condition. The same view was taken by Sheriff-Substitute Glegg in March 1912, when, in a Note attached to an interlocutor declaring that certain privy-middens of this type constituted a nuisance, he said:—

"The evidence leaves no reasonable doubt that a nuisance exists, and will continue to recur so long as the sanitary conveniences are of the kind and amount of those at present in use".

E. HOUSING AND SANITARY REFORM

Though the evils were obvious, reform proved difficult. Local authorities lacked the power to intervene, except through cumbersome and costly private Acts, and were slow to use what powers they did have. There was determined opposition to any restriction of private rights and to all proposals to finance reform by means of local assessment. In 1866, however, Glasgow Corporation acquired limited powers of intervention.

(1) Preamble to 29 Vict., c. lxxxv (1866).—An Act for the Improvement of the City of *Glasgow*, and the Construction of new, and widening, altering, and diverting of existing streets in the said City; and for other Purposes. 11th *June* 1866 –

Whereas various Portions of the City of *Glasgow* are so built, and the Buildings thereon are so densely inhabited, as to be highly injurious to the moral and physical Welfare of the Inhabitants, and many of the Thoroughfares are narrow, circuitous, and inconvenient, and it would be of public and local Advantage if various Houses and Buildings were taken down, and those Portions of the said City reconstituted, and new Streets were constructed in and through various Parts of the said City, and several of the existing Streets altered and widened and diverted, and that in connexion with the Reconstitution of these Portions of the City Provision was made for Dwellings for the Labouring Classes who may be displaced in consequence thereof: And whereas Plans and Sections of the said intended new Streets, and of the widening, altering, and diverting of existing Streets, showing the Lines and Levels thereof respectively and the Lands and Houses to be taken for the Purposes thereof, and Plans of the Lands and Houses required to be taken for the other Purposes before mentioned, and of this Act, and Books of Reference to the Plans containing the Names of the Owners or reputed Owners, Lessees or reputed Lessees, and of the Occupiers of the Lands and Houses, have been deposited with the Principal Sheriff Clerk of the County of *Lanark*, and those Plans, Sections, and Books of Reference are in this Act referred to as "the Deposited Plans, Sections and Books of Reference:" And whereas it is expedient that Provision should be made for the Establishment and Maintenance of a Public Park in or adjacent to the North-east Quarter of the City: And whereas it is expedient that the Lord Provost, Magistrates, and Council of the City of *Glasgow* should be appointed Trustees for the Purpose of carrying the said works and Improvements into execution, and that they should be authorized to raise Money for the Purpose of carrying this Act into effect by means of Rates and on Money borrowed on the Credit of such Rates, and on the Credit of the Property for the Time being belonging to them acquired in virtue of this Act: And whereas the Objects aforesaid cannot be effected without the Authority of Parliament: May it therefore please Your Majesty that it may be enacted.

The following year local authorities were given powers to appoint sanitary inspectors and remove nuisances.

(2) 30 and 31 Vict., c. 101 (1867). An Act to consolidate and amend the law relating to the Public Health in *Scotland* –

Part I. 8. The Local Authority may, and where it shall be thought necessary by the Board [of Supervision for the Relief of the Poor in Scotland] . . . the Local Authority shall, appoint a Sanitary Inspector or Inspectors, who shall be also Inspector or Inspectors of Common Lodging Houses, and a Medical Officer or Medical Officers . . . .

II. 8. In any case where the Existence of a Nuisance is ascertained to their Satisfaction . . . [the Local Authority] may apply to the

Sheriff or to any Magistrate or Justice, by summary Petition . . . and if it appear to his Satisfaction that the Nuisance exists . . . he shall decern for the Removal . . . of the Nuisance. . .

22. In case of Noncompliance with or Infringement of any Decree aforesaid, the Sheriff, Magistrate or Justice may, on Application by the Local Authority, grant warrant to such Person or Persons as he may deem right to enter the Premises to which such Decree relates, and remove or remedy the Nuisance thereby condemned, or interdicted, and do whatever may be necessary in execution of such Decree; or if in the original Application it appears to his Satisfaction that the Author of the Nuisance is not known or cannot be found, then such Decree may at once ordain the Local Authority to execute the Works thereby directed; and all Expenses incurred by the Local Authority in executing the Works may be recovered from the Author of the Nuisance or the Owner of the Premises.

The limited powers of improvements obtained by local authorities under private Acts were augmented by the general statute of 1890.

(3) 53 and 54 Vict., c. 70, s. 4. Housing of the Working Classes Act, 1890 –

Where an official representation [i.e. by the medical officer of health] is made to the Local Authority that within a certain area in the district of such authority either—

(a) any houses, courts, or alleys are unfit for human habitation, or

(b) the narrowness, closeness, and bad arrangement, or the bad condition of the streets and houses or groups of houses within such area, or the want of light, air, ventilation, or proper conveniences, or any other sanitary defects, or one or more of such causes, are dangerous or injurious to the health of the inhabitants either of the buildings in the said area or of the neighbouring buildings;

and that the evils connected with such houses, courts, or alleys, and the sanitary defects in such area cannot be effectually remedied otherwise than by an improvement scheme for the rearrangement and reconstruction of the streets and houses, within such area, or of some such streets or houses, the Local Authority shall take such representation into their consideration, and if satisfied of the truth thereof, and of the sufficiency of their resources, shall pass a resolution to the effect that such area is an unhealthy area, and that an improvement scheme ought to be made in respect of such area, and after passing such resolution they shall forthwith proceed to make a scheme for the improvement of such area.

Until the First World War, local authorities could only condemn and remove slum property; they had little power, and no obligation to provide dwellings. A major landmark was the Royal Commission on Housing in Scotland of 1917–18. Following an exhaustive survey of existing conditions and the obstacles to improvement, the majority report recommended categorically that the obligation to provide adequate housing should rest with the local authorities.

(4) *Report of Royal Commission on the Housing of the Industrial Population in Scotland, 1918*, paras. 2232–2233, 2235, 2237 –

. . . These are the broad results of our survey: unsatisfactory sites of houses and villages, insufficient supplies of water, unsatisfactory provision for drainage, grossly inadequate provision for the removal of refuse, widespread absence of decent sanitary conveniences, the persistence of the unspeakably filthy privy-midden in many of the mining areas, badly constructed, incurably damp labourers' cottages on farms, whole townships unfit for human occupation in the crofting counties and islands, primitive and casual provision for many of the seasonal workers, gross overcrowding and huddling of the sexes together in the congested industrial villages and towns, occupation of one-room houses by large families, groups of lightless and unventilated houses in the older burghs, clotted masses of slums in the great cities. To these, add the special problems symbolized by the farmed-out houses, the model lodging houses, congested back-lands, and ancient closes. To these, again, add the cottages a hundred years old in some of the rural villages, ramshackle brick survivals of the mining outbursts of seventy years ago in the mining fields, monotonous miners' rows flung down without a vestige of town-plan or any effort to secure modern conditions of sanitation, ill-planned houses that must become slums in a few years, old houses converted without necessary sanitary appliances and proper adaptation into tenements for many families, thus intensifying existing evils, streets of new tenements in the towns developed with the minimum of regard for amenity.

Overcrowding

The last census showed that thousands of one-room houses continued to be occupied by families; that overcrowding reckoned even by the most moderate standard is practically universal in the one- and two-room houses; that, in spite of protest and administrative superintendence, domestic overcrowding of houses and overbuilding of areas have not been prevented. To our amazement, we found that if we take overcrowding to mean more than three persons per room, we should, to secure even this moderate standard for Scotland, have to displace some 284,000 of the population. But this is not all. We conclude that, at least 50 per cent of the one-room houses and 15 per cent of the two-room houses ought to be replaced by new houses. In brief, merely to relieve existing overcrowding and replace houses that should be demolished, some 121,000 new houses are required, and, if an improved standard is adopted, as we recommend, the total number of new houses required would approach 234,000. For such gigantic figures our Report submits full justification. On this point the Commission is unanimous . . .

Obstacles to Housing Reform

These, then, are the conditions that cry aloud for redress. But the path of reform is blocked by many obstacles: the failure of commercial enterprise to keep pace with housing needs, the failure of the Local Authorities, both of town and county, to appreciate the full value of their powers, the rapacity of property owners in their claims for compensation, the persistence of antiquated methods of arbitration, the absence of any definite basis for the assessment of compensation, the impotence of the arbiters to check speculative claims, the consequent enormous and deterrent expense of improvement schemes and reconstruction schemes, the impotence of the Local Authorities to control the prices of building sites within the city or of potential building land in the immediate neighbourhood, the absence of a direct obligation on any authority to see that adequate housing is provided for the whole community, the inadequate size, area, and resources of many Local Authorities, the absence of powers to require combination of authorities, the consequent impossibility of effective enforcement of statutes by the Central Authority, the insufficiency of the Central Authority's equipment, the unsatisfactory status of the Central Authority itself—these and their many derivative difficulties of procedure stand in the way of reform. Both commercial enterprise and municipal enterprise have failed to keep pace with the steadily rising demand for more and better house-room . . .

Obligation on Local Authorities for Adequate Housing

But there is an administrative point that is equally fundamental. From the national survey we have conducted, we are satisfied that, in the present unique disorganisation of affairs, the State alone, acting through the Local Authorities, can meet the present discontent. For the time being, commercial enterprise has failed to keep pace with the demand. Doubtless, the climax came with the war; the failure, however, had become manifest long before the war. But whatever its causes, the disorganisation flowing from the war makes an immediate revival of uncontrolled commercial enterprise on an adequate scale impossible. There is, in our view only one alternative; the State itself, through the Local Authorities, is alone in a position to assume responsibility. Here, then, is our primary point in procedure. Hitherto the Local Authorities, though their powers for the provision of houses are extensive, have, for various reasons, been restrained or have refrained from using them to any appreciable extent. We are satisfied that, if those powers are to be exercised on the scale necessary to realise the programme we have set forth, the Local Authorities must be placed under an unmistakeable obligation to maintain a continuous and systematic survey of their housing accommodation, to ascertain how far private enterprise can meet the demands, but, failing provision of houses by other agencies, to undertake themselves—with financial assistance from the State—the necessary building schemes. Without such a definite obligation, exercised under direction of the Central Authority, we are satisfied that, by no administrative machinery known to us, can the necessary houses be provided . . . This matter brooks no delay.

A minority of the Commission, while admitting the magnitude of the problem wished to reserve a larger role for private enterprise in house-building. Nevertheless, the majority's main recommendation, that Local Authorities should be obliged to provide adequate housing, was embodied in the Statute of 1919.

(5) 9 and 10 Geo. V, ch. 60, Part I. Housing Town Planning, etc. (Scotland) Act, 1919 –

1. (1) It shall be the duty of every Local Authority . . . to consider the needs of their district with respect to the provision of houses for the working classes, and within three months after the passing of this Act, and thereafter as often as occasion arises, to prepare and submit to the Scottish Board of Health . . . a scheme for the exercise of their powers . . .
2. A scheme under this section shall specify—

(a) the approximate number and nature of the houses which, in the opinion of the Local Authority, are required adequately to supply the needs of their district;
(b) the approximate number and the nature of the houses to be provided by the Local Authority, and wherever possible the average number of houses per acre;
(c) the approximate extent of land to be acquired and the localities in which land is to be acquired;
(d) the time within which the scheme or any part thereof is to be carried into effect;

and the scheme may contain such incidental, consequential and supplemental provisions (including provisions as to the subsequent variation of the scheme) as may appear necessary or proper for the purpose of the scheme.

The 1919 Act, though leading to some improvement, left each local authority to set its own standards. In 1935 a strict, general definition of overcrowding was laid down.

(6) 25 and 26 Geo. V, ch. 41. Housing (Scotland) Act, 1935 –

PART I

OVERCROWDING, RE-DEVELOPMENT AND RE-CONDITIONING.

Prevention of Overcrowding.

1. (1) It shall be the duty of every local authority before such dates as the Department may, after consultation with the authority, fix as respects their district, to cause an inspection thereof to be made

with a view to ascertaining what dwelling houses therein are overcrowded, and to prepare and submit to the Department a report showing in such detail as the Department may direct the result of the inspection and the additional housing accommodation required in order to put an end to overcrowding in their district, and, unless they satisfy the Department that the additional accommodation required, in so far as it is required for persons of the working classes, will be otherwise provided, to prepare and submit to the Department proposals for the provision thereof...

2. (1) A dwelling-house shall be deemed for the purposes of this Act to be overcrowded at any time when the number of persons sleeping in the house either—

(a) is such that any two of those persons, being persons ten years old or more of opposite sexes and not being persons living together as husband and wife, must sleep in the same room; or

(b) is, in relation to the number and floor area of the rooms of which the houses consists, in excess of the permitted number of persons as defined in the First Schedule to this Act.

(2) In computing for the purposes of this section the number of persons sleeping in a house, no account shall be taken of a child under one year old, and a child who has attained one year and is under ten years old shall be reckoned as one half of a unit...

FIRST SCHEDULE

Number of Persons Permitted to
Use a House for Sleeping

For the Purposes of Part I of this Act the expression "the permitted number of persons" means, in relation to any dwelling-house, either—

(a) the number specified in the second column of Table I in the annex hereto in relation to a house consisting of the number of rooms of which that house consists; or

(b) the aggregate for all the rooms in the house obtained by reckoning, for each room therein of the floor area specified in the first column of Table II in the annex hereto, the number specified in the second column of that Table in relation to that area, whichever is the less:

Provided that in computing for the purposes of the said Table I the number of rooms in a house, no regard shall be had to any room having a floor area of less than 50 square feet.

ANNEX

Table I.

Where a house consists of—	
(a) One room, ...	2
(b) Two rooms, ...	3
(c) Three Rooms, . . .	5
(d) Four rooms, ...	7½
(e) Five rooms or more, . .	10, with an additional 2 in respect of each room in excess of five.

Table II.

Where the floor area of a room is—	
(a) 110 sq. ft. or more, . .	2
(b) 90 sq. ft. or more, but less than 110 sq. ft., . . .	1½
(c) 70 sq. ft. or more, but less than 90 sq. ft., . . .	1
(d) 50 sq. ft. or more, but less than 70 sq. ft., . . .	½
(e) Under 50 sq. ft., . . .	Nil.

Inadequate and poor quality housing have remained notable features of Scottish social life. The result has been a continuing high level of provision of dwellings by public enterprise, and the persistence of low rents charged by many of the larger local authorities.

CHAPTER IX

Transport

A. ROADS

Since the seventeenth century, responsibility for highway maintenance had rested with the Justices of the Peace, who, through overseers, could exact several days 'statute labour' per annum from each tenant, cottar and servant, could levy a tax on freeholders and heritors, and could charge moderate tolls at bridges, causeways and ferries. In 1719 most of the provisions including the controversial ones on statute labour, were reiterated.

(1) 5 Geo. II, c. 30 (1719). An Act for amending and making more effectual the Laws for repairing the Highways, Bridges and Ferries in that Part of *Great Britain* called *Scotland* –

II. And be it enacted by the Authority aforesaid, That the Justices of Peace and Commissioners of Supply for the Time being, in the several Shires and Stewartries in that Part of *Great Britain* called *Scotland*, shall meet and convene at the respective Head-boroughs of the said Shires or Stewartries upon the third *Tuesday* of *May* next to come, and thenceforward upon every such third *Tuesday* of *May* from Year to Year, with power to them or any five of them, to adjourn themselves from Time to Time, and to chuse Clerks, Surveyors and Overseers and all other Officers necessary for putting the Laws in Execution in relation to the Highways, Bridges and Ferries in that Part of the united Kingdom; and if any Clerk, Surveyor or Overseer, who shall be appointed or chosen by the Justices of the Peace and Commissioners of Supply, or any five of them as aforesaid, shall refuse to accept of or take upon them any of the Offices aforesaid, every such Person or Persons so refusing shall be subject and liable to the Penalty of five Pounds Sterling respectively.

III. And be it further enacted by the Authority aforesaid, That the said Justices, Commissioners, or the Officers or Overseers to be appointed by them, shall be and they are hereby authorized and required to call and convene the Tenants, Cottars and other labouring Men within their respective Bounds as aforesaid, to work three Days before the last Day of *June* in the Year of our Lord one thousand seven hundred and nineteen, not being in Seed-time, and likewise to work three Days after Harvest; and so yearly and every Year, until the said Highways, Bridges and Ferries are sufficiently repaired, on such Days, and at such Places as the said Commissioners or their Officers aforesaid shall from Time to Time appoint. IV. And be it further enacted by the Authority aforesaid That every Tenant, Cottar or labouring Man, who shall fail, neglect or refuse to come to work at the respective Times and Places to be appointed as aforesaid, (due Notice being given at the respective Parish Churches where any such Person or Persons have their Residence, upon the Lord's Day immediately preceding) shall be subject and liable to pay eighteen Pence respectively for every such Day's Failure, unless such Person or Persons send a sufficient Man or Men to work for him, her or them; . . .

Statute labour and local taxation proved inadequate for the construction and maintenance of roads. Statute labour was commuted for a money payment and local Turnpike Acts made it possible to raise additional funds by charging tolls on the roads constructed by the Turnpike Trustees constituted under the acts. The earliest was for the county of Edinburgh, in 1713. Other areas obtained acts later: there were about 350 between 1750 and 1844.

(2) 12 Ann. (1713). County of Edinburgh Turnpike Act –

Whereas the Supreme Courts of Judicature, and the chief Officers for collecting and managing Her Majesty's Revenues for that part of Great Britain called Scotland, do sit and meet at the City of Edinburgh, which occasions so great a number of passengers, and many loads and carriages do pass daily to and from the said City, that the Bridges and Highways in the County of Edinburgh, leading to the said City, would become impassable by all persons, horses, and other cattle, if not annually repaired. And whereas the ordinary course appointed by the Laws and Statutes of that part of Great Britain called Scotland, being not sufficient for the effectual repairing and amending the said Bridges and Highways, the Lords of the Privy Council of Scotland did, before the union of the two kingdoms, from time to time, impose and continue a duty to be paid for all Horses with Loads, and all Carts, Sledges, and Waggons passing through the said County to the said City; and directed that the money to be collected should be applied for the repairing, amending, and keeping in repair, the Bridges and Highways in the said County; and whereas the said duty so imposed doth cease on the 2nd day of August 1714; but the said Bridges and Highways will not be effectually repaired at the expiration of the said term; and it being impracticable for the inhabitants of the Parishes in which the said Bridges and Highways lie, to amend or repair the same, except the same or some such other provision be made for raising money for putting the said Bridges and Highways into good and sufficient repair . . . For remedy whereof, and to the intent the said Bridges and Highways may be effectually repaired and amended, and from time to time hereafter kept in good and sufficient repair; it is therefore enacted, that (for the surveying, ordering, repairing and keeping in repair the said Bridges and Highways in the said County of Edinburgh), it shall and may be lawful to and for Her Majesty's Justices of the Peace, for the time being, in the said County of Edinburgh (who are hereby nominated and appointed Trustees for putting this Act in execution), or any ten or more of them, met at one of their Quarter Sessions, to erect, or cause to be erected, a gate or gates, turnpike or turnpikes, in or cross any part or parts of the said Highways or Roads, and to receive and take for every Horse with a Load, passing each and every time through the said County to the said City, the sum of one-sixth part of a penny sterling; and for every Cart, Waggon, or Sledge passing, laden or unladen, each and every time through the said County to the said City, the sum of one halfpenny sterling; which money so to be raised and collected as aforesaid, is and shall hereby be vested in the said Trustees; and the same and every part thereof shall be paid, applied, and disposed of, and assigned to and for the several uses and purposes herein afore mentioned (the reasonable charges expended, or that shall be paid in or about, or by reason of passing this Act of Parliament, being first deducted) . . . Provided always, that nothing in this Act contained shall extend, or be construed to extend, to charge any person or persons riding through the said County, or going in a Coach, Chariot, or Chaise.

The turnpike system was haphazard and the funds raised not always adequate to bring all roads up to the standard required by an industrial society. The contrast between the improved and the unimproved roads became increasingly evident throughout the eighteenth century. In the 1820s a well-known factor of great experience throughout Scotland reflected on the contrast.

(3) George Robertson, *Rural Recollections* (1829), pp. 38–41 –

There are still some of these old roads to be met with in the country, though not much used now as such, and though the ground which they occupied is not yet cultivated. Nothing can be a greater contrast than these with the highways of modern times. Thus, in some places where there was space for taking room, it was not spared. There may be seen four, or five, or more tracks, all collateral to each other, as each in its turn had been abandoned, and another chosen, and all at last equally impassable. In wet weather they became more *lairs*, sloughs, in which the carts or carriages had to slumper through in a half-swimming state; whilst in time of drought it was a continued jolting out of one hole into another. But as there was generally room enough and to spare, in urgent cases the travellers took a new path, insomuch that, impracticable as it may seem, they contrived to get through in one way or other. In cases where the track was confined within walls or hedges on each side, which though rather a rare circumstance, did now and then occur, as there was here no room to flinch, travellers were sadly beset, and had to float through or jolt through with all the patience they could muster. In short, travelling in those times, was a laborious task, exceedingly harassing, and extremely slow.

It was, however, but a small proportion of goods that was transmitted by this mode of conveyance. Nothing was put upon a cart, that could be carried on a horse. Corn and meal, of all kinds, were generally conveyed on horseback, in sacks. Thus, two bolls of meal were *a load*: and hence a load of meal, in market terms, still means two bolls, whether it be in one or more bags. Coals were also conveyed on horseback, in a bag containing three hundredweights; and a load of coals is still understood to be the same weight; whilst a single-horse cart holds, at the least, four of these loads, and in many cases now, six, or even eight loads, or twenty-four hundredweight, is a single-horse draught:—What a vast improvement on the ancient mode of carriage! *Peats*, too, were carried on horseback, universally, in the vicinity of Edinburgh, even in my own time; so also were straw and hay; about fourteen stone, English, or two hundredweight, was a load. It was too bulky an article, to admit of more being laid on; and being equally poised on each side; and hanging down almost to the ground, completely concealed the horse, so that it seemed to be a hay-cock in motion.

There was then a set of single-horse traffickers, under the name of cadgers, that regularly plied on all roads, disposing of many kinds of commodities that were then in demand: as fish, salt, eggs, poultry, and crockery-ware; in fact every thing that was adapted to this mode of carriage. The vehicles in use consisted of various kinds and fabrics, as creels, sacks, panniers: some of wands, and some of wood, as best suited the purpose or the means of the owner, always requiring his ready hand to preserve an equipoise.

In carrying goods from distant towns it was necessary, however, to have a cart, as all that a horse could carry on his back, in a sack or in creels, could not remunerate for the expense of a long journey. A superior kind of functionary was required, who, under the name of the *town-carrier*, had a horse in awkward enough harness, dragging a rudely formed cart through dub and through mire, along these unshapely roads, from one town to another, loaded with many different kinds of goods that were in traffic betwixt the different towns. The time required for this adventurous business was longer, but was unavoidable. It is said, and I can well believe it, that the common carrier from Selkirk to Edinburgh, thirty-eight miles distant, required two weeks to make out his journey betwixt the two towns, going and returning, with a suitable resting time at each to his poor fatigued horse, which had perhaps not less than five or six hundredweight of goods to drag along. The road, originally, was among the most perilous in the whole country: a considerable extent of it lay in the bottom of that district called Galla Water, from the name of the principal stream. The channel of the water itself, when not flooded, was the track chosen, as being the most level, and easiest to be travelled on. The rest of the way, very much up-and-down-hill, was far worse. The townsmen of this adventurous individual, on the morning of his way-going, turned out to take their leave of him, and to wish him a safe return from his perilous undertaking. The same enterprise, with more than treble the loading, is now performed in four days, going and coming.

Travel and road construction in the Highlands had its peculiar problems.

(4) I. Lettice, *Letters on a Tour through parts of Scotland, in the year 1792*, pp. 315–322 –

Fort-William, Sept. 9, 1792

Whilst we were standing on the quay, anxious for their [the horses'] success, as we were not without some apprehension, that they might take fright from the rolling of the boat, betwixt the violence of wind and water; there came down, to join our ferrying party over the stream, a tall, melancholy and gentlemanly figure, completely dressed *a l'highlandoise*, and armed with dirk and pistol. Stepping composedly forwards, and observing our solicitude, very opportunely, to cheer our spirits, he related the incident of two English gentlemen having been drowned three years before, in ferrying over this very water. The boat, however, arrived safe with its charge, to the opposite shore. The men returned immediately with it, for ourselves, and for the carriage; expressing the apprehensions which they had felt at the alarm, and movement of one of our horses, about the middle of their course. Our carriage being put into the boat, tilted it so much, that all who entered, could not restore it to anything like a balance. The difficult passage of our horses, the story just told us by the melancholy gentleman, the boding gloom of his countenance, the wind and tide meeting each other, and causing great agitation in our vessel, a furious storm of rain and hail set in, after a few strokes of our oars, all combined to mark every face with visible signs of uneasiness; and, indeed, an enormous surge in the midst of the current, so nearly overset us, that our feelings, when at length we got safe to shore, were happily, and strongly contrasted to those, which we had experienced on the water.

We landed in that part of the Highlands called Lochaber, celebrated in Scottish song. We did not, however, sing "Lochaber no more," for much were we rejoiced at setting foot upon its solid ground . . .

The estuary of Loch Leven ran on the other hand of this agreeable valley. After we had travelled a few miles, the water branched out into two directions, partly opposite; one branch taking the southwestward by Morvern, through the wildest parts of the Highlands, into the sea, the other toward the north-east, into Inverness-shire, along which lay the military road to Fort William; the route which we were pursuing. Habitations are thinly scattered here: we now and then saw a shepherd's or a herdsman's cot. On the decayed parts of the road, at pretty frequent intervals, we met with peasants repairing, or improving them. Where the base of these mountains runs down precipitately into the water of Lochiel, or Loch Yell, as some of the geographers call it, the road has been cut out of the solid rock, with infinite labour and expence, and made sufficiently wide for the safe passage of meeting carriages; but the greater part of this road, almost from our entrance into Lochaber quite to Fort William, and thence to Fort Augustus, and beyond that toward Inverness, though shaped out of the mountains consists of earth and large stones, rather than solid rock. To have made a road of such considerable length, it being sixty-eight miles to Inverness from Beilichelish [Ballachulish], had otherwise been impracticable. The undertaking, when you consider, that the level is almost wholly artificial, was a very arduous one. The first steps towards its execution were highly daring. The [place on which to stand] which Archimides wanted for the removal of the whole earth, was here as much wanted for the removal of rocks and precipices, hanging directly over the water. And there was no proper access to them for the engineer and his men, but by descending from the ridges of several of the loftiest mountains in the Highlands, and down their most rapid declivities; sometimes, in the tracks of goats and sheep, and often where no footstep of man or beast had ever been set, by clinging to the roots of trees and shrubs, and sometimes hanging to one another in their dangerous descent. When they at last arrived near enough to the bottom to commence their operations, where the ground proved impenetrable to the mattock, pick-axe, or bar of iron, workmen, suspended by ropes among the precipices, were obliged to bore, or undermine the rocks, and then to blow up their solid masses by the application of gunpowder. Notwithstanding the immense labour, difficulty and danger to be encountered in the progress of this work, projected by General Wade, and carried on by his troops, and under his inspection, it was, after ten years, happily accomplished . . .

Government, we understood, allows 8000 *l.* a year for the repair of the military roads of Scotland; a business which employs a considerable number of the peasantry during the summer season, and proves the surest source of their maintenance for the whole year.

These roads are liable to be much broken by the deluges of water, which descend with violence from the hills after rain; and the bridges which are erected at the bottom of every ravine, to let these occasional torrents pass beneath them, are frequently overthrown. This present summer having been unusually wet, we found many parts of the road, especially where the masonry was out of repair, or unfinished, nearly impassable.

In the Highlands the roads built by General Wade were of limited economic value, partly because the routes were chosen for strategic rather than economic reasons. The Highlands, however, saw the first concerted plan for highway development in Scotland. Following an extensive survey by Thomas Telford in 1802–03 (see above, p. 44), parliament made substantial grants towards construction. The state was to pay half the cost; landowners had to raise the remainder, either voluntarily or by assessment. By 1821 about 900 miles of road and over 1,000 bridges had been constructed at a cost of over £500,000, shared between the state and the landlords. Telford supervised much of the work. Though the landlords provided half the cost of the construction of the roads, their upkeep caused anxiety because of the indifference of the local proprietors.

(5) Sixth Report of the Commissioners for the Highland Roads and Bridges (1813). Letter of Robert Brown (former Factor for Clanranald, later for the Duke of Hamilton), p. 36 –

I have had of late occasion to travel on many of the Commissioners Roads in the Highlands, and can safely attest, in general, that they are well executed; and I may add, that if properly attended to, they will be a lasting blessing to this hitherto neglected District, and continue an unparalleled monument of National Munificence.

It gives me pain, however, to remark, that in many cases, if these Roads are left to the care of the Country Gentlemen alone, they will be allowed to fall into disrepair, and every shilling expended on them lost, as the jarring interests and narrow views of some of these individuals will, when the novelty of the thing wears off, prevent their uniting in any common measure, however beneficial; already I know of an instance or two of this.

In short, these Roads must continue to be looked after by the Commissioners, and they should obtain a law in addition to that already enacted, giving authority for the express purpose of watching over and superintending the proceedings of the several Counties, and compelling them to uphold the new Roads in a suitable manner.

In lowland counties, where all the turnpikes were under a single trust, and where the administration was by trustees rather than through tacksmen, toll revenues might be sufficient to keep the roads in good condition —the county of Edinburgh was particularly noted for its efficient management. But in other districts the revenues were inadequate—especially when railways began to compete for traffic—and in 1859 a commission of inquiry estimated the total debt on roads and bridges at nearly £2,400,000. The objections to turnpikes in the railway age were forcibly stated to the same commission.

(6) *Evidence to the Committee on Public Roads in Scotland, 1866*, pp. 189–191: Evidence of William Pagan –

I am a Commissioner of Supply and a Road Trustee in the county of Fife, and also for the Stewartry of Kirkcudbright. I hold the office of treasurer to the county of Fife, and to *Cupar District of Turnpike and Statute Labour Roads.* My attention has been for many years directed to the subject of turnpikes and other roads, and I have written a treatise on the subject of road reform, which is before the Commissioners . . .

I have expressed in my book an opinion that turnpikes are vexations and inequitable. My reasons for this opinion are,—

1st. There is a great expense in establishing tolls and making them effectual. Much labour is occasioned to road Trustees and to both Houses of Parliament, in maturing and passing Toll-bar Acts, and their cost falls heavily on the toll-payers. Houses are required for the tacksmen or their collectors; also gates, tariff-boards, posts and chains, steelyards for weighing, and night lamps. Then there are annual charges for advertising and rouping the tolls, providing tickets, and upholding toll-houses and gates, and their appurtenances. The tacksmen must have respectable annual profits, and the collectors their weekly wages. Where retained in the Trustees' own hands, superintendents of collectors are requisite, they and the collectors being again under the surveillance of the road Trustees, or the road surveyors. Much litigation ensues respecting the meaning of the Toll-bar Acts, the position of gates, rates of toll, evasions, exemptions, and other points. By the time all these costs and charges are defrayed, each shilling levied for toll-dues suffers a serious diminution—the expense of establishment and collection running from 10 to 50 per cent.

2nd. Toll-gates are often unfairly placed—thickly in one part of a county, sparsely in another—and many parties escape the tolls altogether, while others cannot move without suffering toll-bar exactions.

3rd. The multiplication of Trusts, with their special gates, and independent staffs of officers, and separate sets of accounts, causes much expense and annoyance to all concerned.

4th. There is no justice for making ordinary travellers pay tolls, not merely for themselves, but for foot passengers and all the privileged classes to whom the roads are made free by numerous exemptions in Toll-bar Acts, such as mail carts, officers and soldiers on duty, the county police, parochial clergymen, funeral processions, etc., etc.

5th. The exaction of toll dues diminishes traffic—often stops it altogether—and prevents that free intercourse for which roads were intended.

6th. Serious evils and inconveniences arise from time consumed at toll-gates in waiting for the collector opening them, taking his toll, and giving back change, and filling up and furnishing tickets.

7th. The gates, posts, chains, and steelyards are so many dangerous obstructions to the passage along the Queen's highway. Many accidents have occurred to travellers stumbling on turnpike gates with their horses and carriages; nay, valuable lives have often been lost upon them.

8th. Where turnpike and statute labour roads and ancient highways are mixed together, as is not uncommon, there is opportunity and provocation for circuitous driving. Much time is thereby wasted to man, and horses and carriages are worn out, and many extra miles of road are ground down.

9th. The toll per ton frequently runs to fourpence or sixpence, be the distance ever so short, while the railways carry, for the same rate, four or six miles—supplying, as it were horse and cart and driver all that distance—for the same money that is requisite to pass a cart at one toll-gate.

10th. Whatever the amount required for road money, it would be a great convenience were it levied by the year, like statute labour assessment, post-horse duties, and taxes on carriages and horses, and all the obstructions referred to, removed from our public roads.

11th. The toll-bar system bears especially on resident proprietors and tenants. Townspeople suffer also, but in a lesser degree, as, generally speaking, they have railway stations within their bounds free of toll. To through travellers per rail toll-gates are now matters of indifference.

Turnpike and statute labour acts were increasingly allowed to lapse, and road management was taken over by parish and burgh authorities. In 1878 the turnpike and statute labour systems were statutorily abolished, and responsibility for maintaining and constructing roads was transferred to county road trustees (or burghs). On the creation of county councils in 1889, the powers and duties of road trustees passed to them, and on them has fallen the modern problem of adapting the road system to the needs of the internal combustion engine.

(7) 41 and 42 Vict., c. 51 (1878) – Roads and Bridges (Scotland) Act –

4. All Local Acts now in force for regulating, managing, making, maintaining or repairing any turnpike road or statute labour road, or other highway situated or partly situated in any county (including the burghs wholly or partly within the same) in which tolls and statute labour, or either thereof, have not been abolished, shall continue in force until the first day of June one thousand eight hundred and eighty-three, and no longer, unless in the meantime this Act shall be adopted, or tolls and statute labour shall be legally abolished, in such county . . .

11. From and after the commencement of this Act in each county the management and maintenance of the highways and bridges within the county shall . . . be vested in and incumbent on the county road trustees herein-after mentioned, and the management and maintenance of the highways and bridges within each burgh situated in or partly situated in such county shall be vested in and incumbent on the burgh local authorities . . .

13. Within six weeks of the commencement of this Act, the ratepayers of each parish within the county entitled to elect trustees for the purposes of this Act shall meet, and elect by open vote two or more persons of their own number . . . to be such trustees, who shall continue in office for three years . . .

16. The trustees shall divide the county into districts for the purpose of managing the highways under their control . . . and they shall annually appoint for each district such of the trustees as they think fit . . . to be a district committee . . .

32. From and after the commencement of this Act, the whole

turnpike roads, statute labour roads, highways and bridges within each county respectively shall form one general trust, with such separate district management as shall be prescribed by the trustees as herein-before provided; and all the roads, bridges, lands, buildings, works, rights, interests, moneys, property, and effects, rights of action, claims and demands, powers, immunities, and privileges whatever, . . . vested in or belonging to the trustees of any such turnpike roads [etc.] . . . shall be by virtue of this Act transferred to and vested in the county road trustees appointed under this Act . . .

33. From and after . . . the first day of June one thousand eight hundred and eighty-three, all tolls within such county, and within any burgh wholly or partly situated therein, shall be abolished, and the exaction of statute labour, or any payment of money by way of conversion or in lieu thereof . . . shall cease . . .

47. From and after the commencement of this Act, the highways and bridges situated within any burgh shall be by virtue of this Act transferred to and vested in the local authority of such burgh, and such local authority shall have the entire management and control of the same . . .

49. Every district surveyor shall, on or before the thirtieth day of March in each year make up and deliver to the clerk of the board, and to the clerk of the district committee of his district respectively—

(1) A report of the condition of the highways within his district;
(2) A specification of works and repairs proposed to be executed thereon; and
(3) An estimate of the sums required for the purposes of the highways within the district for the year . . .

52. The amount required for the management, maintenance, and repair of highways within each district respectively . . . along with a proportion of the general expenses of executing this Act . . . shall be levied by the trustees by an assessment to be imposed at a uniform rate on all lands and heritages within such district . . . and such assessment shall be paid, one half by the proprietor and the other half by the tenant or occupier . . .

55. The board, subject to the approval of the trustees . . . may from time to time, at a meeting called for the purpose by special advertisement . . . resolve to construct any new road or bridge that

they may think requisite . . . and the expense of construction, so far as payable by the board, shall be raised by an assessment to be imposed and levied as the trustees may determine . . .

The burgh local authority shall have the same powers in regard to the construction of new streets or roads or bridges to be wholly or partly situate within the burgh . . .

75. It shall be lawful for the trustees of any county or local authority of any burgh, respectively, to borrow on the security of the assessments for the payment of debts to be levied under this Act within their respective boundaries . . .

B. WATERWAYS

From about 1790 till the 1840s canals, through the easy and cheap conveyance of heavy goods, made a vital contribution to industrialisation. The advantages of joining the Forth and Clyde had been foreseen as early as the seventeenth century. Work began in 1768 but lack of funds brought a halt before completion in 1775. John Knox summed up contemporary hopes, and also accurately predicted the building of Scotland's other two great canals, later known as the Crinan and Caledonian.

(1) John Knox, *A View of the British empire, more especially Scotland* (3rd edn., 1785), pp. 400 f. –

Of Inland Navigation

The first object which presents itself is the opening shorter communication between the Atlantic and the British Sea; the advantages of which are so obvious, that they may be considered as the groundwork of all succeeding improvements, not only in the Highlands, but over Scotland in general.

That nation admits of three artificial navigations:

1. The Southern navigation, between the Forth and the Clyde.
2. The Western navigation, between Lochfine and the Atlantic.
3. The Northern navigation, between Fort William and Inverness.

Navigation between the Forth and the Clyde.

. . . The work . . . came within sight of the river Kelvin, and six miles from the proposed junction with the Clyde; when the subscription, and a subsequent loan, being exhausted, beyond which the proprietors were unwilling to proceed, the work was stopped in 1775, and hath ever since remained in *statu quo*. The inhabitants of Glasgow, however, by means of a collateral branch, nearly 3 miles in length, have opened a navigable communication from that city to the Forth, and thus the emporium of the north communicates with both sides of the island . . .

Upon the whole, this canal, even in its contracted state, will exceed the most sanguine hopes of the public, in general utility. The distance between the entrance into the Clyde and Forth is, by the Pentland Firth 600 miles; by the canal, scarcely 100. But this disproportion of distance in a sea voyage is trifling, when compared with the delays, the ship-wrecks, the positive and casual expences attending a passage by the Hebrides and the Pentland Firth, or even by Land's End, particularly in time of war, when insurance runs from 15 to 20 per cent. while, by means of the inland navigation, it seldom exceeds 5 per cent.

Respecting the West Highlands; the utility of a short passage between that country and the Eastern seas, need scarcely be mentioned. Hitherto the navigation of the Highlands, and the petty traffic of the inhabitants, have not extended beyond the limits of Glasgow, which was carried on by means of the Clyde, but when the remaining 6 miles shall be completed, a new world will open to their view . . . Those people who have previously been excluded from foreign intercourse with mankind, who have been left to prowl amidst their boisterous shores, at home, will now begin to trade with the various ports of Scotland; with London, Holland, and the Baltic, where the excellency of their herrings will generally command a ready sale.

The benefits to Glasgow and its neighbourhood, from the canal in its present state, almost exceed credibility, of which the annual tonnage to and from that city, of 6 or 7000 *l.* is a strong proof. During the scarcity of 1782–3, the quantity of the grain conveyed thither from England, Germany, and Dantzic by means of the canal, prevented a real famine, and saved the lives of thousands in that populous country. By this communication also, the trade between Glasgow and London at all times considerable, is carried on with great ease and facility, much to the satisfaction of the parties concerned, in those commercial cities.

The same benefits will extend to the populous towns of Paisley, Greenock, Port Glasgow, and the whole Western division of Scotland, when this work shall be completed. The inhabitants of both sides of the kingdom, hitherto estranged to one another, will drop their local prejudices, and become as they ought to be, one people, trafficking and bartering with each other, for their mutual advantage.

Navigation between the Atlantic and Lochfine.

To render the southern navigation still more complete, it will be necessary to shorten the passage . . . from the Hebrides and West Highlands, to Glasgow, Greenock, and other trading towns on that celebrated river. The navigation of the Highlands being greatly lengthened by headlands and other obstacles . . . we cannot estimate the voyage from Cape Wrath to Glasgow at less than 400 miles, or 800 miles outward and homeward. This is a bold undertaking for little open boats, badly constructed, and still worse provided; and if, to the great distance, we consider the almost incessant gales, the numerous islands, lee-shores, rocks, sands, and currents, attending these voyages, we may pronounce them . . . extremely hazardous to the poor natives, whose necessities compel them to such desperate attempts. Nor are these the only difficulties which they have to encounter in their passage to Glasgow. The wind which favoured their voyage to the Mull of Cantire, becomes, consequently, adverse after having doubled that cape; they must then furl the sail, and ply at the oars, through a heavy sea, up the Firth of Clyde, sometimes for several days, before they can reach the intended port. Having disposed of their small assortment of bark, skins, wool, and dried fish; they have, in their return, to combat the same round of difficulties, toil and danger; the whole trip employing four men, from three to five weeks. This traffic, however insignificant, is suspended during the winter season; the navigation becomes then impracticable for open boats, and the people . . . are shut out from all intercourse with the seats of industry, population and affluence. Such is the commerce and navigation of a people inhabiting the richest, and most improveable shores in the British dominions . . .

I am happy to hear that the expediency of this navigation (between the Atlantic and Lochfine) is now generally admitted, and that persons of rank have it seriously in contemplation. It would be still more pleasing, were government to undertake the execution thereof, at the public expence . . .

Navigation between Inverness and Fort William

A third, or northern navigation, of very considerable utility, also claims the attention of the public . . . The proposed line of communication from Fort William to Inverness lies in an eastern direction, and is 53 miles in length . . . Vessels of 9 feet of water might pass from Inverness to Fort William in 3 days; small craft much sooner. The voyage by the Pentland firth is upon an average 2 weeks, sometimes 2 months . . .

Were the proposed line of navigation opened to the great western fisheries, and to all the Hebride Isles, a new species of traffic and commercial intercourse would immediately arise; markets of reciprocal benefit would enliven both shores, and give employment to all those who prefer useful industry to indigence and idleness, of whom there are many thousands in this very remote district . . .

Considering this voyage in a general view, its benefits will extend more or less to the whole southern coast of Scotland, to Liverpool, Bristol, and Ireland. Vessels trading to the Baltic, and which cannot navigate the shallow canal between the Clyde and the Forth, might here find a safe passage during the greatest part of the year. The facility of this conveyance to the army is also obvious. Here is a chain of modern fortresses, viz. Fort George at the east end of the pass, Fort Augustus in the centre, and Fort William on the west; which serve, particularly in time of war, as barracks and magazines, from whence detachments of the army may be ready to sail on the shortest notice. By means of this navigation, therefore, a short, safe, and commodious military intercourse may be kept up between these detachments; and also between the two seas, upon the opposite sides of the island, which no enemy could annoy or interrupt . . .

The accumulated loss sustained by the tedious and hazardous passage round the Pentland Firth, in delays, damages at sea, shipwrecks, captures, extra freight and insurance, amounts, in one year only, to more than would complete the above works of general utility to commerce and navigation; and if to this we add the great object of relieving the distresses of 300,000 or 400,000 people; of bringing them forward into the line of action; and of opening new sources of commerce and wealth within our own island, it is a matter of astonishment that these works have not been completed long ago.

Work on the Forth and Clyde Canal was resumed in the late 1780s and in 1790 it reached the Clyde at Bowling. The Canal did not disappoint its backers: revenue rose from £8,000 in 1790 to £48,000 in 1814, handsome dividends were paid, and by the 1830s over 2,000 passages were made annually including passenger services. On a smaller scale the Monkland Canal, undertaken by the Glasgow magistrates in 1769 in order to break a coalmasters' monopoly, was equally important and successful.

(2) James Cleland, *Annals of Glasgow* (1816), pp. 310–313 – Monkland Canal

This canal affords a cheap communication between the City of Glasgow and the Collieries in the parishes of the Old and New Monklands, distant about 12 miles.

The undertaking was at first suggested to the Magistrates of this City in the year 1769, as a means of securing to the inhabitants, at all times, a plentiful supply of coals. Having employed Mr. James Watt, an eminent Engineer, then resident in Glasgow, to survey the ground, an Act of Parliament was obtained for carrying the measure into effect; the Corporation becoming Stockholders to a considerable extent.

Under the first Act, about ten miles only of the Canal were executed; the first two miles of which, from the Basin to the bottom of Blackhill, are on the level of the upper reach of the Forth and Clyde Canal; the other eight miles, beginning at Blackhill, are upon a level ninety-six feet higher. The communication between these levels was at that time carried on by means of an inclined plane, upon which the coals were let down in boxes, and re-shipped on the lower level.

The Capital to complete the Undertaking was, by the Act, declared to be Ten Thousand Pounds, divided into a hundred shares of One Hundred Pounds each; but this sum was found insufficient, for, besides expending it, a debt of some amount was contracted in executing only the above part of the operations.

The Concern in this unfinished state, produced no revenue, and the Creditors becoming pressing, and a number of the Stockholders having refused to make advances, either for the discharge of the debt, or for the purpose of completing the plan, the whole stock of the Company was brought to sale, and purchased by Messrs. William Stirling & Sons of this City, at the rate of twenty-five pounds a share. These Gentlemen immediately after acquiring the property, proceeded to complete the Canal; and, in 1790, having, along with the Proprietors of the Forth and Clyde Canal, procured a second Act of Parliament, empowering the latter to make a junction between these Navigations, by a Cut from their Basin at Port-Dundas, to the Monkland Canal Basin, built locks at Blackhill, and extended the Monkland Canal to the River Calder, which was introduced into it, and that Navigation made the aqueduct for passing the supplies of water from this stream, and a reservoir formed upon it, to the Forth and Clyde Canal . . .

Coal is the chief article carried upon the Canal; there has latterly been some iron, from the Iron-Works at Calder and Cleland, brought along it, and as the country is favourable for works of this description, the quantity of this article is expected to increase. The only return freight, hitherto, from Glasgow has been manure and lime, neither of them to great amount, but regularly increasing with the extension of agricultural improvement, in this part of the country . . .

The revenue of the Canal, till within these four years, was wholly absorbed by the expenses incurred in the extension and improvement of the undertaking. The gross revenue in 1807, when a dividend began first to be made, was Four Thousand Seven Hundred and Twenty Five Pounds. In 1814, it was Five Thousand and Eighty Seven Pounds. In 1816, it will amount to nearly Ten Thousand Pounds; this increase is chiefly owing to an advance on the tonnage rate, authorized by the Act, but not formerly levied. The ordinary annual expenditure is from Twelve to Fifteen Hundred Pounds.

The Crinan and Caledonian Canals, though great feats of engineering, were costly and unprofitable, and brought disappointingly few economic benefits. Both required state assistance, and were administered by Government commissions.

(3) Forty Third Report of the Commissioners for Making and Maintaining the Caledonian Canal. (1 May 1847–1 May 1848), pp. 3–7 –

The Commissioners have much satisfaction in announcing that the experience of the period which has elapsed since the opening of the canal on the 1st May, 1847, has fully borne out their anticipations of the general stability of the works. The last instalment of the sum which was retained from the contract price by way of guarantee, was accordingly paid to the contractors, Messrs. Jackson Bean, in October last . . .

The total amount of tonnage dues received in the year ending 1st May 1848 has been £3,285 14s. 2d., showing an increase in the first year of opening of above 10 per cent. beyond the highest receipt of any former year. The smallness of this increase will not surprise those who take into consideration the former disadvantageous reputation of the Canal, arising from the uncertainty of a passage in the decayed state of its works, the length of the time necessary to give sufficient publicity to its improved circumstances, and above all the extreme difficulty, even when such publicity is attained, of introducing any change in the habits of the seafaring class. Their general reluctance to incur any pecuniary liability for the sake of avoiding the contingency of a tedious, dangerous and possibly far more expensive passage, is sufficiently notorious, and the Commissioners can only trust to time and experience to manifest the important advantages in point of expedition and economy which are prescribed by the Canal. It is now available for vessels drawing 16 feet of water (about 400 tons), having throughout a depth of 17 feet. A passage from sea to sea is secured by the aid of the steam tugs in from 24 to 36 hours, at a cost which the delay of a day or two in the voyage north about will probably exceed, while instances are not wanting of the delay of vessels on the north coast by contrary winds for weeks and even months . . .

As a matter of public convenience to tourists, and travellers engaged in local traffic, their great resort sufficiently indicates the advantage of the Canal; not less than two, and some times four, and even five passages per diem, along the whole length of the Navigation, were made last season by the passenger steam-boats plying between Inverness and Glasgow, arriving at their respective destinations on the afternoon of the second day. Their charges are such as to bring the opportunity of visiting the Highland districts within the reach of thousands who must else have remained precluded from it; thus almost supplying the place of railroads in a country from which the natural features and the scarceness of the existing population have as yet excluded them . . .

The Commissioners think it advisable upon the eve of closing the large expenditure latterly committed to their care to introduce here a short recapitulation of the amount, and the appropriation of the several Grants by Parliament for the purposes of the Navigation.

In the year 1824 the total amount of the Grants had reached the sum of £947,501; the Canal having been then opened two years with the depth of 12 feet of water only instead of 20 feet as originally contemplated, and for which the dimensions of the locks were calculated. A constantly deficient revenue was the consequence of working at such a disadvantage, under the exclusion of the most profitable class of traffic, and to meet the liabilities that were thus incurred, a further sum of £4,886 was granted in 1830, making £952,387, while the claims to a large amount of the proprietors of land taken along the line of the Canal were still unsatisfied and indeed unascertained.

This state of things continued for 12 years for the last three of which the question of repair was repeatedly discussed by the Treasury and in Parliament, and in the meantime the accruing deficiency had compelled advances by the Bank of Scotland to the amount (including interest) of £26,740. For the reduction of this debt, and without reference to any intention of completing the Canal, a sum of £25,000 was granted in 1841; in 1842 a sum of £27,000 was issued for the discharge of the residue of the debt to the Bank, and also to meet the claims of the proprietors for land taken or damaged along the line; this sum, with the interest since allowed thereon, though not yet wholly applied (a part having been set aside as above mentioned), will have sufficed to meet the purpose for which it was destined.

It is only the sums which have been issued since the commencement of the year 1844, and which amount . . . to £228,000 which have been specially destined to the repair and completion of the Navigation and its appliances. For this object, including the current expenses of maintenance during five years of operations, and including an amount of £5,000 which to alleviate the distress of the Highland districts in 1846–7 the Government permitted to be expended in extra works of utilising the Canal, the Commissioners have an entire belief that the above Grants will be found fully adequate.

Scarcely less essential than canal-building was the deepening and improving of harbours. The most noticeable change was on the Clyde, which was deepened in the later eighteenth century to enable large vessels to proceed upriver to Glasgow. James Cleland, Superintendent of Public Works for the City of Glasgow, summed up the improvements and their effect on trade in his own lifetime.

(4) James Cleland, *Enumeration of the Inhabitants of the City of Glasgow* (1832), pp. 152–153 –

The improvements on the river, and the increase of trade at the Broomielaw, almost exceeds belief. In my own recollection, the Harbour was only 730 feet long; it is now 3340 feet on the north side, and 1260 on the south. A few Gaberts, and these only of 30 or 40 tons burthen, came up to the Broomielaw; now large vessels, many of them 300 tons burthen, from America, the East and West Indies, and the Continent, are often to be found three deep along nearly the whole length of the Harbour. Many of the spaces between the Jettees were formed by eddies into large irregular pools; now, from the under end of the Harbour, for several miles below the City, the river is confined within narrow bounds, and the sloping banks, formed with whin, in imitation ashler, are unequalled in the kingdom, whether the use or the splendour of the effect be taken into account. Formerly, an ordinary flood inundated the under part of the town, to the great injury of its inhabitants; now it requires a very extra-ordinary flood to produce the same effect. Till of late years there were only a few punts and ploughs for the purpose of dredging the river; now there are three dredging machines, provided with numerous buckets and powerful steam apparatus, at an expense of nearly twelve thousand pounds. There was no covering for goods, and but one small crane for shipping and discharging; now the shed accommodation on both sides of the river is most ample, and one of the cranes, for shipping Steam Boat Boilers, and other heavy articles, made by Messrs. Claud Girwood, and Co., may challenge all the Ports in the kingdom for the union of power with elegance of construction. I was present at an experiment when she lifted upwards of *Thirty Tons*. The houses fronting the Harbour extended only to Smithfield, about 650 feet; they now extend to upwards of 3,000 feet. If anything were awanting to show the great increase of trade on the Clyde, the regular advance of dues would supply that want. In 1771, the first years' dues amounted to *L.* 1,021:5:1. In 1815 to *L.* 5,680:4:1, and in 1831, they were let at Public Auction for *L.* 21,350.

The revenues of the estates forfeited after the Jacobite Rebellion of 1745, combined with local capital, financed Telford's great series of improvements at east coast harbours. The Poet Laureate was justly enthusiastic.

(5) Robert Southey, *Journal of a Tour in Scotland in 1819* –

DUNDEE. *Wednesday*, *August* 25.—Before breakfast I went with Mr. T[elford] to the harbour, to look at his works, which are of great magnitude and importance—a huge floating dock, and the finest graving dock I ever saw. The town expends 70,000*L*. upon these improvements, which will be completed in another year. What they take from the excavations serves to raise ground which was formerly covered by the tide, but will now be of the greatest value for wharfs, yards, etc. They proposed to build fifteen piers, but T. assured them that three would be sufficient; and in telling me this he said the creation of fifteen new Scotch Peers was too strong a measure...

BERVIE. *Thursday*, *August* 26 ... We left the coach and descended with them to the harbour, the first of the Parliamentary works in this direction. It is a small pier, which at the cost of something less than 2000*L*. will secure this little, wild, dangerous, but not unimportant port—not unimportant, because coal and lime are landed here from Sunderland, and corn shipped, much being raised in the adjoining country ... The pier will be finished in about two months, and will shelter four vessels. The basin has been deepened. It was highly gratifying to see machinery employed here for the best possible purpose, facilitating human labour and multiplying the strength of man an hundredfold. The stones are lifted by a crane, with strong iron cramps or pinchers; and an iron rail-road is in use, which is carried from pier to pier, wherever it is wanted ... Mr. Farquhar, the Lord of the soil, who has made about 150,000*L*. as a Civilian, advances that half of the cost which Government requires as the condition of its aid with the other. Without national aid the work would not have been undertaken, tho' in such a place and country it is the first step towards improvement ...

ABERDEEN. *Saturday*, *August* 28. ... When R[ickman] and T. returned from their inland expedition, we went to the harbour. The quay is very fine, and Telford has carried out the pier nine hundred feet beyond the point where Smeaton's work terminated. This great work, which cost 100,000*L*., protects the entrance from the whole force of the North Sea ... A ship was entering under full sail—*The Prince of Waterloo*—she had been to America, had discharged her cargo at London, and we now saw her reach her own port in safety—a joyous and delightful sight. The Whalers are come in, and there is a strong odour of whale oil, which would rejoice the heart of

a Greenlander . . . The harbour dues of this year will exceed 8000*L.* . . . Coal and lime are brought to this country from Sunderland, and the lime is carried many miles inland for dressing the land . . .
BANFF. *Monday, August* 30.—Here we rejoined Mr. Telford, Mitchell and Gibb, and went with them to the pier, which is about half-finished, and on which 15,000*L.* will be expended to the great benefit of this clean, cheerful, active town. Lord Fife has begun a similar work at his town of Macduff, the cost has been estimated at 5000*L.*, but is likely greatly to exceed that sum. The pier was a busy scene—handcarts going to and from on the rail-roads, cranes at work charging and discharging huge stones, plenty of workmen, and fine masses of red granite from the Peterhead quarries. The quay was almost covered with barrels of herrings, and women employed in salting and packing them . . .
CULLEN. *Tuesday August* 31.—The works here, of which the whole expense will be about 4000*L.*, are in such forwardness that the pier at this time affords shelter: and when I stood upon it at low water, seeing the tremendous rocks with which the whole shore is bristled, and the open sea to which it is exposed, it was with a proud feeling that I saw the first talents in the world employed by the British Government in works of such unostentatious, but great, immediate, palpable and permanent utility. Already the excellent effects are felt. The fishing vessels were just come in, having caught about 300 barrels of herrings during the night . . .

This whole line of coast is in a state of rapid improvement, private enterprize and public spirit keeping pace with national encouragement, and it with them. Government is to blame for not making its good works better known . . . The money which it bestows upon harbours arises from the remainder of the rents of the forfeited estates; the whole of which rents (till the estates were restored) were designed to be appropriated to the improvement of Scotland. However much the money may have been misapplied during a long series of years by those to whom it was entrusted, the remainder could not have been better applied. Wherever a pier is wanted, if the people or the proprietor of the place will raise half the sum required, Government gives the other half from this fund, as far as it will reach. Upon these terms 20,000*L.*, are expending at Peterhead, and 14,000*L.*, at Fraserburg, and the works which we visited at Bervie and Banff, and many other such along this whole coast would not have been undertaken without this aid from Government . . .

C. RAILWAYS

The first railways, or wagonways, were used to haul coals at collieries or materials on construction sites. The most notable of these was between Kilmarnock and Troon. Horsepower was used; since steam proved inefficient.

(1) *New Statistical Account*, vol. 5, p. 554. Parish of Kilmarnock –

The railway which runs from Kilmarnock to Troon, is another great advantage to the parish. The practicability and usefulness of such a line were long since clearly pointed out. The difference of the respective elevations of the depots is only 80 feet. It was finished in 1812 at an expense of upwards of *L*50,000. It is a double road, constructed with flat rails, resting on blocks of durable stone. Its length is nine miles and a-half. Horse power alone is used, for which 1½d. per ton per mile is paid. The dues are 2d. a mile per ton. We may mention that, in 1816, a locomotive engine, the first of the kind started in Scotland, was tried. It was intended to convey coal to Troon from the Duke of Portland's colliery, but, from its defective construction and ill adaptation to flat rails, it only drew ten tons at the rate of five miles an hour. Since then, no attempt has been made to introduce steam power. As it will in a few years very possibly become a branch of the western railway, several changes may take place in its construction, and it is not unlikely that the only propelling power used will be steam. By means of this railway, there is free intercourse with the harbour of Troon. Quantities of timber, grain, slates, and lime, are brought into the parish, and about 70,000 tons of coal annually conveyed out of it. About 200,000 pass along it in the course of the year. The farmer gets lime cheaply conveyed to his farm,—the landlord's property is increased in value by the facility of communication with the market-town, and the public have a ready means of transport to convenient watering-places.

The early railways were built to carry minerals (rather than passengers) in conjunction with existing canal facilities. An important line was the Monkland-Kirkintilloch, on which steam replaced horsepower in 1832 (2). Though at first built to carry minerals, railways had obvious passenger potential (3).

(2) *New Statistical Account*, vol. 8, pp. 202–203. Parish of Kirkintilloch, June 1839 – *see over*

The first public railway in Scotland, on the modern improved principle, was the "Monkland and Kirkintilloch Railway", which connects the rich coal and mineral districts of the Monklands with the Forth and Clyde Canal near Kirkintilloch. The act was obtained in the year 1824 (5 Geo. IV, cap. 49). The original capital was *L.*32,000; but, by a new act in 1833, (3 Wm. IV, cap. 114) the total capital was raised to *L.*52,000. The northern terminus is at Kirkintilloch, and the south-east at Palace Craig, in old Monkland, including a length, in all, of about eleven miles. The distance between the rails is 4½ feet . . . No passenger waggons are allowed on this railway. It is connected with the Ballochney, and Glasgow, and Garnkirk railways in the south, and these penetrate into all the great mineral deposits in Lanarkshire. Great quantities of coal and iron are transported by this railway to the depot in the Forth and Clyde Canal. The coal is of very superior quality, and is laid down in the town of Kirkintilloch, at the rate of 15s. per waggon of 48 cwt. In 1835, about 49,000 tons of coal, and 3325 tons of pig-iron were shipped on the canal from the railway.

(3) *Mirror of Parliament* (1832), p. 3664. Debate in Parliament on taxing railway travel, 9 August 1832 –

Hume: 'Before the Dundee railroad was established, two or three carts were all that used to find their way over the hills to that town on market day; but since the formation of that railroad, hundreds of country people come into the town every market day . . . The people who now attend the Dundee market would never have gone thither but for the establishment of the railroad . . . I am informed that people are in the habit of travelling by this and other railroads for two pence and three pence each who, but for this mode of conveyance, would never travel at all. I may say that railroads call into existence new markets and new consumers. By saving time they allow a greater degree of industry to be exercised . . . In short, a tax on railroads is a tax on time, industry, and the means of improvement'.

It was only a matter of time before lines were built to England, but there was some doubt on the route to be tackled first. An Edinburgh-Dunbar line was proposed in 1836, but no action was taken until the early 1840s. By 1846 the line had reached Berwick; the Glasgow-Carlisle route was opened in 1848.

(4) *Tait's Edinburgh Magazine*, February 1842, pp. 138–139 –

East Coast Railway.—A meeting was held in Edinburgh on the 14th January, for the purpose of promoting a line of Railway to Dunbar, being the first portion of a railway along the coast to Newcastle: the Lord Provost in the Chair. The large room was nearly full. Mr. Learmonth addressed the meeting. He stated that the line was of very easy construction, and might be made for £500,000, or about £20,000 a-mile. At the lowest estimate, he calculated that above £72,000 per annum would be received for passengers, and £23,000 from goods, or £96,000 in all: from which, deducting one-third for expenses, a clear revenue of £64,000 would be left, yielding 11½ per cent. on the outlay. He adverted to the West coast line of railway to England from Glasgow; and stated the distance to Lancaster, including the branch from Thankerton to Edinburgh, was 202 miles; the engineering difficulties were of the most serious description; and the great proportion of the intermediate country so thinly peopled, that the line could not be made in portions, as no revenue could be expected till the whole line was completed. Taking the expense at £20,000 a mile only, the cost would be upwards of four millions. After several resolutions had been passed, a large committee was appointed. Considering that, with the exception of the first eight or ten miles, the route from Edinburgh to Thankerton runs through Carnwath and other muirs almost totally destitute of population, and that it would cost probably £800,000, there is no chance of the line ever being made. The Edinburgh and Glasgow Railway has cost £30,000 a mile, and we do not think that there is any chance of the western line being made at a smaller cost, or six millions sterling. Truly a magnificent project! Were the line to Dunbar fairly commenced, we have no doubt a company would soon be formed to make a Railway from Newcastle to Berwick, and the intermediate space would then only be thirty miles. Measures are already in progress to connect Newcastle and Darlington by railway; and hence the formation of a railway from Edinburgh to Dunbar will secure the intercourse between Scotland and England by the east coast; for not only will London and the eastern part of England be reached with great ease and expedition by this route, but the middle and west of England, by means of the Carlisle and Newcastle, and other railways. It is, therefore, a matter of the utmost importance to Edinburgh that the railway to Dunbar should be formed; for upon this project it depends whether Edinburgh is to continue retrograde, as it has done for the last quarter of a century, or again spring into new life and vigour. The sum set down for passengers may at first sight seem exaggerated; but when it is considered that the number of passengers on the Edinburgh and Dalkeith railway has been as high as 300,000, and that the whole district from Edinburgh to Dunbar, and for many miles beyond, is thickly peopled, a slight consideration will show that there is no improbability of the revenue estimated being derived from passengers.

The railway boom, beginning in 1845, demanded its own journal. The tone of the first editorial was typical of the boundless—though not entirely unrealistic—hopes and exuberant language of the railway enthusiasts.

(5) *Scottish Railway Gazette*, vol. i, no. 1, 5th April 1845 –

It is at a period when railways and other similar undertakings are giving evidence of a vigorous and happy progress, that we have come forward to record, and if possible to assist in, that progress. There is now hardly a capitalist of any consequence, or a retired gentleman, who has not invested more or less of his property in these great national undertakings, both in Scotland and England, and even abroad . . .

From the progress of Railroads, all parts of the country will become more and more opened up for all purposes. The land of the interior will, by a system of cheap and rapid conveyance, for manure and for produce, become almost as valuable as that upon the coast; the most remote from towns, almost as valuable as that in their immediate neighbourhood; for the difference will only be, that of a cheap and quick carriage. The same results will occur in regard to houses in the neighbourhood of Railway stations; for the artizan can, at a very trifling expense of time and money, bring out his materials, and take home his work, and the man of business as easily join his family, at a distance of ten or twelve miles, as could formerly be done, at a distance of two or three miles. Assuredly there will be an immense progress towards equalizing the value of land; and that of itself will create important study for individuals having capital in want of investment.

Not less important will be the equalizing of the more perishable species of property, the articles of every day's consumption; and the equalizing of industry—the poor man's property. Fish, for example,

—the produce of the sea,—was, a few years ago, inaccessible to any beyond a few miles from the coast. In many places,—it may be said in most,—particularly in Scotland, it is so still. Wherever the railroad goes, that luxury will now be carried; and we need not say that every ton of food taken from the sea is added to the land. On the other hand, the produce of the land, whether animal, vegetable, or mineral, will, with equal facility, be brought to the coast. In this way, not only will the land be enriched, and rendered capable of cultivation, but, a market being created for increased produce, will encourage and reward that production. It is no Utopian vision to say, that the entire country may yet one day be rendered a garden, for it is fast hastening to that consummation every hour.

In a few weeks the same journal offered evidence of success. Most share issues were heavily oversubscribed, which often put the stock at a premium before it had been allotted. Successful applicants profited; unsuccessful ones complained of the allocation.

(6) *Scottish Railway Gazette*, vol. i, no. 2, 12th April 1845 –

Weekly Reports

Edinburgh, April 11, 1845

During the course of the last week there has been a very large amount of business transacted in our Exchange, and at considerably advanced prices. Nearly all descriptions of Railway Shares were, during the early part of the week, eagerly sought after, and sales were made at much higher prices than last week . . .

Speculators are eagerly inquiring after Shares in the Perth and Inverness Railway, the allotment of which will take place next week; from 15/- to 20/- premium is freely offered for Shares in this Line . . .

Glasgow, April 11, 1845

We have to report a continuance of great excitement in our market, and almost all descriptions of shares have been largely dealt in during the week, the majority of Railway transactions having been in the scrips of the newly brought-out schemes, most of which are out on premium . . .

Scottish Railway Gazette, vol. i, no. 3, 19 April 1845 – *see over*

Weekly Reports

Edinburgh, April 18, 1845

. . . The Perth and Inverness Railway came out yesterday at 32s. 6d. premium, and went up to 35s. Speculation has been very strong in the line, and a large number of shares have been sold. To-day prices have rather receded, and it closed at 81s., there being buyers at 80s. It is the opinion of best informed parties, that this Railway has come out at first at too high a premium, and that it will likely decline in price; but much will depend upon what is done in the London and Liverpool markets. Great dissatisfaction is felt at the small number of shares which have been allotted to this city, although the applications were exceedingly numerous, and from parties of the first respectability. It is said that the great amount of shares have been given to parties in London, Liverpool, and other parts of England.

The railway fever, hectic speculation, and numerous far-fetched railway projects naturally attracted satirists. Among them was Henry Cockburn.

(7) Henry Cockburn, *Journal* (1874), vol. ii, pp. 129–131 –

28th November 1845. Britain is at present an island of lunatics, all railway mad. The patients are raving even in the wildest recesses of the Highlands. The ultimate miracles of railways are obvious . . . Distance is diminished twenty-fold. The world is not half the size it was a few years ago. The globe is in the course of being inhabited as one city or shire, everything known to and everything touching everybody. The consequences of the whole human family thus feeling in each thread and living along the line cannot yet be foreseen fully, but there is no reason to doubt that on the whole the result must be good. It will give force to public reason, and thus give great advantages to civilisation over barbarism, and to truth over error.

But in *arranged* countries the change has intolerable present evils—at least in Britain, where the plethora of capital drives the new system on with regardless violence, and where self-interest combines all railway speculators into one corporation, which, with its bursting purse, defies resistance, and respects no feelings but its own . . . Parliament itself, though it unguardedly conceded to injured parties the right of having their compensation adjusted by arbitrators, is itself to an alarming degree a company of railway owners. The outrages of these speculators are frightful. Their principle is, that nothing must obstruct their dividends, which is expressed technically by saying that "the public must be accommodated". This being fixed, all that remains is to ascertain where a line of iron can be laid down horizontally. If the country were a desert, and nothing were to be considered but percentages and engineering, this might be all that required to be thought of; but in a *made-up* country it is the last thing that ought to be regarded. Taste seeks seclusion, and comfort seeks shelter, which implies no great elevation; but railways seek these too. The margin of a loch, the course of a stream, a gentle valley, a wooden plain—these are the railway pastures, for they imply flatness or a gradual rise; and therefore the long domestic happiness or care that may have been enjoyed or lavished upon them are scornfully disregarded. A human bird's nest, a revered ruin, a noble castle, a poetical stream, a glorious wood, . . . all the haunts of long-confiding affection, all the scenes over which taste and genius have lingered, all connected with localities that the heart cares for—what are these to a railway? Must not the public be accommodated? On this phrase the most brutal inroads are making every day, and in the most brutal spirit, on the most sacred haunts.

The large number of small companies which built most of the railway network were soon reduced by amalgamations. The process was evident among some of the earliest railways of the industrial belt.

(8) Report of the Directors to the Shareholders of The Monkland Railways Company, 6th September 1848, p. 3 –

At the General Meeting of Shareholders, held in March last, the then Directors of the Monkland & Kirkintilloch, Ballochney, & Slamannan Railway Companies, were authorised to apply, during the present Session of Parliament, for an Act to Amalgamate the Monkland & Kirkintilloch, Ballochney, & Slamannan Railways, on the terms and conditions then agreed to. Your Directors have much pleasure in reporting that, notwithstanding considerable opposition, the Act has been procured, and that you now meet together, for the first time, under it. Though the opposition caused your Board to accept lower rates than could have been wished, yet, from prudent and economical management, it is anticipated that they will prove remunerative.

(9) 28 & 29 Vict., c. ccxvii (1865). An Act to amalgamate the *Monkland* Railways Company with the *Edinburgh and Glasgow* Railway Company (5 July 1865) –

Whereas the *Edinburgh and Glasgow* Railway Company were incorporated by "The *Edinburgh and Glasgow* Railway Consolidation Act, 1852": And whereas by "The *Monkland* Railways Act, 1848," the *Monkland and Kirkintilloch* Railway Company, the *Ballochney* Railway Company, and the *Slamannan* Railway Company were dissolved, and the several Persons and Corporations who were Proprietors of Shares in the said Companies were united and incorporated into One Company under the Name of "The *Monkland* Railways Company", . . . And whereas it would be of public advantage and Convenience if the *Monkland* Railways Company were amalgamated with the *Edinburgh and Glasgow* Railway Company, and the said Companies are desirous and have agreed that the Undertaking of the *Monkland* Railways Company shall be transferred to and vested in the *Edinburgh and Glasgow* Railway Company on the Terms and Conditions herein-after specified; but these Objects cannot be effected without the Authority of Parliament: May it therefore please Your Majesty that it may be enacted . . .

By the 1860s there were only five large companies (North British; Caledonian; Glasgow and South-Western; Highland; Great North of Scotland), but, in spite of amalgamation, the efficiency of the Scottish railway system was often questioned. Much of the fierce competition between the great companies, especially the North British and the Caledonian, was held to be wasteful; coalowners complained that losses on passenger services were offset by excessive freight rates.

(10) Evidence to the Board of Trade Departmental Committee on Railway Agreements and Amalgamations, 1911. Evidence of Dr. R. T. Moore, representing the Scottish Coalmasters, 8 June 1910 –

17110 . . . The rates in Scotland generally are much higher than those charged for the carriage of minerals in other districts; they are more than double those charged in South Wales, and they are in the opinion of the Coal Masters unreasonably high . . .
17137 . . . The Scotch railway companies have much cheaper passenger fares than the English railway companies. In the last 20 years the Caledonian, for example, has increased its capital by about

15 million pounds for passenger railways which have not been of any service for the mineral traffic, and which have been of very little service to the railway companies . . . Some of these lines which they have made have never been opened and others do not pay any return on the capital spent . . .

17144 . . . The Caledonian have spent large sums of money on the Glasgow Central Railway and upon the Central Station approaches; all these have been rendered less valuable on account of the tramway traffic in the town. Then they spent a lot of money in making a competing line from Paisley to Barrhead. That line they never made; they made the stations and they have not even joined up the rails, and they have never run any trains over it. They made another line of the same sort at Strathaven and Stonehouse, and that does not pay. They also made a line to Ballachulish, away up to the Western Highlands . . .

17152 . . . The Ballachulish line was made in competition with the North British, which had a line to Fort William, and the Caledonian wished to get a competing line up to Fort William. At that time they were anxious to get a railway wherever the North British had one, and the North British were anxious to get a railway wherever the Caledonian had one. This line was made through the Highlands where there are a few sheep, but there is no traffic to pay for it . . .

17296 . . . If the [Railway] Commissioners were satisfied that the reason the Scotch railways were only paying 3 per cent. was on account of the passenger lines, upon which they had thrown away money, lines which they had made and had not opened, I do not see why the Scotch mineral owners should be penalised by the Scotch railway companies in order to pay dividends upon this money that has been thrown away . . .

17299 . . . You rather suggest that the passenger people are getting unreasonably low fares?—That is my opinion.

By the early twentieth century agreements between the five large companies had somewhat restricted competition. But many, including railway managements, still considered inter-company rivalry excessive, and recommended further amalgamation in face of competition from other forms of transport.

(11) Report of the Board of Trade Railway Conference, 1909, pp. 40–41. Statement of W. F. Jackson of the North British Railway Co. – *see over*

When an independent company forms a branch line connecting with one of the larger railways of the country, it is usual for the larger Company to enter into an agreement to supply rolling stock for, and to work the smaller Company's line either for a period or in perpetuity . . .

Since the consolidation of the Scottish Railways, which took place some forty or fifty years ago, the only agreements for working or amalgamations which have been entered into have been of the nature already described, and form no analogy to the case of the amalgamation of two or more large Companies. There have, however, been agreements with the object of confining competition within legitimate limits. Such agreements have, in some cases, accomplished their object by (1) prohibiting the construction of new lines by one Company in the territory served by another, or in territory common to both Companies; or (2) dividing in certain agreed ways, the receipts from traffic, with regard to which there was undue competition, and thus removing the incentive to such competition . . .

The amalgamations which resulted in the five existing Scottish undertakings, simplified the railway arrangements of Scotland, and enabled economies to be effected in working and management, as well as the giving of services and facilities to the traders and the public which would have been quite impossible with a large number of comparatively small railways, and the arrangements which at present exist among the five Companies with regard to routing of traffic and mutual availability of tickets have done something more in the same direction. There is no reason to believe that a further scheme of amalgamation which would unite in one all the railways of Scotland, would not have the same beneficial results as attended the amalgamations which have already taken place.

There would, by such amalgamation of the five railways, be savings (1) in the cost of direction, management, and staff generally; (2) as a result of the common use of working stock and plant; (3) by the discontinuance of duplicate services and stations; and (4) in the cost of advertising and canvassing at present considered needful for competitive reasons; and (5) in the simplifying of the whole arrangements of the Companies, particularly in connection with joint lines, Exchanges of Traffic, Running Powers, &c.

Competition, as between the Scottish Railway Companies, has undoubtedly resulted in considerable diminution of the net revenues of the Companies without anything like equivalent advantage to the traders or the public . . .

Such competition, is however, not by any means the only form of competition which prejudicially affects the Scottish Companies. The smallness of the country, and its extensive seaboard and navigable waterways, make shipping competition a formidable factor, as vessels can reach all the most important centres . . . and also most of the secondary centres . . . This competition becomes more and more formidable as time goes on. It has the double disadvantage, from the railway point of view, of not only abstracting traffic from land routes, but of taking principally the bulk traffics which yield the best net results by giving good wagon and train loads, with limited handling and clerical service.

There should also be mentioned the increasing competition to which railways are subjected by tramways and various forms of motor traction . . . Continuous tramway journeys are possible in Scotland, extending to no less than 20 or 30 miles, and this form of competition is always in the more populous districts, its effects are the more keenly felt by the Railway Companies.

If, therefore, the Scottish Railways are to be maintained as efficient factors in the maintenance and development of the trade of the country, relief must come to them from some quarter, as, with their capital commitments, the ever-increasing demands of labour and requirements of the Board of Trade, and the formidable water and tramway, &c., competition they have to meet, with the consequent decreasing and even vanishing dividends, it is impossible they can continue to find money to meet their absolute needs, much less to provide for development. Amalgamation, with its possible economies, would afford a very substantial contribution towards the relief thus required.

Complete amalgamation, however, came only with nationalisation in 1948. Recently, in face of air and road competition, the scope and functions of railways have been thoroughly reviewed: it has been proposed to close over 200 stations and halts, and to withdraw over 500 uneconomic passenger services. But modern freight services are likely to remain important.

(12) British Railways Board, *The Reshaping of British Railways* (1963), pp. 13–16 – *see over*

Air transport is not competitive in terms of speed for inter-city distances of less than 200 miles, nor is it competitive in terms of cost except while operating as the minority carrier able to keep a high load factor by creaming from the total flow. This restricts the routes over which air competes seriously with rail to the London–Manchester, London–Newcastle and London–Scotland routes.

On the Scottish routes, air makes quite serious inroads into the loading of day trains, and will continue to do so. Even though trains may be speeded up, they will not match city-to-city transit by air over such a distance, and erosion of daytime rail traffics between London and Scotland will probably continue to the point where some trains will have to be withdrawn. On the other hand, sleeper trains between London and Scotland continue to attract a satisfactory level of traffic, and there is good reason to suppose that they can be improved and increased . . .

Competitive railway building in the past led not only to duplication of main arteries between some of the principal cities, but also to duplication of passenger stations and all the ancillary facilities . . . which go with large terminals. Very little has been done, so far, to rationalise the main line passenger services which use alternative routes and terminals, but it is clear, in many cases, that concentration on selected routes and stations would provide equal or better services and permit substantial economies . . . The Caledonian, the Glasgow and South Western, and the North British Companies left a legacy of four large terminals in Glasgow . . . The future of all these is being determined, and . . . discussions are already taking place with civic authorities who are most anxious to collaborate in the development of sites which will be released by concentration schemes . . .

Today, rail stopping services and bus services serve the same basic purpose. Buses carry the greater part of the passengers moving by public transport in rural areas, and, as well as competing with each other, both forms of public transport are fighting a losing battle against private transport . . .

Ownership of private transport is as common in rural areas as in towns. For example, the ownership of cars in the north of Scotland is 11.7 per 100 of the population, which equals the national average.